Education and social control:
A study in progressive primary education

Education and social control:
A study in progressive primary education

Rachel Sharp
Department of Sociology
Macquarie University, Australia

and

Anthony Green
Institute of Education
University of London

with the assistance of
Jacqueline Lewis

Routledge & Kegan Paul
London and Boston

First published in 1975
by Routledge & Kegan Paul Ltd
Broadway House, 68-74 Carter Lane,
London EC4V 5EL and
9 Park Street,
Boston, Mass. 02108, USA
Set in 10/12 Press Roman by Autoset
and printed in Great Britain by
Unwin Brothers Limited
ISBN 0 7100 8160 X (c)
ISBN 0 7100 8161 8 (p)

Contents

Preface   vii

1 Sociology and the classroom   1
2 Theoretical considerations   15
3 Mapledene Lane: the school and its environment   36
4 The school ethos   47
5 The teacher's perspectives   68
6 Social stratification in the classroom: an ideal type   114
7 Social stratification in the classroom: dimensions of variability   128
8 The social structuring of pupils' identities: some examples   137
9 The child centred ethos as an accounting system   166
10 The parents   196
11 Summary and conclusion   216

Appendix: a note on methodology   228

Notes   235

Bibliography   241

Index   251

Preface

The interests reflected in this book are both theoretical and political, and may be crystallized into two major themes, the one centred on sociological theory and methodology, the other on infant education and substantive issues therein.

The substantive focus is upon the 'child centred' approach to education and, more specifically, upon the application of methods grounded in this approach in three classrooms in the infant department of a particular school. Our intention was to attempt to study and demonstrate some of the more or less subtle ways in which wider social structural 'forces' impinge upon or influence the pedagogy and other social processes at the level of the classroom and the school. We have tried to illustrate some of the structures of the broader context of the teachers' practice which tend to lead to consequences which belie both their moral commitments and the causes they appear to have adopted and profess. In doing this we are attempting to pin-point some of the paradoxical features of the teachers' practices and the sources of those paradoxes. Our stance is essentially exploratory rather than verificatory.

The child centred teacher sees him, or herself as engaging in a radical critique of the authoritarian-élitist assumptions of the more formal, traditional approaches to education. He does not wish to subordinate the child's individuality to some predefined social requirements or impose 'high culture' upon the child in an arbitrary fashion because these would frustrate the realization of the child's inner potential. We attempt to show some of the ways in which the well-intentioned 'radical practices' of the progressive educator produce effects very similar to the hierarchical differentiation of pupils characteristic of formal methods. Whilst laying emphasis upon the freedom of the child, the teacher who has adopted the ideology of child centredness may well find himself unwittingly constrained to act in ways which pose serious problems concerning the efficacy of accommodating to and encouraging the 'spontaneous development of the child from within himself'. In our explanation of these and other phenomena which we have researched, what is being suggested is that the child centred educator, with his individualistic, voluntarist, and psychologistic solution to the problem of freedom fails to appreciate the ways in which, even in his own practice, the effects of a complex, stratified industrial society penetrate the school. It is suggested that the radicalism of the 'progressive educator' may well be a modern form of conservatism, and an effective form of social control in both the narrow sense of achieving discipline in the classroom and the wider sense of contributing to the promotion of a static social order generally.

The second theme explored in the book concerns the adequacy of certain theoretical developments in sociology generally and recent developments, in the sociology of education in particular. We refer to the group of perspectives, which, very loosely we admit, we categorize under the rubric 'sociological phenomenology'. Sociological phenomenologists present themselves as radically opposed to traditional orthodoxies in sociology and make a claim to be holding a humanist perspective which does not denigrate man's individuality and spontaneity, or reduce actors to the mere passive effects of social structures. They reaffirm the significance of human action, and see social structural formations as the dynamic creations of constitutive human subjects who, through a continuous process of interpretation and negotiation, make and remake their social worlds. In this approach to understanding social phenomena there is a preoccupation with consciousness, the ethics of human freedom, and a denial of the theoretical possibility of structural determinations in the social world. Social structure therefore becomes, for the sociological phenomenologist, the mere reification of concepts created by the social scientist (or anybody else for that matter) in search of an object. Under the guise of theoretical novelty and radicalism this approach often tends to overlook the fact that it is grounded in a long history which presents as its most significant recent source the forms of idealism found in the Kantian and Hegelian traditions. For all its reflexivity, sociological phenomenology appears to be unwilling to trace the conditions of its own existence. It does not, and perhaps cannot enquire, for instance, into why it should be that this particular brand of neo-idealism should capture the imagination of social scientists at this particular time.

The major ideological link between our interests in child centred educational thought and practice and sociological phenomenology is to be found in their underlying commitments drawn from the traditional assumptions of liberalism. Both the sociological phenomenologists and many who look to child centredness as offering solutions to fundamental social and philosophical problems can be integrated in the liberal tradition. Their concept of man is individualistic, voluntarist, and creative; their concept of society is reductivist, consensual, and utilitarian. Our book attempts to chart some of the theoretical and practical implications of this, by focusing upon a rather narrow empirical setting (a primary school), in order to demonstrate that liberal ideology in this context fails to take account of the wider social context. Any notion of human freedom and self expression must be situated in such a way as to highlight one of the key features of modern society, what appears as the freedom and self-determination of a few occurs within the context of its denial to the many. A social-historical treatment of liberalism shows that it is now generally carried by, and certainly supports the interests of those favourably entrenched within the socio-economic structure. Although at certain times, liberalism may have seemed to offer a basis for the criticism and undermining of the dominant hegemony, we argue that radicalism requires the jettisoning of certain basic liberal assumptions which have preoccupied educators and those who have tried to theorize about education for so long.

Education and Social Control can thus be read as a piece of critical sociology. We make no claim to having provided a complete or adequate theoretical alternative to the current paradigms in education and sociology. Though we do not claim the exclusivity of proposing yet another 'new direction' in social thought, we intend in part to convince the reader of the need to look again at the way in which problems have been generated and solutions proposed within sociology and education.

It is important to be clear that our substantive analysis, of which three classrooms in a primary school are a cornerstone, does not involve a direct personal critique of the subjects of our observations, be they teachers, parents, headmasters, or social workers. To them, of course, we owe a great deal for allowing us to observe their activities in the classroom and school, and with them we share a concern with the educational process and the well-being of the children in their charge. However, certain ethical problems have to be faced here as in any scientific activity; in this case, the problem that in observing and attempting to develop explanations of social structural phenomena, the identities and motives of those whose activities constitute aspects of those social structures may appear to be impugned. To obviate personal identification the names of all persons and places are changed. We do not, however, fall back on the truism that knowledge is its own reward as a solution to this problem, nor, what is a facet of the same perspective, that it is up to the reader, given his own value commitments, to take or leave the work according to its perceived pragmatic utility to him. To our subjects we want to stress that a humanist concern for the child necessitates a greater awareness of the limits within which teacher autonomy can operate, and to pose the questions; 'What interests do schools serve, those of the parents and children, or those of the teachers and headmaster?' and 'What wider interests are served by the school?'; and, possibly more importantly, 'How do we conceptualize "interests" in social reality?'. Therefore instead of seeing the classrooms as a social system and as such insulated from wider structural processes, we suggest that the teacher who has developed an understanding of his location in the wider process may well be in a better position to understand where and how it is possible to alter that situation. The educator who is of necessity a moralist must preoccupy himself with the social and other preconditions for the achievement of his ideals. Rather than affirming a separation of politics and education, as is done within commonsense liberal assumptions, the authors assume all education to be in its implications a political process.

However, having made this clear, it is not assumed that to bring about change in the educational institutions it is a sufficient condition merely to spread the word to schoolteachers and change their minds. This is very probably a necessary condition but not a sufficient one. Just as we try to describe and explain social structural phenomena which constitute our critique of the often naive voluntarism and individualism of sociological phenomenology and shallow child centredness, so we argue for the need to develop theories which can inform the political actions by which egalitarian moral concerns can be realized.

This book is intended not simply for sociologists, but for all those who share an interest in education. The authors are aware that some of the language used, especially in chapters 1 and 2, where we are forced to deal with the concepts and perspectives developed by the theorists under scrutiny, is quite technical and thus may be rather daunting to those who are not familiar with sociology as a discipline. Such readers are advised to start at chapter 3. In this and subsequent chapters the theoretical problematics outlined in the first two chapters are gradually unfolded.

As to the origins of the work, it arose out of a project initiated and directed by Rachel Sharp and completed in collaboration with Anthony Green, who worked on the project from its inception in 1969, and Jacqueline Lewis, who spent the academic year 1970-1 assisting with the fieldwork (see the appendix on methodology, p. 231). We have outlined above the main themes which have informed the work and although Sharp and Green take joint responsibility for it, we feel that it is necessary to acknowledge the very real contribution made by Jacqueline Lewis and our colleagues and friends, for their critical support and encouragement. A special acknowledgment is due to the members of the Tuesday evening seminar; Grenville Wall, Roger Harris, Tony Cutler, Nat Saunders, John Ahier, Vic Sharp, and Peter Seaman for their critical comments on chapter 2, and for the no doubt manifold, but unrecognized influences they have had upon the formation of our ideas; to Noel and Jose Parry, Felicity Roos, Daphne Johnson, Felicity Phelps, Margot Streberny, Mike Flude, and Eileen Green for their reading of various drafts, and especially to Peter Seaman for his detailed and very helpful comments on the almost-finished product; to the students of the B.A. Sociology of Education course at Middlesex Polytechnic for their unwitting assistance in the development of certain themes; and perhaps most importantly, to the staff, parents, and pupils of Mapledene, without whose tolerance and forbearance we would have been unable to do this work.

1

Sociology and the classroom

The theoretical perspective in this study has developed against a background of what some might define as a paradigmatic crisis in the sociology of education. Kuhn (1962) defines a paradigmatic crisis within science as a situation when the prevailing consensus within the community of scientists begins to break down, when normal science is no longer capable of solving the sorts of problems which scientists consider important, when established conceptual frameworks and methodological procedures become the subject of critical scrutiny. Whilst Kuhn fails to provide an adequate account of the genesis of such a paradigmatic crisis, nevertheless his description of the phenomenon seems highly applicable to the present situation in the sociology of education.

The sociology of education has emerged as a sub-area of specialization in sociology, relatively unaffected by major controversies within its parent discipline. To some extent this is explicable in terms of the institutional framework within which the study of education proceeded. Developing in specialized university institutes and schools of education relatively isolated from established academic departments of history, philosophy and psychology and more recently sociology and economics, the study of education has tended to be preoccupied with the policy concerns of the practising educator and sometimes insulated from the wider theoretical controversies which go on within its contributory disciplines.

This trend has been reflected in the development of the sociology of education as an academic discipline, the problems of the specialization reflecting more the current preoccupations of the policy maker than the generic problems within mainstream sociology. To some extent this has been facilitated by the failure of mainstream sociologists to consider the study of education as of major sociological importance. Unlike their intellectual founding fathers, particularly Durkheim, modern sociologists have often relegated the study of education to a lower status area, not worthy of systematic study. As a result, the prevailing traditions in the sociology of education, structural functionalism on the one hand, and positivistic empiricism on the other, have not received the same sort of critical scrutiny that such perspectives have been exposed to within mainstream sociology.

The structural functionalist approach, using a holistic model of the social system, has tended to analyse educational structures and processes in terms of their contribution to basic system requirements. Major preoccupations have been the analysis of the role of education in socialization, social selection, role allocation, and social control seen from the systems perspective, and predicated on the maintenance of ongoing social equilibrium. As many critics have pointed out, such an approach frequently operates with an over-integrated view of society unduly emphasizing those aspects which are deemed to be the functional requirements of the social system. These accord with established interests in the social structure which may be in direct opposition to the interests of other groups in the system (Lockwood, 1964; Gouldner, 1959; Gouldner, 1971). Moreover a tendency to use an over-integrated view of structure may go hand in hand with an over-socialized concept of man. In this view man is conceived as an atomistic unit responding to reified system requirements. This dehumanizes and fails to give credence to the role of man as an active subject in the historical process (Wrong, 1961; Turner, 1962).

On the other hand, however, the empiricist tradition has engaged in a series of 'fact finding' and 'head counting' missions, producing a great deal of statistical information about, for example, differential class chances for educational attainment, but offering little by way of explicit theoretical or conceptual breakthroughs for interpreting such data. This tradition, where it is not guided by either an explicit or an implicit theory, reveals the inherent weaknesses of an inductive approach to theorization. However, many of these empiricist studies are guided by structural functionalism which influences the formulation of the problems to be studied and the areas within which solutions can be sought. An underlying value consensus is assumed and structural malintegration, whilst it is not ignored, is treated as a temporary, dis-equilibriating factor rather than as a central feature of a stratified society. Methodologically, this tradition tends to engage in positivistic 'fact finding' procedures with arbitrarily imposed categories for differentiating data. It fails to do justice to the complexity of social reality, which cannot be 'grasped' by merely reducing sociologically significant characteristics of men to their external and 'objective' indicators.

Against this background, however, a new perspective is emerging (Cicourel, 1973; Garfinkel, 1967; Filmer, 1972; Keddie, 1971; Esland, 1971; Young, 1971). It is difficult at the moment to give a 'name' to this new tradition since there are a number of strands and subcategories, variously called symbolic interactionism, phenomenological sociology or ethnomethodology, whose proponents would be anxious to argue for the distinctiveness of their perspective. Nevertheless, without wishing to engage in essentialist debates over nomenclature, what seems to be held in common by all of them are, first, their common heritage in German Idealism, developed in social science in the work of G.H. Mead, M. Weber and A. Schutz, and second, their substantive concern with the problem of subjective meaning as basic for an understanding of the social world. For the sake of brevity we will call the approach 'sociological' although recognizing that we run the risk of over-generalizing.

The present authors are, however, critical of this new perspective which, they suspect, may be developing as a new orthodoxy within the sociology of education. This orthodoxy is premised upon an uncritical acceptance of certain idealist assumptions about the nature of man and society which they regard as misleading.

It is proposed, in this chapter, to illustrate the present state of paradigmatic uncertainty within the sociology of education by critically analysing various approaches which have been taken towards a particular substantive area of study relevant to the authors' own main interests; the area of classroom interaction. In this chapter, whilst attempting to give some brief overview, we will trace the development of what, we have suggested, may well be emerging as the new dominant perspective. In the following chapter we will proceed to make some broader observations on these idealist tendencies within the discipline and, in so doing, explain our own perspective.

The literature which relates to our interests in both sociology and social psychology is immense and wide ranging in its substantive concerns although quite narrow in its theoretical and methodological pre-occupations. The substantive issue in which we are primarily interested concerns the relationship between the construction of pupil identities and the practice of the teacher within the context of social structure in the classroom, school and the wider society. Much of the research which relates to these issues is social-psychological rather than sociological. Without becoming involved in boundary disputes in this area of the 'knowledge industry' of education or claiming to offer an exhaustive overview, we wish, nevertheless, in this brief appraisal of some examples of work in this field to highlight the limitations of such approaches.

An important feature of the relevant literature illustrating the general tendency in educational theory mentioned previously is its explicit or implicit problem of policy orientation (Seeley, 1966) particularly with respect to the 'good teacher' and the 'good classroom' situation. Frequently this work is set within a structural functional model (Parsons, 1959; Getzels and Thelen, 1960; Dreeben, 1967; Young and Beardsley, 1968), at the intra and extra classroom levels; such a model largely takes for granted and contributes towards the dominant institutional arrangements of education and underplays the possible structural determinants of these processes.

Moreover, the dominant epistemological stance revealed in the American literature and in the growing British work on classroom interaction is that of positivism and empiricism. These themes can be found, for example, in all the most important textbooks or readers in both America and Britain which claim to provide an overview of the substantive area (Gage, 1963, 1968; Morrison and McIntyre, 1972; Yee, 1971). These views are especially illustrated in texts where methodological innovations such as the use of video tapes for collecting data are advocated or used (Adams and Biddle, 1970). The main problem of these researchers appears to be the accurate recording of 'facts' rather than the prior issue of clarifying the conceptual schemes operating behind the collection and recording of these 'facts'. Although improvements in the technology of classroom research are of central importance, it is accepted by us as axiomatic that what is crucial to the knowledge so produced and eventually fed back into the common sense of educational practitioners is the way these 'facts' are ordered and interpreted. Thus the theme of this chapter is not so much to chart the accomplishments of the available research showing just what substantive issues have been researched (e.g. Withall, 1960; Boocock, 1966) and illustrating the appropriate variables, but to look at the conceptual frameworks within which these 'findings' are generated. With this in mind, there follows a brief review of some major stances taken to social interaction in the social structuring of the classroom and the school.

Getzels and Thelen (1960) present an almost classically Parsonian perspective on classroom interaction illustrating the dominance of the structural-functionalist tradition in the sociology of education. Thus

> within this framework, then, the class may be conceived as a social system with characteristic institutions, roles and expectations of behaviour. The class as a social system is related to the school as a social system, which in turn is related to the community as a social system and so on. Ideally, the goal behaviours of one system are 'geared into' the goal behaviours of the other related social systems.[1] Within the class itself, goal behaviour is achieved through the integration of institutions, the definition of goals and the setting of expectations for the performance of relevant tasks. In performing the role behaviours expected of him, the teacher 'teaches', in performing the role behaviours expected of him, the pupil 'learns'.

This is their setting of the 'sociological' or 'nomothetic' level of analysis; that is to say, social structure is a normative phenomenon, and sociology is firmly rooted in normative analysis. They contrast this level of analytic abstraction with the 'individual', that is to say with the 'psychological' or ideographic levels when examining any specific role performance. Thus it becomes necessary to look at both role expectations and need dispositions when attempting to understand the behaviour and interaction of 'specific role incumbents'.

This approach takes as its main concern the intersection of society and personality both as it is problematic for the explanation of social behaviour and as the focus where different levels of analysis need to be distinguished. It is unable to conceive of conflict and lack of integration as a consequence of social structural phenomena, of, for example, divergent interests generated between groups and individuals as they compete for scarce resources. Conflict arises merely as a result of a lack of integration between personality and the normative order, that is, malsocialization. Within this kind of approach society consists of a unified order, according to a dominant value system and it is inconceivable that major tensions, or indeed any tensions can be the result of anything other than personal recalcitrance against this dominant hegemony. Thus its view of socialization tends to be one of a passive actor being socialized into a consensual institutional framework rather than one which allows the actor to participate in his own conceptual construction of the world and his own fate as a project. This latter view is central to the interactionist approach to action and social structure which is often proposed as an alternative to structural functionalism (Blumer, 1962; Bolton, 1963) and which has greatly influenced social phenomenology. The latter will be considered in greater detail in the next chapter.

The behavioural image of man and social structures which is exemplified by much of the literature in the sociology of the school and classroom interaction is grounded in the positivistic projects of control and prediction. Here the social system is either seen as a 'pattern of stimuli' which schedule or trigger off the responses of organisms which have been socialized to react in given ways to certain given stimuli, or as a transcendent supra-individual system in equilibrium. In the Parsonian model there is a tendency to combine the two (Parsons, 1951). From the symbolic interactionist and social phenomenological perspective the critique of these positions centres on the view of human conduct as *behaviour*, i.e. as consisting as purely of responses to external environmental or internalized stimuli. Whilst accepting part of the thrust of this criticism and thus of the image of man implied, we would suggest questions also need to be posed regarding the equation of social structures with normative factors. Structural factors other than the merely symbolic may be features in interaction. It is crucial to consider the ways in which elements of the interactive situation may well not be acknowledged or understood by the actors involved but that such factors nevertheless structure the opportunities for action in ways which are more complex than has sometimes been thought.

When considering the generation of pupils' identities, for example, the pupil's opportunity structure for acquiring any particular identity relates not merely to the teacher's working conceptual categories in her or his consciousness, but also to facets of the structure of classroom organization which has to be understood in relationship to a range of extra-classroom as well as intra-classroom pressures which may be or may not be appreciated by the teacher or the pupils. It is important to attempt to understand classroom social structure as the product of both symbolic context *and* material circumstances. The latter factors tend to be underestimated both in structural functionalism and in social interactionism and social phenomenology. We will discuss this below.

Most work on classroom interaction takes on an empiricist position towards theory building, clearly illustrated in the opening remarks by Withall (1960) to a long review of the literature. Though apparently accepting Lewin's dictum of a need for theory—'there is nothing so practical as a good theory'—he proceeds to set this within the context of Jahoda's (1958) attitude to the concept 'mental health', namely, that a multiple criterion approach is needed to better understand, control and predict variables in these global phenomena . . . all encompassing and relatively meaningless concepts have to be broken down into manageable, discrete, describable operations of behaviour . . . this necessitates specifying, describing and quantifying the behaviours of teachers and learners under defined and described conditions.

Here we have, briefly presented, the whole gamut of a positivistic orientation rooted in a fundamental atheoretical empiricism.

However, not all classroom research has been atheoretical. The extensive body of research which stems from the original studies of Lewin, Lippet and White (1939) on the 'climate' or 'atmosphere' of social groups is certainly guided by a theory. Nevertheless, we question the adequacy of the guiding theoretical perspective for the empirical work which ensued. 'Climate' refers to the dominant attitudes prevailing in a pupil group towards their teacher and is generally conceptualized dichotomously as either democratic or authoritarian. However, the main orientation of the research problems has been that of assessing the extent and direction of learning, productivity and morale associated with these types of leadership and control. This type of research typifies the social engineering orientation of much positivistic research in American social science and though purporting to be concerned with group dynamics, it rests heavily on individualistic premises.[2] Moreover, the adoption of a concept of leadership grounded in personality and exchange theory (with its reductivist assumptions) does not go far enough in generating adequate theories to explain classroom phenomena and accounts in part for the inconclusiveness of these researches and the failure, in their own terms, to provide useful information for pedagogy (Anderson, 1959). It is doubtless true that in several ways the teacher is the classroom 'leader'. However, the empirical realization of this leadership in the classroom is not unproblematic but is influenced by features, both internal and external, which situate the leader's actions. Thus in the extra-classroom context account must be taken of the colleague vocabulary and rhetoric which constitute important aspects of the ideological concerns in the political structure of the school. As a sociological phenomenon, leadership at this level cannot merely be explained by the analysis of the leader's personality. The effective leader cannot be understood as a rational 'economic man' abstracted from his situation, choosing the technically most efficient means to achieve his desired goals. Rather, effective leadership must be analysed in terms of the total pattern of the material and ideological environment which socially structure, in this case, the teacher's opportunities to perform and to lead and selectively influence modes of classroom control. Thus rationality encompasses both aspects of individual choice and action, and aspects of the actor's situation. In the narrowly defined classroom context, the practices of the teacher are not merely a function of her personality. However 'democratic' she may be, as indicated by her response to questionnaires, or through recording the main aspects of her spoken control, or her descriptions of her classroom organization and teaching methods, it is possible to chart social structural features which have come to influence specific styles of leadership. These are historically generated not merely as a consequence of past social interaction in the classroom but in the wider patterning of social relationships in the social structure of which she is a part.

At both levels the social psychological basis of these researches gives rise to blind spots which a broader theoretical orientation might go some way towards illuminating. Thus much work in group dynamics on leadership overlooks the implication that it is concerned with power but ignore conflicts, as well as the generation and manifestation of power and its legitimating ideologies in the contexts studied. We do not overlook the fact that much of this work has shown that leadership is specific to context rather than merely to personality, and has thus moved somewhat away from the earlier personality or 'great man' approach. Nevertheless, in the work on teaching and classroom leadership this is seldom acknowledged, possibly because, given the age and obvious social inferiority of their clients, teachers seem to have overwhelming power. This has dulled sensitivity to the wider sociological basis of their power and the constraints upon it. These matters will be brought to the reader's attention in our own study.

This discussion leads us to the consideration of another and quite closely related body of research which will be briefly reviewed to illustrate some further issues in and weaknesses of research in this area: Kounin's work (1958, 1961a, 1961b, 1970) on the 'ripple effect'. The general intention of this programme of research was to delineate what it is that teachers do that makes a difference to children's behaviour. Whilst the social climate studies attend to classroom culture and so are oriented in some respects to ideological features of these situations, the work under discussion tends to remain relatively behaviourist. Attempts are made to relate objective variables such as teachers' 'desist techniques' to children's behaviour as 'effects'. These are posited as relations of cause and effect. The sophisticated concept of 'ripple' refers to the phenomenon of the teacher's influence being related to pupils other than the particular one she is addressing or attempting to control. In a sense this is an advance on the notion of 'climate' in that it involves a measure of dynamism and clearly implies consequences which are not intended by the primary actor on whom the research focuses as a causal variable, the teacher. However, it is the 'empiricist', 'scientific' perspective and its consequences which are the main object of our critical concern. This perspective involves an ideological commitment to the cumulative and progressive notion of science which, we suggest, in the case of social science becomes the enumerating and compounding of the 'findings' and failures of common sense. These are generated by the method of correlating variables which are thought 'significant' to the problem. What occurs is a piling up of 'findings' rather than an accumulation of knowledge which might benefit from alternative premises. Criticism from within these approaches tends to be on methodological rather than conceptual or theoretical grounds. Issues of sampling and observation oriented to improving methods of acquiring and processing the 'facts' are the main concern. Our central point is that the programme of researches carried out by Kounin and his colleagues show few examples of *theoretical* displacement or disconfirmation.

Thus their work to date (1970) can be summed up briefly. From the initial discovery that there was a ripple effect in kindergarten classrooms and the later observation that these did not occur in the adult-child relationships at summer camps, they write:

> These findings taught us that studies of adult-child relations, of which discipline is one facet, cannot be separated from the milieux in which they occur and the major roles of central adults in their milieux. . . . In contrast, (with findings in simulated and real classrooms) interviews with high school students about their actual classrooms showed that qualities of desist techniques did not relate to ripple effects. Ripple effects were related to students' degree of motivation to learn the subject being taught and their liking for the teacher (p.142).

As a theoretical breakthrough this amounts to saying that the observed behaviour of discipline and its effects need to be seen in the context of the meanings and motivations of the actors in the situation.

This does little more than account for the behaviour by adding plausible 'commonsense' interpretations. What it omits is any attempt to provide an account of these milieux in terms of their different historical generation and of the different types of political relationships found in these milieux between adult and child. If the meanings and motivations of actors in different situations vary then this is a problem to be explained. It is necessary to relate explanations of social meanings to wider societal parameters. There is a sense in which this type of study illustrates one of the key weaknesses of much work done on classrooms. Whilst it may be useful from an analytical point of view to differentiate different levels of analysis—the classroom from the school, the school from the community and so on—it is important to avoid reifying this analytical distinction and treating the different levels of analysis as theoretically distinct. The social processes which occur within classrooms, whilst they may not merely reproduce mechanically wider societal processes, are certainly not autonomous from them.

A methodological innovation in Kounin's programme of work did lead, for them, to the possibility of theoretical advance. When they used 'ecological', naturalistic, observational techniques, i.e. adopted video-taping, they found that the earlier discovered effects disappeared. There was no relationship between 'desist techniques' and 'children's reactions', in terms of reactions to 'specific desists', or to the overall amount of deviancy and 'deviancy contagion' present in the classroom. While Kounin asserts 'that this latter learning involved unlearning on my part', in the sense of having to replace the original questions by other questions, his rejection of 'disciplining techniques', in favour of 'classroom management in general', adding the variables of 'work involvement' to that of 'deviancy', represented very little by way of conceptual, theoretical or methodological reformulation. The problem for them still remained one of correlating the teacher's action with children's behaviour, taken at the surface level of 'overt signs of involvement and deviancy'. Again we have static empiricist social psychology masquerading as a theoretical advance.

Finally we will mention the more sociological approaches to aspects of classroom social structure relating to labelling and the notion of the self-fulfilling prophecy as a feature of the organization of pupil identities. The main theoretical premise, rooted in symbolic interaction theory, locates the teacher as the central organizing actor in the classroom, as in many of the works previously cited, in particular that her expectations have real consequences. This was demonstrated, though not without major problems of interpretation,[3] by Rosenthal and Jacobson's (1968) experimental study which aimed to show that if teachers were led to expect certain pupils to improve in their school work relative to their previous performances, then the children would show improvements despite there being no objective grounds for this expectation, as indicated by an IQ measure. Though to some extent the experiment was a 'success' in these terms, it is unfortunate first, that the authors were unable to show how the improvements had occurred because they had no ongoing observational data; and, second, that from their own theoretical position the finding is anomalous in that at the end of the study the teachers were unable to remember which children were expected to improve, unless one accepts entirely their mechanism of unconscious effects.

The study by Rist (1970) presents an indication of some of the features of classroom management which are implied but not investigated by Rosenthal and Jacobson. Here the material ecology of the classroom rests upon and generates stratification as infant schoolchildren sit at tables which are hierarchically evaluated by the teacher. There is a move by Rist away from the simple social psychology which rests upon personality theory. He shows the way in which, at least to some extent, the social identities of the pupils are defined by the material and social conditions of the classroom and the activities of the teacher. We see the need to expand this type of work in situating and differentiating the idea and structure of self-fulfilment. The implication of this point will be explored in the accounts of our substantive research.

Recently, the sociology of education in Britain has received a stimulus from various 'phenomenological' approaches. Probably the most useful starting point at which to locate the initiation of these developments is with the Manchester studies. Hargreaves and Lacey were particularly concerned to develop studies which went beyond what had emerged as the mainstream of the sociology of education at that time. They noticed, along with others, that the neo-positivist, Fabian perspective which charted the structured inequality built into the educational system, and which linked it with the wider class structure, enabled little to be said of the intra-school processes. These processes mediate the link between education and society but are explained autonomously, that is, from within the school itself. The researchers, therefore, undertook case studies drawing inspiration from American organization theory, and theories of labelling and subcultural (youth cultural) formations.

Their works, particularly that of Hargreaves, were well received at the time and set the stage for more recent 'new directions' in the sociology of education, in the work of M.F.D. Young (1971) and, of special concern to us, that of Esland and Keddie. The latter, along with various other closely related writers and researchers, claim a basis for their theoretical and methodological concerns in the phenomenological sociology of Alfred Schutz. Although they would cite differences between themselves and the earlier symbolic interactionist orientation of Hargreaves and Lacey, it would seem that they have much in common and that all owe a debt to the synthesis made by Berger and Luckmann. The idealist interest in the social construction of reality in consciousness is the critical linking factor, and is also evident in Hargreaves's later work, particularly *Interpersonal Relations and Education* (1972). Here it will be useful to pick up the theme of the self-fulfilling prophecy once more.

The general issue we wish to raise is about their treatment of the self-fulfilling prophecy. It is that the most important condition of its existence appears to lie in the reified and reifying consciousness of those who, like teachers, possess power (although exactly what the latter entails is rarely made explicit). This means that the processes whereby prophecies are fulfilled tend not to be investigated, nor indeed are the conditions for the generation of such prophecies greatly elucidated beyond such ideas as that it is 'economical' for people like teachers to stick to the categories of pupils once they have generated them (Lacey, 1970). Hargreaves notes that there are two conditions for the fulfilment of prophecies: either (1) the teacher alters his behaviour towards the child or (2) the teacher communicates his expectations to the child, which the child then adopts and acts out as part of his identity. However, a close scrutiny of Hargreaves's accounts reveals that his central tendency is to explore the latter process, despite his noting with Nietzsche the implicit criticisms of idealism that 'success is the greatest liar'.

Along with this goes Hargreaves's main practical and, crucially, moral invocation for the teacher to 'avoid premature categorization'. Our main line of critical attention does not deny that the interaction process in which actors generate mutual identities, in which reality definers are able to impose their definition upon others, is important. Rather it stresses that by operating purely at this level of analysis the orientation is too narrow to generate sociological accounts of the social structure of the classroom, because it has to assume, rather than make problematic, the power of reality definers or, even more narrowly, ignore it and assume that interaction occurs on a basis of democratic negotiation between interested parties who are political equals.

In the work of Esland and Keddie reification is a critical issue. As is implicit in the approach of Hargreaves's sociological phenomenology, social organizations are viewed as the achievement (accomplishments) of their members in interaction with each other. Reification occurs, for them, at two levels. First, it is the crystallization and objectivation of expectations within a community of interactors, i.e. the routine, taken-for-granted world they mutually inhabit as an epistemic community. Second, reification is the illegitimate (to them) phenomenon of crystallized typifications of pupils held by teachers. Keddie recognizes and illustrates the different categories of pupil (A stream, C stream and Bs ambiguous in between) and attempts to analyse the discrepancies between the professional context of staffroom commitments and the classroom context of pedagogic styles. She does not, however, offer a very clear explanation of the origins of these two contexts. For instance, in the Educationalist Context, what are the bases of the range of ideology to which the teacher would give verbal support? In the Teacher Context, what is the basis of the C stream teacher's opportunity to operate within this perspective? To what extent are her findings related to the wider societal context? Is it possible to conceive of the teacher, faced with material problems of classroom management, operating radically differently? By setting the problem up as merely one of inconsistencies between different levels of conscious perspective the analysis can offer little more from within these theoretical boundaries than an appeal for consciousness reform within the circumscribing structure of limited material possibilities for action.

In the study which follows we hope to illustrate an alternative approach to reification. We will suggest that there is more to reification than merely explaining it by reference to the content of social actors' perspectives. We will explore the apparent paradox that whilst the infant teacher has a fairly clear awareness of the problem of the self-fulfilling prophecy—'It's always dangerous to give a dog a bad name'—nevertheless, in her substantive practice some children are reified as being 'really thick', 'really bright', 'really peculiar'. The sociological question is not merely to describe such instances and illustrate the inconsistencies in the teacher's view of her role (Educationalist v. Teacher Contexts) but to ask at the level of teacher consciousness: 'To what problems are these viable solutions for the teacher?' This approach will then lead to a systematic attempt to socially situate the classroom and intra-classroom processes within the wider structure of social relationships.

In conclusion, we are not suggesting a return to the naivety of much of the work done in the 1950s and 1960s on social class and educational opportunity, which, to some extent, the more recent work has exposed. On the other hand, we are unable to accept the theoretical and methodological assumptions which recent British approaches have adopted. Whilst we may be sympathetic to their desire to escape from what they see as the anti-humanism (Young, 1970) of a structuralist and materialist approach, by focusing their attention on the consciousness of social actors they have narrowed the scope of sociological enquiry to a point where the kinds of explanations they can offer for social processes are found seriously wanting. Nevertheless, given the growing popularity of their approach to social processes not merely in the sociology of education but in sociology generally, it seems appropriate to consider in greater detail some of the strengths and obvious weaknesses of social phenomenology.

In so doing it will be possible to articulate the theoretical perspective which we have adopted in our substantive work. It is to this that we now turn.

2
Theoretical considerations

In chapter 1 it was suggested that sociological phenomenology[1] is rapidly emerging from the present crisis in the sociology of education as the new orthodoxy.

Whilst not wishing to deny that this perspective has been responsible for many fruitful insights both in resuscitating debates which are of fundamental significance to the social scientist—structure and consciousness, holism and individualism, causality and meaning—and in the critique of established research procedures, the authors share many reservations about the claims being advanced that this 'new tradition' provides a completely adequate basis on which to build an understanding of the social world. In particular, they are concerned lest premature commitment to the new perspective should obscure the very important issues which need to be discussed.[2]

The approach which will be advocated in this study requires an awareness of the crucial issues involved without advocating premature commitment to either side of the debate. However, the authors take the view that many of these issues are by no means new but have long preoccupied social scientists and philosophers, and that in many cases it is not possible, given existing social metaphysics and ontologies, to overcome the inevitable dualisms and polarities which characterize the terms in which the debates are articulated (Brodbeck, 1958; Braybrook, 1965; Emmet and MacIntyre, 1970; Natanson, 1963; Gardiner, 1959). Thus, whilst the authors will attempt to develop some of their reservations held against the search for meaning in social life not simply as a substantive area to study but as the source of explanations, they do not pretend to be suggesting a completely water-tight alternative which is logically closed and transcends all previous formulations. Rather the intention is, by clarifying some of the key problems, to suggest the directions in which intellectual and theoretical work ought to be moving and to illustrate some of their ideas in what is an essentially exploratory study.

In this chapter the intention is, first, to outline the theoretical dilemmas for which the concern with meaning in social life is seen to be a solution and to specify some of the key ideas which seem to be important in this perspective; second, to make some critical comments about the perspective in the light of its claim to be a theoretically adequate basis on which to build a new sociology and as a series of guiding principles for research; third, in the light of this discussion, the authors will attempt to spell out their own reformulated perspective which has informed their studies of teachers in classrooms.

The thrust of the main argument of the chapter depends upon the view that phenomenological sociology is primarily concerned with a social-psychological and not a sociological problematic. This is not to suggest that sociologists do not need a social psychology, or that, within its own terms, the phenomenological perspective compares unfavourably with alternative formulations, such as social behaviourism or Freudianism. The point is, rather, that although specialization at a particular level of analysis may be both desirable and inevitable, the different levels of analysis, the psychological and the sociological, should not be confused. Moreover metatheories and theories developed at different levels of analysis should be compatible and logically consistent with each other. Theorists working at their respective levels should also be able to articulate the points at which the various levels of analysis link up and interpenetrate.

Sociologists, unfortunately, frequently fail to articulate the basic psychological assumptions and theories on which their sociological formulations depend. Similarly, psychologists have often avoided explicating the social assumptions which their theories presuppose. In recent years Talcott Parsons is one of the few social theorists who has systemically tried to develop over-arching conceptual frameworks which enable him to link the different levels of analysis and explore the theoretical implications of the articulation of the sociological and the psychological (Parsons, 1951). However valid may be the criticisms of his particular formulations, at least one can applaud him for recognizing that a given change of direction in sociological theorization necessitated some modifications at the psychological level of theory building (Black, 1961b;

Scott, 1963). There are, however, far too many theorists within both sociology and psychology who, operating at one level of analysis, rely on certain assumptions about the nature of man or society which are either unexplicated or perhaps inconsistent with the main body of ideas being developed at the other level.[3]

Nor is the problem resolved by a systematic reduction of one level of reality to another. Some sociologists, for example, would see man as basically the player of socially prefabricated roles into which he is forced to fit. Little credence is given to the acting subject; human freedom and creativity is an illusion; the only ontological reality is society. The psychological problematic has been resolved through a systematic sociological reductivism[4] (Wrong, 1961). Similarly there are those who see social life as purely a screen on which private motivations and individualistic urges are projected. Thus, the methodological individualist would argue that all social life is ultimately explicable in terms of the actions, intentions and world views of individuals and the social has no ontological or epistemological significance (Homans, 1964; Watkins, 1959). In this formulation the social has been reduced to the psychological. It is, of course, interesting to speculate on the possibility of categorizing the actions or intentions, thoughts or whatever, without invoking a social context which alone gives them meaning (Wittgenstein, 1953; Winch, 1958).

Neither of these solutions is satisfactory. Both fail to take account of the problem of emergence, that societies reveal structures and processes which are not reducible to the simple sum of the actions of individuals looked at *qua* individuals (Durkheim, 1951) and that the social scientist has to begin to develop a perspective which enables him to develop the connection between macro sociological and historical processes on the one hand and individual biographies on the other[5] (Sartre, 1964). It is necessary to situate the individual in a social context, to be able to say something about that context in terms of its internal structure and dynamics, the opportunities it makes available and the constraints it imposes, and at the same time to grasp that essential individuality and uniqueness of man that evades any total categorization.

Such aims presuppose a preoccupation with some of the crucial central issues in the philosophy of the social sciences—those concerning holism and individualism, free will and determinism, causal analysis and understanding, subjectivity and objectivity. It has already been noted that a complete resolution to these dilemmas will not be forthcoming here. Indeed it is doubtful whether such resolutions could be forthcoming given the frequently incompatible ontological, metaphysical and epistemo-logical assumptions which the varying theoretical stances on these issues presuppose. Nevertheless a self-conscious awareness of these issues will sensitize the analyst to some important problems with which an adequate theory must come to terms.

One of the basic considerations which preoccupies the social theorist concerns the problem of the explanation of social regularities, the debate centring around, on the one hand, a view of social regularities as causal relationships and inter-connections, and, on the other, as logical relationships at the level of meaning (Winch, 1958; MacIntyre, 1962; Weber, 1949; Rickman, 1967). The former emphasizes the thing-like status of social reality. This does not necessarily imply that society has an ontological existence over and above individuals but that societies exhibit regularities like those in the material world, accessible to understanding and explanation through the same logical procedures as those in the natural sciences. Thus Durkheim advocates the treatment of social facts *as* things. On the other hand it is possible to view society as a network of human meanings, a 'texture of interrelated consciousnesses', the task of sociology being the interpretative understanding of this 'structure of intelligible human meanings'. This requires a methodology appropriate to its object and different from that necessitated by the structure of the physical world.

Now it may well be the case that these differing metatheoretical positions are fundamentally irreconcilable, that an integration between materialism and idealism, or explanations at the level of cause, and at the level of meaning is in principle impossible. However, even if this were the case, this has not prevented theorists from continuing to be preoccupied by these dilemmas and proffering so called 'solutions'.

Sociological phenomenology offers one such 'solution'. It seems, however, that far from overcoming these dualisms and dichotomies, its 'solution' lies firmly within the idealist tradition. The influence of major thinkers in the idealist school, Kant, Hegel, Husserl, Dilthey, Weber, Simmel and Mead, is clearly discernible in the modern proponents of phenomenological sociology. Their idealism may be illustrated by looking at some of their basic tenets and assumptions.

The sociological phenomenologist is opposed to any kind of mechanistic interpretation of human behaviour, rejecting all forms of determinism whether biological, psychological, social or cultural.[6] He operates with a creative view of man but stresses the importance of the social context of other actors in the development of mind, consciousness and the self. Man is a free and creative constructor of his own projects (Mead, 1934). The essential quality of man which frees him from the determinations of the material world is his ability to engage in symbolic communication, the significance of which is to be found in the process whereby men through symbolic communication learn to take the roles of the other, making indications to others and themselves, rendering their environment meaningful and a context for self-creativity. In these terms social structure is seen as a human, indeed, an intellectual construction, the result of the network of consciousnesses of people which acquire in their socialization a 'sense of social structure', and through their interpretative action in the social world reproduce it (Cicourel, 1970).

By consciousness, the phenomenologist does not refer to some entity, the contents of which are amenable to scientific investigation like objects in the physical world. Rather, consciousness refers to the relationship between the knowing subject and the object world around him (Edie, 1965). The contents of consciousness refer to the particular way in which reality 'out here' is constituted in the mind, which of the various stimuli coming from the external world the self will attend to, and how the external world is subjectively structured and organized or how, to use the ethnomethodologist's terms, 'negotiated reality is accomplished.'

Moreover, given the relationship of conscious social actors to each other, consciousness and the self are never fixed and static. Man is always, whenever he participates in social relationships, open to continual socialization, modifiability or transcendence. Society is 'an open horizon for man's ongoing self-realization'. Identity is never fixed, once and for all (Strauss, 1958; Rose, 1962; Berger, 1967). Because of the significance accorded to voluntarism, creativity and indeterminacy, human experience is always ultimately idiosyncratic and unique even though there may be some intelligible structure in the relationship between human actors, given shared elements in their social experience.

In this tradition we have a focus on the dialectical relationship between man and society. Society affects but does not determine human activity. Social action is not the mere mechanistic expression of social structure. Social structure is not a system of relationships over and above the individuals who compose it. Society is a process of creative interpretations by individuals who are engaged in a vast number of concerted interactions with each other. It is this which we label the social structure (Hiller, 1973).

Whatever the basis of interaction the knowing subject is forever in a dialectical relationship with himself in terms of the interaction of the I and the me, and with the social structure of interrelated interpreting consciousnesses. This fundamental tension between the self and others means that society should be seen as continually in process, a process which results from the stream of creative interchanges between conscious knowing subjects and the boundary conditions of their social and non social environments. Since institutional structures result from and are stabilized by the creative interpretations of social actors, they are open to continual transformation and change (Berger and Luckmann, 1967).

Clearly such an approach to social reality is very different from one which sees societies as embodying mechanistic or causal relationships. The stress which this perspective lays on the creative knowing subject and his ability through symbolic communication with others to create both himself and his world brings the individual right into the forefront of history and society. The rejection of mechanistic determinism makes the search for causal regularities either at the psychological level or at the social inappropriate. Moreover the perspective avoids any tendency to reify the social structure (Filmer et al., 1972). The message of the phenomenologist is that we must dereify society and see it in terms of interindividual transactions and accommodations. Sociology must proceed through the exploration and interpretation of human meanings for this is what constitutes society, a human and intellectual construction fashioned by consciousness in its intersubjectivity.

The task for the sociologist is therefore to provide an ongoing description of the flow of phenomena in the consciousnesses of social actors. It would involve attempting to explicate and elaborate the taken-for-granted features of everyday activity, teasing out the interpretive procedures and surface rules in everyday social practices (Garfinkel, 1967). It requires that we explore the way in which social actors define their situations, their subjective typifications of themselves and others and the rules which define how reality is subjectively constituted and experienced in interaction settings. Moreover a static analysis would be rejected in favour of a stance which enabled one to grasp the ongoing negotiated and processual character of reality definition as social action is accomplished and social actors generate adequate performances during the negotiation of their own status and role behaviour in situated settings (Cicourel, 1973; Becker et al., 1961).

The basic preoccupation of the sociological phenomenologist is thus with the subtle texture of meaning which constitutes social reality. The essential idealism of the perspective becomes apparent given the focus on the knowing subject's construction of the 'external world'. Indeed, the 'external social' world is a mere subjective construction of the 'constituting consciousness'.

Before making some critical comments about this perspective the authors want to emphasize that their stance towards social phenomenology does not rule out as unimportant the actors' definitions of the situation, the structure of typifications they employ to make sense of their experiences of the world. Sociological explanation of what people do must be framed in terms which include the actors' subjective point of view. Nor does it necessitate adopting a model of man which de-emphasizes intentionality, human purposes, goals, projects and so on. What is being rejected, however, is the view that focusing on levels of subjective meaning is all that the social scientist needs to do.

The social world is more than mere constellations of meaning (Gellner, 1956). Although we can accept that the knowing subject acts in the world on the basis of his understanding, that there is always a subjective factor which enters into knowledge of the world, it does not follow from this that the world possesses the character which the knowing subject bestows upon it, that the objects which we know in the social world are mere subjective creations capable of being differently constituted in an infinite variety of ways (Lichtman, 1970). The phenomenologist appears to be putting forward what we could argue is an extreme form of subjective idealism. Where the external objective world is merely a constitution of the creative consciousness, the subject-object dualism disappears in the triumph of the constituting subject (Hindess, 1972). In addition, any form of sociological phenomenology which argues for the primacy of the knowing subject necessarily invokes Wittgenstein's argument against an individualistic epistemology and the possibility of a private language. Such a position can only degenerate into scepticism or relativism since there are no means for distinguishing between things seeming to be the case to the actor and things *being* the case. We want to maintain such a distinction although we accept that the social world is meaningful to those who act therein. This does not mean, however, that we equate systems of meaning with the totality of social life or the meaning of action to the actor as the only meaning that can be given to the act.

There are, however, other tendencies within phenomenology as it has been applied to the social world (tendencies which could be called social Kantianism) which accept Wittgenstein's private language argument and his view of the meaning of action as constituted by the context of activity, but narrow the conceptualization of the context of action to merely cultural phenomena like language and normative rules. In our perspective, although language, normative systems and ideas are obviously constituents of the context of action, they are not synonymous with it. There may be other relevant aspects of the context of action which need to enter into sociological explanation.

Both forms of sociological phenomenology are far closer to philosophical idealism than Weber, who is often acknowledged as one of the intellectual forerunners of the movement. In spite of Weber's search for meaning, (even) he came to see social structures and their regularities as something other than mere constellations of meaning (Parsons, 1963). If we look, for example, at Weber's preoccupation with capitalism, although he was concerned to capture the weltanschauung of those who adhered to the protestant ethic, the importance of his contribution was that he saw the institutions of capitalism as both unintended consequences of the protestant mode of being in the world, and as a configuration which by the logic of its own functioning narrows the range of possibilities open to men, giving rise to a level of sociological problem which cannot be resolved merely by looking at how the individual defines the situation and how he acts therein.

We do not agree, therefore, that the starting point for sociological enquiry should necessarily be the subjective categories of social actors and that social scientific conceptions of social reality should merely be what Schutz describes as second order constructs, i.e., constructs of the constructs of the acting subject (Schutz, 1962b).

Our position depends heavily on the Marxian notion that the problem of how a society understands itself in the forms of social consciousness which are operative in the society and which permeate the consciousness of individual social actors, needs to be distinguished from how the society exists objectively (Marx and Engels, 1964). Simply to dwell on the surface structure of consciousness, as the phenomenologist seems to advocate, may mask the extent to which such consciousness may conceal and distort the underlying structure of relationships (Lukács, 1971; Godelier, 1972). In the same way that Marx was against starting his analyses of society and history at the level of consciousness but rather sought for the basic societal structures which regulate interindividual action, so we need to develop some conceptualization of the situations that individuals find themselves in, in terms of the structure of opportunities the situations make available to them and the kinds of constraints they impose.

The actors may be conscious of these constraints but need not necessarily be so. They may be subconsciously taken for granted, or unrecognized, but the situation will present them with contingencies which affect what they do irrespective of how they define it. Thus the social observer cannot necessarily base his understanding of the social world simply on the flow of consciousness of the actor. His view of the situation may be very different from the actor's, although both frames of references may be necessary components of a full explanation of the stream of events.

The position which we are advocating raises the (highly problematic) issue of the relationship between men's consciousness of their situation and the social reality in which they are embedded. We have noted how the phenomenologist makes the social structure an idealist construction, the creation of man's minds. Cicourel, for example, seems to equate men's 'sense of social structure' with the social structure itself (Cicourel, 1973). At the other extreme the mechanistic materialist sees ideas as mere mechanistic emanations from the base of materiality having no real autonomy from the social structural formations which give rise to them.[7] In rejecting both these extremes it is important to stress that none of the intermediary positions (put forward by such writers as Lukács, 1971; Korsch, 1970; Goldmann, 1969; Althusser, 1970; Godelier, 1972) has satisfactorily overcome metaphysical dualism in a way which leaves no room for ambiguity. Vague terms like 'ideas mediating reality', the 'dialectical interplay between consciousness and the world', or 'the coincidence between consciousness and reality' still leave many of the issues unanswered. Since there is as yet no satisfactory theory of ideology which clearly articulates the mediation of ideas and the social context in which they arise, it is important to avoid taking up a position which involves a premature resolution of as yet unresolvable theoretical dilemmas. Suffice it to say that an adequate theoretical perspective must be able to take into account human coherency and the creative power of individuals in acting in and transforming the world—and the relationship between conscious activity and objective reality (Goldmann, 1969).

One of the problems we are faced with, however, is that the debate about the relationship between 'consciousness' and 'reality' has been conducted at a highly abstract and philosophical level. We are suggesting that some insights might be gained by bringing the debate down from the formal level to substantive empirical reality. This is not to advocate an empiricist approach to the resolution of fundamental metatheoretical issues. Such an attitude would be absurd. Rather it is suggested that thought about particular empirical problems might help to clarify one's conceptualization of the philosophical problematics.[8] It is on this premise that our own work has proceeded.

One of the substantive issues in our own work, for instance, concerns the relationship between teachers' conscious perspectives and their situation.

The phenomenologist, however, although he stresses the social nature of mind has not developed an appropriate perspective within which he could investigate the relationships between man's social being and mind. Mind always seems to be treated as an independent variable. In the study of society, on the other hand, there is surely a wide range of problems which might necessitate treating mind as a dependent variable (Gellner, 1956). We want to be able to ask whether certain kinds of structural arrangements are conducive to the development of certain kinds of consciousness, whether the world view or systems of meaning of the acting subject are limited and shaped by the structural arrangements in which the individual is located. Now the phenomenologist would accept that there is a social distribution of knowledge, but we would argue that the problem is not simply whether the individual has been exposed to certain ways of typifying the environment in his epistemic community but would want to render problematic the relationship between the content of typifications and the context in which they emerge. If we do not have a framework which makes problematic the relationship between men's social being and the contents of their minds any congruence in mens' beliefs and typifications have to be treated as merely accidental or contingent (Brewster, 1966).[9] The phenomenological framework does not enable us to pose the question of why it is that certain stable institutionalized meanings emerge from practice rather than others or the extent to which the channelling of interpreted meanings is socially structured and related to other significant aspects of social structure.

Some tentative answers to such questions may depend upon an exploration of the relationship between knowledge and interests. Although Schutz was concerned to relate knowledge and interests his main preoccupation was with the subjective aspects of defining the situation where the actor's biography and present choices between his various interests jointly determine which elements of the situation are relevant to him. We would argue that Schutz's notion of interests is inadequate and seems to neglect the extent to which interests are socially structured around men's relationship to the material world (Habermas, 1972; Lockwood, 1964). We want to be able to explore the way in which the social construction of reality may be related to the social structuring of 'objective' reality. A notion of objective reality presupposes a very different answer to the question of how society is structured. We have already seen how the phenomenologist sees the structuring of society as

basically the result of the creative processes of interpretation of social
actors in interaction sequences. But for us, the social world is structured
not merely by language and meaning but by the modes and forces of
material production and the system of domination which is related in
some way to material reality and its control.[10] Indeed, we would want to
suggest that the intellectual construction of social reality, the structuring
of language and meaning is affected by the relationships of domination
and subordination in society (Dreitzel, 1970) and the differential location
and hence different interests of groups within the social structure
(Lockwood, 1956, 1964; Dahrendorf, 1958). The conscious active
interpretations and definitions of social actors take place within a context
of givens, psychological, social and material. It is for this reason that we
want to suggest that the relationship between ideas and the substratum of
reality should be treated as significant sociological problematic.

The sociologist should therefore go beyond the phenomenological
preoccupation with human meanings and the actions with which they are
logically connected. To stop there would be unnecessarily limiting and
not enable the analyst to evolve any movement beyond the purely
descriptive or illustrative level of enquiry.[11] We do not accept the
methodological individualist's position that the focus of study should
always be on the individual, his actions, intentions, projects, or that
social explanations should always be phrased in terms of some knowledge
acquired about individual phenomena. Although we accept the truism
that society consists of individuals, the methodological consequences of
such a truism are by no means trivial and necessitate taking up a
methodological stand in favour of holism (Gellner, 1956; Mandelbaum,
1955). The individual can only be understood in terms of his
embeddedness in a societal context, giving rise to a level of problem which
is emergent from and not reducible to our knowledge of individuals
(Lukes, 1968). Indeed, we would go further than this and suggest that the
individual may not always be important or even relevant in the course of
historical and social change.[12] The task of the social scientist therefore,
far from attempting some hermeneutic understanding of the individual
acting subject in all his idiosyncrasy and uniqueness should be to look
behind the level of immediacy in order to try to develop some sociology
of situations, their underlying structure and interconnections and the
constraints and contingencies they impose.

As Dray has argued (1967), if we accept what seems to be
Collingwood's (1954) approach to explanation in the social world, which
in many ways rests on similar assumptions to sociological phenomenology

then we are forced to the view that once we have related the action to the actor's intentions, world views and projects, then we have explained the action. But to postulate a logical connection between belief or meaning and action does not necessarily imply that we can explain what actually happened. We need to supplement our analyses of subjective meaning with some conception of the actual structure within which the individual is embedded (Gellner, 1962). Otherwise we risk the charge of complete relativism, of not being able to say why the historical individual perceived the situation in that way, whether he correctly perceived it or was mistaken, or alternatively why the outcome of the actor's behaviour may have been very different from what he intended. Sociologists in the past have frequently observed that some of the most interesting sociological problems emerge where there is no congruence between man's definition of the situation and his intentions, and the outcome of his actions (Merton, 1957). We need to explore these kinds of concrete cases if we are to fully grasp the complete texture of social life and the consequences it has for individual action.

In other words the observer must make a distinction between the meaning of the situation as it appears to the actor, and the meaning of the situation to the observer and the distinction will be in terms of the conceptual framework which the latter employs to render that situation comprehensible.

Without a careful analysis of the actor's situation and the kind of constraints on action imposed there may be a danger of overemphasizing or reifying a one-sided and partial view of man stressing 'freedom' and 'creativity' instead of seeing these as themselves social products of particular kinds of circumstances. The phenomenologist with his ahistorical categories may be guilty of just such a reification. He premises his empirical analysis on a philosophical view of man which stresses the active rather than the passive elements of human endeavour. Now although such a philosophical notion may be an essential prerequisite of doing any sociology at all, one must beware of translating a philosophical premise about man into a quasi-empirical proposition purporting to describe actual men in interaction everywhere. For the phenomenological sociologist mutual interaction among free creature social actions becomes the archetype of social interaction everywhere. Such an approach is very similar to and perhaps a constituent part of the liberal democratic approach to freedom and democracy. In liberal democratic theory, in spite of the affirmation of the value of the individual and the importance of his freedom, there is a failure to take account of the social constraints on freedom arising from the particular way in which society is organized.

Our perspective, on the other hand, would want to treat freedom, rationality and creativity as historical products.[13] We would not want to rule out of consideration those historical conditions where the dialectic between what Mead called the 'I' and 'me' disappears and men become reduced to 'me's', where for all practical purposes they are treated by others not as free and equal self-determining agents, but as things. This brings us to the weaknesses of the phenomenological account of reification and objectification (Brewster, 1966). Although the phenomenologist accepts that the world may sometimes be experienced by man as objectified and reified, as an external facticity bearing down on him with its constraining power, the implication of his position seems to be that this occurs as an essential by-product of man's participation in the social world but that dereification is possible simply through the processes of reconstruction of our thoughts which envolves the acting subject realizing the socially objectified world as essentially a human product (Berger and Luckmann, 1967).[14]

We would reject this view in favour of one which enquires into the social distribution of opportunities to be self-determining and creative and the conditions under which men begin to experience the social structure not as a field for self-realization but as objectified.[15] An adequate theoretical framework should aim to explain why in certain kinds of contexts there are limitations on men's freedom and creativity, and why the constraints of the given are so powerful; thus rendering the view of society as continually in process, open to reconstruction and continual modification, as an ideological illusion. Moreover there may well be social situations where, for whatever reason, the individual may find it very difficult to give a meaning to his situation or his actions at all, or where he is completely constrained to do things irrespective of how he defines the situation. Such situations must be just as much a part of the sociological problematic. It would seem that a view of man which emphasizes his ability to transcend his environment, and a view of society which sees it as nothing but the emanation of intersubjective processes has lost sight of the sociological phenomenom of externality and constraint. Society ceases to be the external force that can condition people's actions and guides not simply with its culture but with its apparatus of control.[16] Although determinism may be inappropriate as a generalized perspective this does not mean that social reality never affects the individual as if it were a mechanistic determining force, especially those at low levels of the social structure, far from the mechanisms of power and control.

We argue therefore that the correct perspective should enable one to ask the question 'Under what historical conditions can men break through the structure of determinations?' Such a perspective retains the model of man as active, with intentionality, while socially locating him within a context which may resist, block or distort his projects. To realize his values as an acting subject who seeks to control his situation, he faces the constraining effect of others in this situation, the institutionalized consequences of his and others' actions, the sanctions that can be used against him, and the conditions of his non-social environment. His beliefs about the situation may not necessarily be compatible with the structure of possibilities inherent in the facts. As Lukacs (1971, p.126) argued, 'In so far as the principle of praxis is the presumption for changing reality, it must be tailored to the concrete material substratum of action to have any effect or to impinge upon it to any effect.'

The phenomenologist, preoccupied with micro contexts, seeing social actors as men coming together with their differing realms of meaning, constructing together through a process of reinterpretation and negotiation a new intersubjective structure of meaning, seems only to be capable of 'grasping' a limited type of social encounter, that between free and equal partners in a truly 'liberal' society. This raises the question of the implicit value orientations and ideological biases of phenomenology when applied to the structure of the social world. Is there not a connection to be drawn between its one sided view of man, as free, self-realizing, co-operative, and the political world view of liberal democracy? Perhaps the phenomenologist has internalized the liberal democratic version of society as if it were a true description of how society is organized and how it holds together? He tends to accept as a given the basic macro structure of a modern industrial society, its socio-political and ideological features and then proceeds to concentrate only on micro levels of interaction, dyadic social interchanges between patient and doctor, teacher and pupil, deaf mothers and children, etc. The focus of attention is definitely the individual in face to face encounters (Dreitzel, 1970), and 'Society is dissolved into its settings'. What is lacking is any systematic attempt to conceptualize these encounters in terms of their context within the structure of society. And the macro-structure, in so far as it structures the distribution of resources and power, may materially affect the interactions of individuals at the micro-level, setting the objective limits and conditions to their experience. The phenomenologist, with his stress on mutuality and negotiation, may be performing an ideological function in the sense that the constraints of the structure, the oppressive face of social reality, may be masked. This links us with the point mentioned previously that the phenomenologist has a one sided theory of motivation and over-generalizes from an atypical condition of man which may only be found at certain levels of the social structure or in certain socio-historical circumstances. This one sidedness may be consequent upon his preoccupation with the problem of meaning to the neglect of man's relationship with the material world. In any case the structuring of social meanings in society may in itself be related to and a constituent of the social structuring of material reality. The significance of this point can be demonstrated if one looks at the way in which the phenomenologist treats the problem of negotiation[17] of meaning. What he seems to underplay is the extent to which the negotiation of meaning in social situations takes place within a context of material and other givens where certain things are non-negotiable. In many cases not all parties to interaction have equal power to define the terms of the debate, to define the parameters of 'acceptable social reality'. As Bachrach and Baratz have argued (1963), the very form of the debate, its questions and problematics and the procedures which determine their solution, may reflect the differential power of some to define reality for others. As P. Cohen has suggested,[18] the negotiability of meanings is an empirical question and may be closely tied in with the material conditions of men which circumscribe the field of their possibilities and their ability freely to negotiate an acceptable social reality.

In the same way we would want to take a critical stance towards the linking up of the phenomenon of common or joint actions with the issue of intersubjectivity of meanings. We want to question McKinney's notion of 'rational' action (McKinney, 1970), where he defines a rational action as action within an unquestioned and undetermined frame of typifications of the situation, 'rendering rational behaviour within an organizational context as dependent upon socialization into an existing knowledge at hand'. The thrust of this conception is to make meaningful and rational action occur only within a framework of shared culture or consensus. We would argue that joint actions may occur for a variety of reasons, duress, compromise, self-interest, inertia, as well as conformity with consensual definitions of the situation. It must not be assumed that all 'reality tests' are or need to be shared amongst the social actors who engage in face-to-face interaction for an ongoing social structure to be maintained. Social interaction may proceed intact, there being for each actor positive feedbacks, fulfilling the requirements of personal reality tests, without this implying communality at the level of meaning. What may appear to be rational co-operative activity may in fact be a situation of sustained mutual misunderstanding or deception. Alternatively there may be autonomy of meaning and behaviour generated as latent or unintended consequences of the common vocabulary available as distinct from the common meanings.

All these points require that we take a critical stance towards intersubjectivity and the surface structure of meaning and try to develop a framework which can look beyond the level of immediacy at the structure which lies behind it. This should not imply that we need only produce theories of 'objective' reality, but that we should see the 'objective' world 'out there' as on the one hand mediated by consciousness and, on the other hand, setting limits to the boundaries of objective possibility. Phenomenology with its failure to situate men and its idealist tendency to disembody mind deprives the student of society of some of the tools whereby a dialectical exploration of the relationship between structure and consciousness might be developed.

We now turn to the implications of these remarks for the theoretical orientation which we have taken to the empirical aspect of our work.

The perspective which we are advocating is one which attempts to situate teachers' world views and practices within the context of social and physical resources and constraints which they may or may not perceive, but which structure their situation and set limits to their freedom of action through the opportunities and facilities made available to them and the constraints and limitations imposed on them. However, although we want to emphasize the structural constraints of the larger system of social relationships in which the individual teacher is embedded it does not follow from this that what the teacher does in each and every instance is wholly determined by these objective relationships. This would denote a form of structural determinism which would reduce men's actions to stimulus-response chains. Our view of man is one which sets him as more than merely a responder to certain fixed stimuli in his environment proceeding on some mechanistic and determinate destiny but acting within a context which cannot be intended away by consciousness and which narrows the range of likely ensuing behaviour.

We would not want to accord absolute autonomy to consciousness for two reasons. First, in the case of teachers we want to argue that there will be an affinity (Weber, 1948) between consciousness and structure in the sense that given types of structure can only accommodate certain ranges of content for consciousness. For example, one would expect a stratified society to coexist with institutionalized forms of social consciousness which include a notion that there is a structured differentiation between men in terms perhaps of intelligence, desert, needs, etc. Second, we want to suggest that the objective possibilities of a given situation may render the social action of teachers very different from that which they intend.

The physical context of action, the structure of time and space resources available to the actor, has often been written off as trivial in the exploration of social structure but in our view is an important factor in the situation (Bennett and Bennett, 1970). We will take up this issue in connection with the analysis of classroom processes where the sheer numbers of children with whom the teachers have to deal, given the fact that scarce resources for distribution reside mainly in the teachers, present constraints on action and lead to consequences that the teachers may not recognize as primarily the result of the material conditions in which they are trying to function. We will take up this idea in relationship to Schutz's notion of a contemporary/consociate continuum when trying to explore the problem of children's career structures in the classroom. In Schutz's formal discussion he tends to underplay the material structuring or situating of this as an empirical phenomenon. While Schutz sees the contemporary/consociate continuum as related to remoteness in the subject's mind of the other social object, to us it is related more closely to the appropriateness of the knowledge of the other as an object to work with and upon in the context of immediate constraints, of which purely physical ones are no less important than the social. The sociological problem for understanding the actor's knowledge about another is found in the practical difficulties this other poses in this context, rather than in pure descriptions of the subject's consciousness. We are thus able to pose the sociological problem—rather than the purely social psychological question of the reification of the other's identity to the subject—and to see this problem as related to the subject's inability to apprehend satisfactorily, for his praxis, the other in his uniqueness and to motivate him accordingly. Thus the imposition of certain events and situations may well feed into the actor's system of relevancies. In the case of being confronted with other-social-actors-with-whom-we-have-to-deal, as a teacher is when she has to deal with children in a classroom, these 'others' may take on the constitution of being 'imposed' on the teacher because she cannot constitute them within her system of relevancies given the material structure of opportunities which the situation yields her for achieving some genuine degree of intersubjectivity with all her pupils.

Other significant aspects of resource and restraint which constitute the teacher's situation which can be more clearly seen as social, arise from the expectations of her by other actors in the situation such as other teachers, the headmaster, the wider structure of professional colleagues outside the school, the parents, local authority officials, or social workers, and so on.[19] Some of these expectations may well take the form of reified institutionalized expectations about teachers' behaviour in certain communally defined situations which are highly legitimated and/or taken for granted. Thus when looking at teachers' practices we will need to explore the structure of expectations regarding their activities, the ideological and social context in which they work and their own orientation to them. Yet although it may be possible to identify such institutionalized expectations, for the observer they pose problems regarding their generation, social transmission and whence they derive their power. In the context of this study it will not be possible to answer all of these questions. Nevertheless, we will need to look both at the normative structures embedded in consciousnesses and at the structure of material and political relations which generate the system of control which lie behind these institutionalized expectations—which can, if need arises, be brought to bear on those who challenge the rules. This structure of control may be perceived by the teacher but it may be unchallenged to the extent to which it is accepted as legitimate, taken-for-granted and presupposed and hence not necessarily problematic or pertinent to the actor's consciousness.

Our emphasis on seeing the actor's consciousness in terms of the actor's embeddedness in a context of social and physical resources and constraint results from the fact that resources, whether the material and physical power to coerce others or have access to facilities for the achievement of one's projects, together with the institutionalized power to direct, are unequally distributed in society generally and have implications for the analysis of social processes in the kinds of micro situations we have been investigating. Thus certain individual actors, or categories of actor in our study have wider discretionary power to act *vis-à-vis* others. This power may in some cases be direct, or more usually, mediated through institutionalized norms and rhetorics. This unequal distribution of power is significant both as a crucial variable in the explanation of the differential contents of consciousness and for understanding the outcomes of action.

For our approach, therefore, we have found it necessary constantly to broaden the perspective beyond the immediate situation to examine the parties' respective situations in a wider structural context, which differentially makes available structural supports and resources that each can bring to bear to support their activities, legitimate their projects and facilitate their actions.

The problem of power has been taken up by us in the study with respect to three main substantive issues. The first issue concerns the political structure of staff relationships in the school. Here the position of the headmaster as a reality definer in the situation will be explored in relationship to the perspectives and practices of the teachers. Of particular concern will be the extent to which, within the parameters of acceptable practice he defines, the three teachers differentially manage to negotiate some autonomy at the level of their classroom practice. We will, in this connection, make problematic the issue of intersubjectivity between the teachers over how the situation should be typified and explore the role of the child centred vocabulary not merely as a means of communicating common structures of typifications to the participants but also as a rhetorical (Spencer, 1970) and presentational (Goffman, 1959) symbol of commitment to the underlying structure of political relationships in the school. We will investigate the extent to which behavioural conformity is achieved by some through the fear of constraint rather than through internalized role expectations and an adherence to consensual meanings, whereas a level of behavioural autonomy is achieved by others through the use of the common vocabulary which may serve to gloss over possible differences in goals or orientations and conceal them from significant (i.e. powerful) others.

The second level at which power relationship will be investigated concerns the relationship between the teachers and their pupils and the role of the teacher in the social structuring of pupils' identities. Here we will see how the teachers' processing of the pupils is related to the structure of material and social constraints on the one hand and to the available 'knowledge' which dictates how the situation should be defined and how the teacher should act within it, on the other hand. We will attempt here to see how the phenomenon of stratification in the classroom and the concepts we develop to analyse it can be seen as the linkage between both aspects of consciousness and as an entry point into the analysis of the totality of the classroom situation and the wider structure of which it is a part. The power of the teacher to process pupils has to be linked with the objective structure of possibilities which the situation presents, leading to consequences which may be very different from what the teacher intends. We will also explore the extent to which the teacher's power is mediated by the particular roles which pupils play and the teacher's available knowledge to categorize them and manage them in a context which requires some maintenance of social order.

Finally, we will explore the interrelationships between teachers collectively and their clients, in this case the parents. We will want to look at the totality of the teachers' situation in the school, particularly the interests they cherish and the threats they feel themselves subject to. We will suggest connections between the ideology of the staff, the vocabulary of motives (Mills, 1963) and operational philosophies (Strauss, 1964), on the one hand, and the opposed interests as perceived by their clients, on the other. We will make problematic both the surface structure of the differential meaning systems which each group adheres to, and the underlying structure of their interrelationships which may be related to the differential distribution of power.

In all of these substantive issues the problem of power will be seen to be crucial. We need to see the actors in this situation not as free and equal participants engaged in the social interchange we call education, together negotiating and building up in an open context some mutually acceptable definition of reality, but in terms, frequently, of actors with varying degrees of power to define reality for others, not necessarily in terms which others accept as legitimate but which define for others the parameters of negotiability, and the conditions under which constraint will or will not be used.

Such a view goes beyond a definition of power as referring simply to the ability which some have to define reality for others (Keddie, 1971). What seems to be crucial is whether in the last analysis one can control others and bring sanctions to bear against others, irrespective of their definition of reality. And the ability to do this derives not from language, the system of symbolic meanings itself (Berger and Luckmann, 1967), but from the distribution of power and authority in the macro structure. The precise relationship between different forms of power is empirically problematic in any given situation. Although all forms of power may be sustained ultimately by force, at the lower level, empirically, in stable situations, far more subtle forms of power may be in evidence. Nevertheless it is ironic that idealist notions of power which reduce it to the ability to define reality for others, whilst they may be premised on an idea of human freedom in fact deny it completely. Human creativity and freedom necessitate a notion of force sustaining power such that when ideological legitimations are called into question the opponent's actions can be constrained irrespective of how he defines reality. As the existentialists have pointed out, man can be existentially free even when being forced by circumstances to march to his death!

Chapter 4
relate to text

Thus the ability of the headmaster to influence the actions of his teachers, the ability they have to process pupils, the ability of the teachers collectively to protect themselves against the felt threats of parents, lie not merely in their linguistic and conceptual superiority but in their position in the power structure, which supports them. If they are linguistically and conceptually superior it is only because those who have power in the macro structure define it to be so and have given them available sanctions to reinforce their definition of reality against others. Power is thus not just the transfer of communications, information and symbols but also the force which lies behind those symbols. Such issues will again be related to the question of intersubjectivity and the use of the child centred vocabulary not to communicate intersubjective meanings but as devices to maintain social control.

This study does not claim to provide a comprehensive theory of the specific role of education in advanced capitalist formations. Nevertheless the examination of a particular substantive series of problems within a school has to be conducted within some wider conception of the social location of the educational system and the functions it performs for the wider structure of which it is a part. The authors are aware, however, that within the present state of theory such a conceptualization must necessarily be a crude one. It does not seem to follow, however, that there is no point in conducting a study of classrooms in advance of a water-tight metatheory since an understanding of lower level processes may contribute towards a better understanding of the social structure and the wider system of interconnections it embodies.

In our conclusion we will make some tentative suggestions as to the broader role which 'progressivism' may play in sustaining a particular set of social relationships in the context of an advanced industrial society where mass demand for education has outstripped the educational and occupational opportunities available. Whilst we are aware of the broader implications of the work, it should be stressed that the main focus of analysis is a particular school operating in a given social and material environment.

We go beyond and are thus critical of the teachers' constructs. Unlike the phenomenologist, we employ a concept of false consciousness and implicitly highlight in critical fashion the falsity, where it is substantively incorrect, and naivety, where it is superficial, of the actor's consciousness. We try to generate explanations of structures latent to the totality as they recognize it and thus go beyond phenomenological description which tends to be based squarely on the subject's here-and-now.

3

Mapledene Lane :
the school and its environment

Mapledene Lane was a Junior Mixed and Infants' school completed in the
late 1960s on a large new local authority housing estate. The inhabitants
of the estate had mainly lived in poor accommodation previously in
various parts of the city and had been allocated housing here through slum
clearance schemes or by virtue of their high priority on the council's lists.

The estate was considered large by local standards. It consisted of three
main types of accommodation: terraces of houses with garages and small
gardens round the edges of the scheme, several large four-storey blocks of
maisonettes and a number of high rise tower blocks containing one and
two bedroom flats. In the centre of the estate there were a few shops, a
church, public house, several supermarkets and a community centre
which provided a meeting place for an apparently thriving community
association, a playgroup and other activities.

The physical position of the estate accentuated a feeling of cultural and
social separation from its surrounding area. It was flanked on one
boundary by a large main road, and on the others by a canal, playing
fields, open scrub land and factories. On one side it was bordered by
terraces of mainly owner-occupied housing with long neat back gardens
which had high fences or roads separating them off from the estate
inhabitants. The inhabitants on the estate often spoke of their sense of
being isolated and cut off from the rest of the borough. They frequently
expressed the view that they were looked down upon and treated as if
'we're only from the estate so we can be pushed around' as one parent put
it. No local public transport went through the estate and the residents had
to walk quite a distance out of the estate to catch buses.

This sense of isolation is partially explicable by the fact that the type of housing which bordered the estate could be considered a typical suburban development of the late 1920s and 1930s and was different in terms of its social class composition from that of the estate. The inhabitants of Mapledene Estate were mainly working class with very few non-manual workers, whilst the surrounding areas seemed to be more lower middle class in composition.

Although we did not have access to any hard data on the social class composition of the estate, it was 'common knowledge' at the school that the parents were all working class. Nevertheless, a closer study of the estate would doubtless reveal a complex social structure and indeed both the teachers whom we talked to at the school and the inhabitants whom we met on the estate operated with fairly complex and differentiated typifications of the various categories of people who lived there. It is assumed, however, that such differentiation which occurred tended to be intra-class rather than inter-class, which renders the school particularly interesting given the frequently found preoccupation with somewhat crude comparisons between social classes rather than within them, when analyses of the social distribution of achievement are undertaken.

The school itself had been built some time after the first housing units had been completed and some of its first pupils had been reallocated from other schools in the surrounding area. When the school first started it was in temporary accommodation on the site of a nearby school, and when the new buildings were completed in 1968 the school 'proper' had started. It consisted of eight classes covering the full age range from five to eleven. The four bottom classes were vertically grouped, parallel classes containing five, six and seven year olds in each. The other four classes comprised one set of two parallel, vertically grouped classes containing the younger juniors with a few top infants, and two end-on older classes for the older age ranges. The school was 'bottom heavy' in the sense that there were proportionately far more children in the lower age ranges. This phenomenon reflected the fact that the typical occupants on the estate were young families with small children. Although we have no accurate information on the demographic structure of the community the evidence seems to suggest that it was an unbalanced community where the proportion of young married couples with children was unduly high. Such a situation was reflected in the fact that the school itself was about to be considerably enlarged and during the period of observation there was some discussion about the need for an additional primary school to cater for the needs of the estate. The possibility of an additional school on the estate was a salient issue among the staff of Mapledene Lane. Fears were sometimes expressed regarding the possible undesirable consequences of having an additional estate school which might compete for pupils and provoke dissension among the local inhabitants. The headmaster and staff of Mapledene had put forcibly to the local authority the view that if there were to be another school it should be an infants' school which could work in close co-operation with Mapledene rather than compete with it. The rationale behind such a view will perhaps become more apparent later in the text when the school's ideology and relationships with the local community are discussed at greater length.

Mapledene Lane itself was a single-storey modern building situated in the centre of the estate. Though not completely open plan it is perhaps architecturally typical of primary schools built in the late 1960s and its layout and design reflect the 'new' approaches to primary education which 'official' thinking in the Department of Education endorses. The classrooms were light and spacious, grouped in a nonsymmetrical way around a central area housing the assembly hall which was also equipped as a gymnasium. There was a separate dining area with the school kitchens alongside, a TV area, an inner court yard and a few wide corridors which also served as play spaces or quiet teaching areas. The classes did not give the impression of being closed off and isolated from each other. Many of them were interlinked and their large picture windows overlooked a paved terrace which separated them from other classrooms. The overall feeling the visitor experienced when he walked around the school was one of relaxed informality. The teachers and the pupils, although based in one classroom, were not confined there and as the headmaster informed us, the children were allowed to move freely according to their needs from one area to the next.

The school was well equipped with the materials and audio-visual equipment one might expect in a modern primary school; TV, tape recorders, sand and water trays, play equipment, pottery kilns, painting easels, display boards, musical and cooking equipment, and so on. The walls were generally covered with pictures, murals, collages, examples of children's writing, etc. The environment was bright and colourful giving an impression of busy activity. The staff had their own comfortably furnished staffroom with a sink and cooking equipment at one end, and their own cloakrooms. The headmaster had a separate office adjoining that of his secretary, next door to the staffroom. He did not confine himself to his own room, however. He was frequently to be seen walking round the school, talking to the teachers or joining them for coffee in the school breaks or lunchtimes.

There were eight teachers, all in their twenties. At the beginning of the observation period there were no men on the staff, besides the headmaster, but in the second term another man joined the staff, an experienced teacher from a school nearby. Several of the staff had been at the school since it started, the others arrived when the school was enlarged. The teacher turnover had been low by the average standards of the Education Division and the headmaster felt himself fortunate to have what he considered to be a very stable staff of above average enthusiasm, commitment and competence.

Besides the teaching staff there were also two welfare assistants, one of whom joined the school halfway through the research. These assistants, as well as making tea and coffee for the staff during break, performed a variety of functions. They would help the younger children dress before and after PE sessions and at the end of the day, take home children who had become ill and hear children read, particularly from the younger classes. One of the welfare assistants was specifically designated to supervise children who were engaged in play activities in the area outside the infant classrooms, and to help groups of children with needlework and various other handicrafts.

The headmaster had been teaching since the end of the last war and held a previous headship elsewhere. He was recruited to Mapledene to establish the school. He was well known among teachers in the neighbourhood and was regarded in the borough as somebody who was attempting to implement the 'new approach' to primary education in his school. During the research period he gave talks in the locality to teachers and others about various aspects of modern primary education and visited other schools to discuss educational matters and so on. Moreover Mapledene itself was regarded by others as something of a show piece. There were frequent visits to the school by various people with an interest in 'progressive' primary education from other schools and local colleges of education, and the headmaster seemed to enjoy expounding the school's 'approach' to these and other interested people.

Having briefly described the school, its context, its structure and personnel, it is necessary to make some general reference to the climate of educational opinion in which the school operated. We will take up some of these points in greater detail when we consider the headmaster's and the teachers' perspectives. For the moment, however, we wish to describe some important elements of the trend of educational thinking as a background against which to analyse certain important social processes in greater detail.

Bernstein and Davies (1969) have shown in their sociological review of the Plowden Report that the 'progressive', 'child centred' approach has become something of a 'semi-official ideology'. Howdle (1968) has traced the development of this approach in British education concentrating particularly on the Froebelian and Montessorian strands, whilst Blyth (1965) gives an account of the introduction of the 'developmental' tradition into British education and its interplay with the older 'elementary' and 'preparatory' traditions.

The general features of the philosophy of the developmental tradition have sometimes been traced back to Plato, but more usually it is educational theorists and practitioners like Rousseau, Froebel, Montessori, Pestalozzi, Dewey and others who are regarded as the fathers of what Entwistle calls the 'child centred' approach. Whilst there may be significant differences in orientation between such writers, there seems to be a nucleus of ideas upon which all would agree which relate to the view that the child should be allowed to develop his own inner potential rather than have ideas and techniques from the adult world imposed upon him, thus denying the child's own integrity and inner being. Rather than focusing attention upon the preparation of the child for adult life, treating the child as nothing but an adult in the making, or allowing the child only the minimal necessary education in terms of the skills required for adult functioning, the child centred approach aims, by treating the child as a unique subject with its own needs and interest, to extend to the child as large a measure of autonomy as is consistent with a liberal democratic view of society.

This philosophical tradition, though it has received few contributions from British philosophers, has informed various 'experiments' in the education of young children in this country. Whilst the work of people like J.H. Bradley at Bedales, E.B. Castle at Leighton Park Quaker School, A.S. Neill at Summerhill and Kurt Hahn at Gordonstoun are well publicized, there is a long tradition of lesser known examples which make up what is sometimes known as the Progressive School Movement. Whilst many of these experiments took place outside the state system, some of the key ideas have filtered through into the state system and form a background to official reports and legislation in this century with the endorsement of 'progressive' thinking in government reports on the primary school in 1931 (HMSO, 1931) and the Plowden Report (HMSO, 1967).

This approach is also endorsed in the present training of primary school teachers as W. Taylor has illustrated in his book *Society and the*

Education of Teachers. Taylor has traced the values underlying teacher education. He notes the diffuse nature of the teacher's role and links this with the child centred approach whereby the teacher assumes 'responsibility for the socialization of the child rather than simply his instruction'. He quotes evidence which seems to suggest that British trainee teachers[1] are more 'child centred' than their American counterparts and refers to the anti-intellectual stance of teacher training where emphasis is placed upon the expressive rather than the rational intellectual aspects of teacher-pupil interaction.

It might be useful at this stage to elaborate a bit further on some of the themes which seem to constitute the 'progressive child centred' approach to primary education. These themes are sketched out in ideal typical terms without trying to suggest that there will not be a high level of variation and subtle differentiations between teachers and educators who in general terms would subscribe to this tradition.

To some extent this 'enlightenment' can indeed be seen as a reaction against the excessively didactic authoritarian approach in, for example, the 'payment by results' era. We have suggested that the new focus of attention is epitomized in the 'progressive's' claim to being 'child-centred' as an expression of the concern for the 'whole' child. It is no longer a case of children being rigorously drilled, of inculcating 'facts' regarded as sacrosanct, but of schooling being adapted to the requirements of the child. The child is no longer regarded as an 'empty vessel' to be filled by the teacher, but to a large extent as an arbiter of his own education. He is allowed to follow his own interests; in exercising his right to 'choose' he acquires self-control and responsibility.

In order to develop the child's potential to the full it is, therefore, considered essential that his schooling be made relevant, and that this can only be achieved by removing 'artificial' disciplinary barriers (e.g. 'knowledge does not fall into separate compartments'–Plowden), thereby allowing the child to pursue whichever aspect of the situation appeals to him. The curriculum is thus based on 'problem solving' rather than subject areas. The child is presented with a challenging and stimulating environment and encouraged to find out for himself without waiting to be told the answer. In short, learning by doing.

For, 'Proficiency in learning comes not from reading and listening but from action, from doing and experiencing' (J. Dewey); as 'When they learn in their own way and for their own reasons, children learn so much more rapidly and effectively than we could possibly teach them' (J. Holt); because 'Knowledge which is acquired under compulsion obtains no hold in the mind . . . then do not use compulsion but let early education be a sort of amusement' (Plato).

The aim then, is to allow the child free expression in order to foster what is individual in each human being. For, 'the purpose of teaching is to bring ever more out of man rather than put more into him' (F. Froebel). The emphasis is on emotional as much as intellectual development:

the subject matter became now rather the ostensible occasion of an educational activity deeper and richer than itself: and insistence upon facts, and upon rote learning, retired before the demand that what mattered most was the development of appropriate knowledgeable behaviour in a social context, rather than the equipping of persons with knowledge for possible future use (L.R. Perry).

Central[2] to progressive child centred philosophy are the concepts of 'readiness', 'choice', 'needs', 'play' and 'discovery'.

Briefly, it is believed that given an invigorating setting, when the child is 'ready', he will 'choose' what it is that he 'needs'. This selection is believed to be facilitated through 'play' which sets in train the 'discovery', or learning processes.

The essential point is that the child must be 'ready'—emotionally and socially well adjusted before he is considered cognitively receptive:

There can be no more question of teaching them 'how' to read, write or do sums before they have made their own efforts through spontaneous activity, than there can be of teaching babies to walk before they have made attempts to stand and crawl (E.R. Boyce).

This is an emphasis which finds psychological substantiation in Piaget's work on the stages of children's conceptual growth, although Plowden concedes that Piaget is not 'primarily an educationalist' and that his 'thought which influenced the 1931 Report and our own, is not easy to understand'.

Furthermore, it is considered that 'play' not only facilitates the desired social/emotional adjustment when children share and co-operate in their games, but is also a means of making education 'relevant' to children. For instance, the manipulation and control of construction toys, Lego, building bricks, etc., is said to stimulate the development of concepts such as capacity and number: 'Wide ranging play and satisfactory play is a means of learning, a powerful stimulus to learning, and a way to free learning, from distortion by the emotions' (Plowden). Thus it is intended to make 'work' as much 'fun' or intrinsically satisfying as possible, so that the child will want to find out for himself why things are as they are. It is important that he himself initiate the 'discovery' process because, 'In Math(s) certainly, and very probably in all subjects, knowledge which is not genuinely discovered by children will very likely prove useless and will soon be forgotten' (J. Holt). However, it is stressed that the child is not expected to rediscover the extant body of knowledge by himself: 'We do not ask or expect a child to invent the wheel starting from scratch . . . . (nevertheless) a child does not need to be told what wheels are and what they are for in order to know. He can figure it out for himself, in his own way in his own good time' (J. Holt). It is apparent that much reliance is put on the child's discretion, his ability to choose without the 'need' to be *told* because 'it is not always possible for us to know what a child requires but he will take what he needs from what we offer and reject the rest' (L. Ridgeway, I. Lawton). The tacit assumption is that 'what we offer' will more than cover the child's (unknown) 'needs'.

The recommendation that the child be left free to choose is seen to be based, on the one hand, on a belief that he is able to make an informed choice to satisfy his particular 'needs', which leads to the suggestion that, 'we could well afford to throw out most of what we teach in school because the children throw it out anyway (hence) we can *afford* to throw away our curricula and our timetables' (J. Holt); and on the other an acknowledgment that the teacher is often ignorant of what the child 'requires'. Thus it would seem that the child is accorded greater percipience than the teacher. 'In short, the school should be a great smogasbrod of intellectual, artistic, creative and athletic activities, from which each child could take whatever he wanted and as much as he wanted, or as little' (J. Holt).

It is evident that the aim of progressive education at a structural level is to provide children with 'free' access to stimulating materials and experiences from which they may select as and when they require. This is said to be most easily achieved by operation of the 'integrated' (or 'free') day in a 'vertically' (or 'family') grouped class.

The integrated day is seen as the most appropriate framework for fostering intellectual and social integration. In Perry's terms:

the (child-centred) model acknowledged that experience was a continuum for the pupil, that is, that learning and development were going on all the time; this led to criticism of the older (traditional) models, rigid classroom and subject divisions and its neglect of the learning opportunities provided by other aspects of the school situation.

Thus it is believed that undue compartmentalization of knowledge is avoided by dispensing with set 'periods' for specific 'subjects', although there may be special areas allocated for different activities—a nature table, for instance. Consequently the syllabus and curriculum are extremely flexible, if they are employed at all, any number of activities being in progress at a given time. However, although 'in some jargon, this kind of situation is called instructive, (this) is misleading . . . because there is always a kind of structure to what is presented in a class' (Hawkins, in Holt, 1969).

Taking the 'River Thames' as a topic, the children can be encouraged, for example, to find out about its geological formation, its historical, geographical, agricultural, industrial significance, the biological life it supports, etc. Each child is free to follow up, often in the form of a project, what is of particular interest to him without being confined within a single disciplinary rubric. Moreover, children having the same interests are able to pursue them together since they are allowed to move from one activity, or class, to another at will.

Vertical grouping is recommended in preference to the horizontal class where children are categorized merely on the basis of age because it recognizes that children of the same chronological age may be at different stages of intellectual and emotional growth. Within a mixed age range, theoretically, it should be possible for each child to operate at his own 'level', to the benefit of advanced and slow alike who can 'be themselves and develop in the way and at the pace appropriate to them' (Plowden).

It is also felt that by providing more of a society in microcosm (or 'family') children will adapt to school life, learn to co-operate, and assist each other, more readily. The older children will 'mother' the younger, who will have before them the older children as exponents of the type of behaviour expected from a school child and upon whom they can model their own actions. Thus it is held to be especially important for reception classes to be vertically grouped, and also larger classes, where older children can help the teacher with younger ones.[3]

Without wishing to gloss over the complexity of the 'progressive, child centred approach', it is suggested that the following quotation from Plowden (p.187, para. 505) sums up the ethos of modern primary education quite well.

A school is not merely a teaching shop, it must transmit values and attitudes. It is a community in which children learn to live first and foremost as children and not as future adults. In family life children learn to live with people of all ages. The school sets out deliberately to derive the right environment for children, to allow them to be themselves and to develop in the way and at the pace appropriate to them. It tries to equalize opportunities and compensate for handicaps. It lays special stress upon individual discovery, on first hand experience and on opportunities for creative work. It insists that knowledge does not fall into neatly separate compartments and that work and play are not opposite but complementary.

The assumption is being made that these ideas constitute part of the context of ideas within which the school is operating. However, although they have received official endorsement in Plowden we recognize, as did the teachers at Mapledene, that they are only held by a 'progressive' minority.

There is also the notion of 'compensation' developing alongside the idea of child centredness. With the recognition that children from lower social strata tend to achieve less well than those from the upper levels of the hierarchy, recent educational thinking has begun to focus upon the need to compensate for the deprivations inherent in the lower social class environment which are thought to be 'responsible' for the lower class child's lower attainment. Official thinking is moving away from the idea that equality of opportunity can be achieved by merely presenting the child with formal opportunities; something must be done to alter the conditions which lead to the continuation of class disadvantages. This involves intervention through compensatory education programmes and other social policies. The Plowden Report endorses such a view with its advocacy of educational priority areas:

Although standards will rise, inequalities will persist and the potential of many children will never be realized. The range of achievements amongst English children is wide and the standards attained by the most and the least successful begin to diverge very early. Steps should be taken to improve the educational chances and attainments of the least well placed and to bring them up to the levels that prevail generally. This will call for a new distribution of educational resources (p.55, para. 146).

More recently the government's commitment to a nationwide system of preschool nursery education with priority of development in the 'problem' areas of large cities again reveals its acceptance of the necessity to compensate for cultural disadvantage.

These two notions, 'child centredness' and 'compensation', will be further explored as they are constituted in the structure of the teachers' perspectives and in their classroom practice. It is proposed now to consider in more detail the school ethos especially as this is expressed and articulated by the headmaster himself.

4

The school ethos

This chapter will be concerned with depicting the school ethos but to some the suggestion of a school ethos might involve undue reification. Nevertheless in our encounters with people who were not part of Mapledene Lane, i.e. social workers, officers from the local education authority, parents of the pupils, as well as other teachers who worked in the area, they all referred to the school as if it had a distinctive ethos. Certainly those teachers within the school itself were aware that the school had an identifiable ideology about its role and practices in relationship to its clients.

Nevertheless, philosophies are carried and articulated by individuals and although it would be inappropriate to identify the school ethos as synonymous with the perspective of the headmaster, that his views greatly influenced the practices of all the teachers could not be denied. He was the most powerful reality definer in the situation. It was rare for anyone publicly to question his views on educational matters and such controversies which did occur were generally over minor administrative matters or issues of interpretation rather than involving any radical critique of the underlying assumptions of his world view.

It is proposed, therefore, to summarize the substance of two interviews with Mr McIntosh, the headmaster, using extensive quotations from the transcripts, because it is felt that the views expressed in these interviews go some way to capture his perspective, although in a non-situated way, and provide a background against which the social processes within the school can be analysed.

However, the data found in these interviews do not speak for themselves. The use which can be made of the data depends upon the developing theoretical perspective which was emergent throughout the period of observation in the school. The data themselves reflect that perspective, in that the kinds of questions posed to the headmaster relate to the theoretical and substantive preoccupations of the researchers themselves. The headmaster's perspective portrayed in his own words has to be related to the social context in which he and the researchers were placed. In these interviews, which were conducted towards the end of the field work, he was 'in the hot seat'. That is to say, a definite interview situation had been arranged beforehand and he was aware that he was going to be cross examined about his general approach to education in Mapledene Lane. Nevertheless, the fact that the interviewer had interacted with him over the course of a school year and had frequently had the opportunity both to observe him in practice and to converse with him, provided some constraint on the situation which may be reflected in the data. This constraint operated in two major directions. In the first place, in both preliminary and follow-up questions the researcher's attempts to probe in a very open-ended way without pre-categorization, in order to allow the headmaster to speak for himself, were often thwarted because both the headmaster and the researcher had often talked about such issues before and, therefore, a naivety, adopted for methodological reasons, would have significantly affected rapport. Second, there were obvious pressures on the headmaster to present himself, in the interviews, in a way consistent with his perception of how he had previously presented himself to the observers. This may have affected the conduct of the interview and in his substantive discussion of the issues raised.

The data thus presented here do not purport to be complete and self-sufficient, to portray in some final form all the nuances of the headmaster's perspective, but merely to serve to illustrate elements of his views on a number of areas in which the researchers were interested. However it is inevitable that some distortion is involved by presenting the substance of these interviews to illustrate his perspective. The headmaster could only reply to questions which were put to him; he may well have had important views on issues which are relevant to the analysis but which he was never given an opportunity to speak on. However, had he done so, the analysis might have needed substantial modification. Such issues are involved in any approach to scientific theorization and are not peculiar to participant observation and qualitative research procedures in the social sciences alone.

Nevertheless, our integrity as researchers does require us to make explicit some of the preoccupations underlying the particular form of the questioning which took place, which centred around five major issues which are not separate but interlink at many stages. First, we wanted to explore how the headmaster characterized the school's functions and aims, and why he defined the school's role in the way he did. Second, in the light of the former, we wanted him to characterize the school's approach to pedagogical methods, and to see (a) how he would describe them (b) how he would differentiate them from other possible approaches and (c) how he would justify them in terms both of his aims and of his perception of the material which had to be processed. Third, we wished to get him to articulate how he characterized the clients—the pupils and their parents—both factually and evaluatively, and the actual and ideal relationships which could obtain between the school and its clients. Fourth, in the light of the preceding, we wanted him to explicate what he found problematic in the situation, to articulate what he saw as the specific difficulties and problems presented and the possibility of overcoming them. Finally, we wished to explore with him how he saw his own role as headmaster *vis-à-vis* other significant social actors in his role set; pupils, teachers, parents, social workers, etc.

From an analytical standpoint, however, the researchers were particularly interested in the extent to which his perspective revealed any logical inconsistencies, internal contradictions or ambiguities, not in order to depict a man confused, but because their developing analysis of the situation had suggested that given certain pressures on him some inner contradictions and ambiguities would be inevitable.

Mr McIntosh distinguishes his school from others more formally and traditionally organized for the

> 'care and concern shown to individual children' . . . the actual teaching
> techniques are based on this . . . we are here to look after the
> children—it's their welfare that concerns me and I'd put that as a
> priority. I don't see the prime aim of the school as a learning
> institution although I realize that I'm paid to do this . . . and I have
> an obligation to see that my children become literate and
> numerate . . . but I feel that the child himself, his well being and his
> welfare must be our first concern.'

This concern for the child as an individual has implications for pedagogy:

'Our aims will surely determine our methods . . . We are concerned, as a general principle, with trying to develop each child, and we would use mathematics or what could loosely be described as English, art and everything else, to do this . . . You see, the aim is trying to develop a child and help him to mature and become a person rather than that he should be a good user of adjectives or doer of long multiplication sums. That he should be confident and capable to take a role in society . . . To have his curiosity satisfied and so on.'

Mr McIntosh makes a clear distinction between the present needs of the child and some less clearly defined future needs:

'The methods probably tend to meet the needs, the current needs of children—whereas in schools more formally set up, more traditional in their outlook, the focus seems to be on some long term goal, like getting children through the 11+, or getting a good job . . . We tend to say—Dick needs . . . because we *know* about Dick, we've spoken to the health visitor and we know all about his background and so on . . . many schools wouldn't find it necessary to go into the children's background so deeply, and indeed some head teachers would say—what has that got to do with school?'

In this connection it is important to mention that the headmaster has institutionalized strong relationships with local social workers who are involved with families working on the estate in order that the school should be provided with as much information about the families as possible. Thus, as the headmaster explained, they are in a position to keep a special watch on those pupils whose family circumstances rendered them 'at risk'.

The approach to education is justified through developments in psychology:

'The work of Piaget has opened many people's eyes that the stage of childhood is a distinctive stage and children are uniquely children—they are not mini adults—their minds don't work in the adult way.

In addition, social change has brought new demands on the school. He claims that his views are based on:

'The awareness that educationalists have that we live in a rapidly changing society and that the skills, knowledge, facts, that were once considered an absolute must for every school boy, are now no longer to be considered so. We see a generation of youngsters growing up and taking jobs which they may have to change three or four times in their working lifetime, so what is it that schools need to be providing? They need to help children to be adaptable so that they can weather the changes when they come . . . I think we are trying to . . . more broadly base the curriculum . . . and that's what causes people a lot of misgivings . . . there's a departure from what we could call the sanctity of the 3 Rs . . . After all that is what school was about—now we see our role as teachers in a much wider way . . . We see education as much more broadly based.'

When asked which of the aspects of the school's programme he regarded as absolutely essential to the new approach, he responded thus:

'The vertically grouped classes are not essential—but we did it because I was very anxious to, I almost said force, the hand of the teachers, to ensure that it would be difficult to take the class as a class . . . Each child has got an individual learning pattern . . . I've tried to think of as many ways as I could of encouraging teachers to regard their children as individuals . . . So if you divide up the age groups and introduce vertical grouping then it is perfectly obvious that you can't do with a five year old what you can do with a seven year old . . . so it forces teachers to look at their seven year olds as a much smaller group—and indeed, as is happening around the school, as individuals. With regard to the integrated day, this is an absolute must and, indeed, if we did not have the integrated day we would not have the system. The integrated day serves to make children reasonably independent and self-reliant . . . The strongest principle of growth is freedom of choice . . . every time you choose you grow up a little bit . . . the antithesis . . . if you never make children make decisions then they become very, very, immature . . . and so we encourage children to make choices.'

This does not mean that the integrated day is synonymous with pupils choosing what they want to do all the time:

'The best teachers are aware of what their children are doing . . . if there is a need to divert the child from something then the best teachers do it . . . how they do it depends to a very large extent on the skill of the individual class teacher . . . but I wouldn't like anyone to think that we don't have some kind of structure . . . we are aware that children must learn to read if it is humanly possible . . . we are aware that they must acquire some mathematical concepts . . . and we try to force the issue by some teachers trying to arrange . . . this group will do this . . . this group will do that . . . but within that kind of situation there is room for the child who says . . . I want to write a story of how I went up my nan's, or I want to draw a picture of my uncle's caravan and that sort of thing . . . what goes on in the school tends to be not so much teacher dominated. Teachers aren't the fount of all knowledge—teachers aren't stacked up with facts and all that sort of thing—teachers are *instigators* of learning. They are organizers of children's environment so that children can learn.'

This approach to pedagogy presents problems for the teacher:

'The problems are immense . . . the hard part, I find, is being able to satisfy the needs of so many children . . . how can you satisfy 35-40 children often wanting that number of different things at much the same time . . . it's done by constantly encouraging children to do it by themselves . . . all the time you are trying to help the children to help themselves, rather like getting a trolley in a supermarket and going round.'

However, in this school,

'The difficulty with us is that we have too many children who are not wonderfully stable for one reason or another and it is these children who find this kind of thing rather difficult because many of them are crying out for more direction . . . "please tell us . . . you tell us, Miss, what you want to do and we will do it." But we've considered this in the staff room and we've come to the conclusion that, whilst we might be sympathetic here and sometimes pander to this . . . in the long term these are children who need our way . . . You organize the children so that they can see some kind of purpose here . . . you've got to let them see some end results and that it's not chaotic . . . You've got to try to ensure that they don't become like butterflies flitting from one thing to another and really you find this very markedly among the younger children . . . but as you go further up the school you find children sticking to things for much longer.'

The headmaster thinks it is a problem to ascertain what all the children's needs are, given the number of children in the class:

'Because children tend to be past masters at concealing things . . . they tend only to say what you want them to say . . . In the more traditional approach, there was never any need to find out what the children's needs were . . . good spellers had the same spelling tests as bad spellers . . . With the way we do things at least, here is a chance that in the hurly burly of the day a child will reveal his needs . . . one of the nice things about the little children is that because their needs are so simple they are revealed so readily . . . you've only got to watch a child with the sand running through his hands to realize that he has very simple needs.'

A child's needs can be ascertained 'by what he does, what he says . . . what he seems to lean towards'. When the interviewer asked him 'supposing he leans towards things that you don't want him to lean towards . . .?', his reply was,

'What he leans to, might well be what he very much needs to do . . . When we're discussing very young children using play material . . . we, as teachers, don't see play material as means of filling in children's time . . . we see play material as means of extending children's experiences . . . One of the most common questions that I'm asked is—"How long would you let a child play then?" . . . and the glib answer is—"As long as he needs to" . . . but I don't have that kind of courage . . . but this is what all my instincts now tell me to say . . . but I just haven't that kind of courage . . . and I prod and prompt. It would require a great deal of courage to watch a child going on and on and on without attempting to divert him to the more serious business of learning . . . but I think that those so called progressive schools that adopt that sort of policy have probably got a very good point—because when they do come to it . . . they come to it with zest and probably make up all the . . . You see, one of the things that has turned me against the traditional approach is the memory of all the wasted hours in the classroom when children went through a kind of hoop—a circus routine which meant nothing. I would like to think that school is a satisfying place, a place that very much fills up their lives and comes very close to home in importance in their lives.'

He was asked whether he would always adopt the same pedagogical approach regardless of the type of pupil he was teaching. He replied,

'I think it was Plowden that said there is no right way for all children all the time . . . one must try to find what is right for most of the children most of the time . . . this is what I feel about this approach. If I were in a middle class area, I think I would use fundamentally the same kind of approach . . . you see one of the things that has happened in this school is that the staff stand well with the children . . . They like us.'

There are, of course, some pupils about whom he worries but he is

'More and more convinced that where children are not taking advantage of this kind of approach the reason must be sought outside the school . . . I have enough evidence to show that children do prosper and get on and learn in this kind of way to be quite confident . . . In a traditional school the tender, withdrawn child tended not to stick out like the proverbial sore thumb, but in this one he does . . . Children learn by doing . . . and children who don't seem to have enough confidence to get cracking and do something—these are the kids who worry me—who are so tense and apprehensive . . .the extraverted ones . . . the children who are confident, reasonably relaxed kids . . . these are the kids we can help, these are the characters who derive intense benefit.'

With regard to the former he

'would think we must first of all have a look . . . see what background information we can get on him . . . there will undoubtedly be a very good reason why . . . and, of course, the tragedy is in the school, of course . . . is that children are what they are before they even get here . . . if I sit here long enough I could talk myself out of having any influence on children whatsoever . . . because there's no doubt about it . . . the educational attainments of children are determined entirely by their backgrounds . . . the ultimate destiny of a child is determined by his home background and his parents' aspirations . . . this is what decides things no matter whether he goes to a traditional school—a progressive one or what have you.'

He admits to being pessimistic:

'I am pessimistic . . . I was at my most confident and best when I was getting children through the 11+. That's when I really felt that I knew what I was doing—I felt I knew all the answers . . . It's only when I rather shamefacedly put these things to one side and started to consider individual children and the needs of each child . . . my downfall began round about 1962, I suppose, when I went on a course when we considered child development in some depth.'

For Mr McIntosh feels strongly that

> 'Home is the deciding factor and there's a lot of evidence, surely, to
> show that where parents' aspirations are high—then often the
> achievement of their children are high . . . in a working class area one is
> constantly aware of the low aspirations that the parents have, the
> evidence of open evenings—when the parents' opening gambit is "Does
> he cheek yer?"—or "Does he give you any lip?" Middle class parents
> wouldn't start like that . . . they'd say, "How is his reading?"—or "Is
> his spelling all right?" . . . or something like that.'

Mr McIntosh notes that his experience in this school has forced him to
return to first principles but he is more than ever convinced that

> Children's attitudes to life, learning and the world around them is
> determined by those who are closest to them . . . and it isn't
> teachers . . . it's determined by mother and father . . . and if these
> aren't present, whoever substitutes for them.'

However, he admits to being pleased with his pupils' behaviour:

> 'I think that what I am impressed with here is the way the children
> behave in school in contrast to the way I hear they behave outside
> school—mind you, I've no direct knowledge of the way our children
> behave outside school . . . we don't have any discipline problems at
> school.'

When the interviewer asked him whether he gets the support he is looking
for from the parents who are largely working class, his reply was as
follows:

> 'In many ways what I'm trying to do here . . . or what I'm trying to do
> with children I do best in this kind of area . . . because the aspirations
> of most of our parents are not as high as those you would find in a
> middle class school and one of the difficulties that those of us who try
> to run reasonably progressive primary schools have is that . . . this
> inbuilt conservatism that exists in all people . . . and middle class
> people are successful people . . . and they can't see that their children
> would be successful unless dealt with in the way that they were dealt
> with . . . working class people, such as I deal with here, don't have the
> same aspirations and therefore to some extent I don't have the
> pressures that I would have if I tried to the same thing in a middle class
> area.'

At the same time, however, the children's background presents problems for the teachers:

'The number of my parents who will take the trouble to take the children to the library are very few . . . Our children don't have a pattern to emulate that would be helpful to us . . . the skills of reading and writing are not widely used . . . much of what we do here in a school like this is compensatory education, we are trying to make up for, and compensate for, this kind of deprivation.'

The headmaster described how there had been strong opposition to the teaching methods from a group of parents when the school first started. He explained this in the following way:

'I am absolutely convinced that the school was used as a whipping boy . . . that the parents were very, very unsettled . . . they had run into financial difficulties . . . parents were utterly frustrated . . . they had nothing on which to vent this frustration and they turned on the school. Each time we interviewed a parent and really got down to it we found it was nothing to do with the school at all . . . It was another problem . . . and to some extent this still exists . . . on the rare occasions when we do have to interview a parent who is hot under the collar for some reason we find that nearly always it's . . . "My husband hasn't been home for three nights" or something like that . . . but what I've said about the aggressions and frustrations of the parents being directed against the school is accepted by all branches of the social workers . . . it came up only about a fortnight ago at a lunchtime conference which I attended of the FSU (Family Service Unit) and it was said by one of the social workers as if it was taken for granted . . . I think that is right.'

He does not feel, however, that those who complained and caused trouble in the early days were entirely the ones who were experiencing domestic or other stress:

'The thing snowballed . . . there were one or two people in this kind of position who became hysterical and who transmitted this to others . . . there were a handful of hot heads who got very hysterical and they did a great deal of damage.'

He tried a number of measures to reassure parents. He held

'parents' meetings at which I tried to explain to them my vision . . .

tried to point out that the world is changing and you're not fitting your children best for this new world by giving them the same kind of things that you had . . . I'm not at all sure, though, that you can convince parents through talking . . . I was trying to make an intellectual appeal . . . but I see now that our parents probably either got the wrong idea or remained utterly unconvinced. However we very, very sensibly resisted the pressures of the parents . . . it wasn't easy, and the staff supported me very loyally in this . . . I refused to relent and refused to give in or to make any kind of concession to traditional or retrogressive methods and we persisted in what we were trying to do . . . let's remember too, that while we were being attacked all the time by a group of parents, we were also being attacked by a group of older pupils who found it extremely difficult to accept this new, this different way of doing things—and there were a group of pupils who were being extremely disruptive . . . and of course, to some extent they were being supported by their parents . . . the common thing that parents said was that the children were bored . . . of course behind this they meant that we hadn't given the children a lot of sums to do or English exercises to do . . . we tried to assess the needs of the children and to meet them as far as we could . . . and this paid off hands down . . . because we have won the children.'

Generally he seems very satisfied about the way the school's policy has developed:

'If we have achieved any success here . . . and I think we have . . . and the more I look around and the more I see, I think we have nothing to be ashamed of here . . . our standards in all the measurable things would compare favourably with schools that are run differently, and the standard of behaviour of children in school is in the main quite good . . . we've achieved this through the children . . . we have won the children . . . and the children have won for us quite a number of the parents.'

However, the difficult relationships with parents in the school's early period did dampen the staff's enthusiasm to involve the parents more:

'We talked about community schools—schools being used by the community and having close links to it . . . also we talked about involving parents more and more in what their children were doing. This was very much in our mind . . . this part of our role tended to get pushed to one side under this kind of pressure—staff said—"No fear—I wouldn't dream of . . . Fancy having Mrs so and so in the classroom".'

Relationships are, however, starting to improve:

> 'We will bring parents into the school . . . I'm certain that to get the
> parents involved with the non-academic aspects of the school . . . is the
> way to do it . . . if you can get fathers or mothers to come into school
> and work with a small group of children they see that the place is not a
> blackboard jungle at all and that although there appear to be a number
> of children milling about, it's in a kind of framework of a secure kind of
> order . . . it's reasonably orderly.'

He wants to limit parents' involvement, nevertheless, to non-academic
activities:

> 'At the moment I prefer to preserve that area for the teachers . . . we've
> got a lot of evidence to show that parents and non-professional people
> can do the children a lot of harm and unintentional harm.'

He takes mathematics teaching as an example and says:

> 'Oh dear, it's difficult enough with teachers, isn't it . . . who themselves
> were the victims of poor maths teaching . . . and who need almost to be
> psychoanalysed and have a lot of this removed again if you're going to
> help children . . . you need to have taken a great deal of trouble to find
> out what are these basic principles to get hold of and I've tried to
> encourage my staff to push these basic principles with the children
> rather than sums to be got right and ticks to be acquired.'

Unfortunately, from his point of view parents will persist in giving their
children 'sums' to do at home.

> 'I think that they feel that they all want to help their children, don't
> they? . . . they want to help their children to get on . . . this is what
> they tell me . . . to get on means getting a good job . . . get a better job
> than they themselves have and enjoy a better life . . . I think a lot of
> them would like their children to do what you and I do with a certain
> amount of ease . . . which is talk. This is what they would really
> love . . . They think doing what you're told in school . . . getting
> your sums or your spellings right helps toward this end . . . I feel sorry
> for parents. I really do . . . because so much of what they do is
> misdirected and it's now widely recognized that working class mothers
> do not prepare their children well enough for school . . . subordination
> of the child to the authority of the school is what they earnestly believe
> to be the pathway to success . . . middle class mothers don't have any

qualms about that . . . they know that the best way to prepare the
children is to get them to use the toilet properly . . . to do up their
buttons . . . and laces and encourage them to be inquisitive . . . they
encourage their children to be active and get up and make things and
indeed they give them materials in the preschool days which encourage
this . . . it's quite clear that working class mothers see toys not as a
means of extending children's experience but as a means of keeping
them quiet and out of the way . . . stopping them from doing anything
that will be faintly annoying or upsetting to adults . . . I think that our
parents do this kind of thing because they think they are doing the best
thing for their children . . . but we have to be careful not to undermine
the relationship which the mother has with the child.'

In the long run, though:

'I would hope . . . that children who have been the recipients of
reasonably progressive education would, themselves, become better
parents.'

That, however, may be a long term solution. In the meantime he is
pressing for the establishment of more pre-school provision in the area:

'The next step beyond that is to introduce universal nursery
schooling—to introduce some kind of pre-school education—you see,
vital attitudes are laid down very easily . . . With pre-school provision
we could help children to use materials differently . . . and we could
give them what good parents would and do automatically give their
children . . . The main plank in my platform is . . . that if we had such a
unit that it could well be a focal point for the meeting of young
mothers . . . it is in that stage when the children are very much babies
when the question of their academic prowess and the ability to read
doesn't come into it then those of us who are professional child
raisers . . . and let's face it, that's what we are . . . we could spread our
influence and advice more in that sort of setting. But we already have
made a dickens of a lot of converts in school . . . I'm prepared to accept
that there are a lot of parents who aren't quite sure of what goes on in
school . . . but the number of parents who are definitely anti is very
small indeed.'

Mr McIntosh recognizes that this approach to education obviously
depends upon the attitudes and quality of his staff:

'I have to put a great deal of trust in the people at the Town Hall and I have to trust them that they will find me people who will fit into the school community . . . They wouldn't send me anybody whom they didn't think would fit in . . . but I would certainly encourage anybody who didn't support the principles that I hold to move on . . . you see . . . I've been a head before and one of the things I discovered here is that the biggest menace is the traditional formal teacher . . . because parents' attitudes to education die very hard . . . and no matter how interesting the things which other teachers do . . . there's still a hankering for getting their children into that class where they do *proper* work . . . where there's none of this messing around . . . it's all very nice . . . it makes a lovely exhibition . . . but basically learning your tables and doing ten words spelling on the blackboard and writing about them . . . this is what it's all about really . . . and the parents want their children to be in the classrooms with the traditional teachers.'

On the whole he is very satisfied with the quality of his staff. Of course, he recognizes that there are variations between them but:

'The main aims, the main principles are everywhere there right throughout the school . . . As a group of people they are above average as teachers . . . I find them very pleasant and helpful, and I've no reason to think that they are not completely loyal . . . they're certainly the pleasantest group of staff that I've ever worked with.'

Taken together they help to provide an educational environment which he can feel proud of:

'I find the words formal and informal dirty words nowadays but I think you know what I mean, that there's no rigidity about the set up—by not having this rigid set up, kids who are in acute distress, and let's face it, we have got a great number who are really in distress, there's no other phrase for it . . . and their distress is caused by their home conditions . . . this kind of setting enables them to withdraw, opt out . . . they are not brought into conflict with a timetable or with a teacher who is determined to teach addition or decimals if it kills her . . . these clashes are constantly being avoided here . . . and so children who have difficulties . . . they find relief here . . . the brightest sparks . . . they are freed from the drudgery of having to tag along after Dick or Harry in the class and they swing along in their own way doing the things where they find satisfaction.'

His view of the school, especially *vis-à-vis* those children 'in distress' is of an

> 'environment where perhaps they can find some sort of relief here . . .
> We have the largest number of children at risk out of any school in the
> city . . . We have a history of domestic instability . . . and the number
> of kids at risk reflects this . . . but everybody tells me when they come
> into the school this fact is not apparent . . . So I am led to believe . . .
> that the school itself has become a great socializing institution, if you
> like, . . . a civilizing institution . . . so that the children when they come
> here, they conform to the norms that we have . . . The children like
> school, they believe in it, they think it's good . . . the sort of things we
> do here appeals to them . . . It seems to meet their needs . . . this is
> what they want . . . the school is run the way they want . . . it's a kind
> of community association for kids and they like it and they will stand
> up for it—and if threatened, I daresay, they would man the
> barricade . . . but they certainly never let us down . . . In that sense we
> are meeting the needs of both those children who are in distress and
> those who are not.'

Mr McIntosh feels that with his pupils their emotional needs are
paramount:

> 'I think this is where we would probably part company with more
> traditional, more formal schools, in such schools perhaps the head
> teacher would think it was no part of the function of the school to meet
> the emotional needs . . . that the school was here to hand on a certain
> culture, a certain way of life, along with a lot of skills, information,
> knowledge and that sort of thing . . . and that the emotional needs of
> children having nothing to do with the school . . . we don't take that
> view, we try to see children as whole people with emotional needs,
> intellectual needs, physical needs and so on. It's become almost
> platitudinous now but we try to treat the education of the whole child.'

Of intellectual and emotional needs, he argues

> 'The two have got to be met simultaneously for any good and lasting
> result to ensure . . . one of the things that parents are constantly
> saying—He should be made to do things . . . Now we don't share that
> view at all . . . we've long since realized that the things that you can
> make them do are hardly worth the doing and the things that are worth
> doing are the things you can't make anybody do . . . and so we try to

win the children to what we believe . . . and this is what we try to
do . . . all round the school, it varies a bit depending on the constitution
of the group . . . we've got a lot of children of poor intellectual
calibre . . . this is revealed by our reading difficulties . . . their low
intellectual ability combined with a lot of other things.'

In trying to summarize the headmaster's perspective we could argue
that it involves a fusion of, on the one hand, a child centred perspective
towards education, whilst, on the other, a social pathology view of the
community from which his pupils are drawn. He sees the school as dealing
with seriously deprived children who are both emotionally and
cognitively underdeveloped and thus the school has to provide a
socializing environment, or as he puts it a 'civilizing force' which can
secure a supportive context in which the children can develop. Although
the school has an obligation to produce numeracy and literacy, the
teaching of these skills is not its prime aim. The main concern is with the
developmental needs of the whole child, encouraging him to be
self-confident, responsible, with initiative and adaptability which will
enable him to function in adult society. The perspective adopted is that,
by seeing to the present needs of the pupils, their long term needs will be
taken care of. Formality and rigidity of structure as aspects of classroom
organization are rejected in principle because children, as individuals,
have idiosyncratic features of personality, attitudes, and techniques of
learning so that rigid uniformity would be inappropriate. Moreover,
childhood has its own requirements and adult-imposed knowledge may be
dysfunctional for the child's present needs. This perspective is situated
within a view of the world as being characterized by rapid social and
technical change which no longer requires children to possess bundles of
arbitrary knowledge but to be capable of innovating, of being adaptable,
able to make decisions, etc. Moreover, whilst the pedagogy advocated is
justified as being suited for all children, it is regarded as particularly suited
for 'these children' who require a therapeutic environment, one
characterized by concern and informality if they are to transcend the
emotional problems they possess. Nevertheless, there is an underlying
pessimism regarding the role that the school can play in counteracting the
adverse effects of home environment, for children's personalities and
attributes are acquired very early on in life, in the home, and there is little
the school can do if a satisfactory pre-school life has not been
experienced. This pessimism, then, is associated with what could be seen
as generally low expectations regarding the pupils' educational prognosis.

Before proceeding to some discussion of the position of each of the three teachers studied *vis-à-vis* the school ethos as defined by the headmaster, some comments will be made about various areas in which the headmaster's account of the school ethos revealed ambiguity, confusion and in some cases obvious contradiction. Such ambiguities reflect conflicting pressures on the headmaster's structural position as well as some inherent ambiguities in the ideology of child centredness itself. We will return to attempt a further sociological analysis of these ambiguities in a later chapter.

The first ambivalence worth discussing relates to what the headmaster sees as the prime aim of the school. On the one hand he does not define the school as primarily a 'learning institution', by which he seems to mean concerning itself with the transmission of the skills of literacy and numeracy. For example, when discussing various kinds of external pressure on the teachers' freedom to operate in the way they feel fit he acknowledges that others, particularly parents, may put a greater emphasis on reading and writing, but he holds a much broader conception of the school's role: 'I feel that the child himself, his well being and his welfare must be our first concern'. Yet in spite of this, he has to acknowledge that whatever else he may do he has to teach children to read and write: 'I realize I'm paid to do this', he says.

Now this ambivalence is at the heart of many of the so-called contradictions in his thought, for example, that related to the defence of his school's methods *vis-à-vis* supporters of more formal or traditional approaches to pedagogy. When attempting to justify the efficiency of his approach, he does so in terms of what we could call traditional criteria regarding the pupil's achievement in literacy and numeracy and good behaviour.

> 'The more I look around and the more I see, I think we have nothing to be ashamed of here . . . Our standards in all the measurable things would compare favourably with schools that are run differently and the standard of behaviour is, in the main, quite good.'

Although wanting to stress not simply the differences in methodology but also in the aims of the school compared with a more formal one, he is unable or unwilling to specify criteria for evaluating the school's success which involve rejecting what he could regard as traditional criteria.

In the same way, although he wants to stress the importance of play as an educational device, it is quite apparent that within his perspective there is a hierarchical evaluation of the different types of possible activities

which children can be involved in, in terms of their educational
significance. For example, when discussing how far he would go in letting
children do what they wanted he argues:

> 'It would require a great deal of courage to watch a child going on and
> on without attempting to divert him to the more serious business of
> learning.'

On the one hand he wants to argue that children should be free to choose
to do what they need to do—but their choices will be differentially valued
by the teacher. Such an ambivalence relates very closely to the
uncertaintly in his conception of the teacher's role *vis-á-vis* the pupils. Do
children need therapeutic freedom in which to pursue their interests
without teacher interference or do they need the security of structure? At
what point does or ought the teacher to intervene? On the one hand he
says:

> 'The best teachers are aware of what their children are doing . . . and if
> there is a need to divert the children from something then the best
> teachers do it . . . but I wouldn't like anyone to think that we don't
> have some kind of structure.'

On the other hand there is an equation of the child's needs with what the
child does, with the implication that one should not interfere.

> 'What he leans to might well be what he needs to do . . . I'm asked,
> "how long would you let a child play?" and the glib answer is, "as long
> as he needs to", but I don't have that kind of courage, but this is what
> all my instinct now tells me to say.'

Such a statement reinforces the supermarket attendant image of the
school teacher he talked about in which the teacher arranges the context
but within it the child takes what he needs from the situation. Between
the Scylla of arbitrarily imposed structuring by the teacher which violates
the integrity of the child's developing consciousness, and the Charybdis
of a *laissez-faire* permissiveness which may lead to anarchy, how does the
teacher decide to intervene? From the headmaster's account there are no
unambiguous guides beyond what 'the good teacher knows'. But how
does he know and what criteria does he operate with? No objective
procedures are offered to guide the teacher in decisions of this kind. The
same kind of ambivalence is noted in connection with the issue of his
evaluation of working class life styles and patterns of existence. How can
one integrate a belief in children being given free choice and developing in

their own way, when built into the very notion of being an educator is the idea that one is involved in a process of transmitting beliefs, attitudes and values which children, when left on their own, would not necessarily acquire? Such an issue also raises the question of the consistency of the headmaster's beliefs in the primacy of the influence of the home background and his pessimism regarding the role of the school. We could ask, if home background is all-important, why is it that so much stress is laid on the importance of the school's approach and its ethos and methods? Does it really matter which methods are used since background explains all? But again the headmaster's account certainly seems to suggest the contrary, these methods are better than other methods—and the school has been successful presumably in compensating for the effect of bad backgrounds. Nevertheless, there is a hint that the headmaster is not being entirely consistent: whilst background may explain failure, it is the school's approach which explains success.

Another point worth emphasizing in connection with the headmaster's evaluation of the children's background is the headmaster's ambivalence regarding the parents' aspirations. On the one hand, he argues that perhaps it is easier to adopt child centred approaches in a working class area because the parents have low aspirations for their children; on the other hand, he explains the fact that most of his parents try to help their children through assisting them with reading, writing and sums because they want their children to get on, do better than they did—get a better job—all indicators not of low or no aspirations or interest in education but precisely the reverse. Such an ambivalence is only resolvable by arguing either that the parents do not have the right kind of aspirations, or that the methods they use to achieve their aspirations are inappropriate. Both sentiments are, as we have seen, expressed in the headmaster's accounts—but again how can we equate this with the headmaster's belief in freedom of choice? Why cannot children be allowed to aspire towards the things they, or their parents, think are important, or adopt methods that they decide are instrumental for the pursuit of their goals?

Again, this ambivalence comes out in the interview when he quotes the Plowden Report's arguments that schools have to adopt methods which are most suitable for most of the children most of the time. From his own account, however, we suggest that there is an inconsistency between his view that an individualized approach is necessary towards each child, his own observations that some of the children are crying out for structure, to be told what to do, and yet his reluctance to give them what they seem to want and his apparent support of these methods for all kinds of children, regardless of social class or other differences between them. Why is it that a child centred approach does not permit a high level of differentiation in methodology and pedagogy to take account of the prior experiences to which the children have been exposed? The headmaster would reply that within his approach the teachers would differentiate their treatment according to their assessment of the individual needs of each child. But then he admits that one of the very real difficulties associated with the methods is precisely the problem of how, in a large class with so many children, it is possible to identify what each child's needs are. Such an ambivalence explains his statement that, 'with the way we do it, at least there is a chance that in the hurly burly of the day a child will reveal his needs'.

A further inconsistency in his position over children's needs can be illustrated by referring back to the point he made about 'children being past masters at concealing things' when discussing the problem of coping with large classes. Yet a moment later he argued: 'one of the nice things about little children is that because their needs are so simple, they are revealed so readily . . . you've only got to watch a child . . .'.

These ambivalencies have been gone into at some length for they provide an important indicator to some of the relationships which exist between the headmaster's ideology, on the one hand, and some of the conflicting pressures and constraints on his position, on the other. Many of these ambivalancies have been revealed elsewhere in various commentaries, usually by philosophers, on some of the internal philosophical and theoretical contradictions within that body of thought that we could loosely call the 'child centred progressive' approach to education. Nevertheless, the implication of some of these commentaries seems to be that such contradictions and logical inconsistencies are merely the result of woolly thinking and with a little more logical clarity and philosophical expertise, the confusions and ambiguities could be ironed out. Such an approach is questioned here. Although the authors have carried out a critical dissection of the headmaster's perspective they want to disavow a judgmental stance towards the inner contradictions they have revealed. From their perspective as sociologists, they would suggest that such inconsistencies may well be indicators of diverse and conflicting constraints on the position of the educator which pose interesting questions regarding their explanation on the macro level, and have important implications for actors in the way they function at the micro level.

Having both outlined the school ethos as expressed by the headmaster and referred to some of the problematic areas within the school ethos, we now turn to an examination of the perspective of the three teachers who were central to the investigation.

5

The teacher's perspectives

In this chapter an account will be presented of some important dimensions of the teachers' perspectives on their work but before commencing this project some clarification of concepts is necessary.

At various points in the discussion we make reference to the concept of teaching ideologies. We will define a teaching ideology as follows: A connected set of systematically related beliefs and ideas about what are felt to be the essential features of teaching. A teaching ideology involves both cognitive and evaluative aspects, it will include general ideas and assumptions about the nature of knowledge and of human nature—the latter entailing beliefs about motivation, learning and educability. It will include some characterization of society and the role and functions of education in the wider social context. There will also be assumptions about the nature of the tasks teachers have to perform, the specific skills and techniques required together with ideas about how these might be acquired and developed. Finally, the ideology will include criteria to assess adequate performance, both of the material on whom teachers 'work', i.e. pupils, and for self-evaluation or the evaluation of others involved in educating. In short, a teaching ideology involves a broad definition of the task and a set of prescriptions for performing it, all held at a relatively high level of abstraction.

The content of the ideology will be a function of a complex of interrelated factors of which the following might be the most important: the image of teaching which the teachers formed whilst they, themselves, were pupils; second, the cognitive orientations and ideological commitments built into the course of professional training they receive; and third, the complex of experiences which teachers have encountered when faced with the practical exigencies of doing the job. Moreover, the teaching ideology will be embedded in a broader network of social and political worldviews whose determination, in the individual actor, derive from the socialization experiences undergone.

The task of ascertaining teachers' ideologies is more difficult than that encountered by Strauss when examining psychiatric ideologies (Strauss *et al.*, 1964). With psychiatry, the existence of 'schools' of psychiatry makes it comparatively simple to discern the dimensions and boundaries of the major ideological orientations. But even there, in spite of knowledge about the possible dimensions along which psychiatrists' beliefs could be measured, there was not complete conceptual clarity. With teachers, however, the situation is exacerbated by the fact that there are no professional groupings which differ clearly in terms of their outlook and approach to teaching methodology, thus compounding our problems of conceptualization.

Nevertheless, it is important to stress that we are not attempting to grasp in all their complexity and subtlety all features of the teachers' ideologies, but are more concerned with a lower order of beliefs which form part of what we define as the teachers' 'perspectives'. Ideologies are not static, deterministic systems of beliefs which prescribe their own application in specific situations. Hence we use a concept of 'teaching perspectives' to distinguish between ideas of the actor which exist at a high level of generality, which we here call teaching ideologies, and those sets of beliefs and practices which emerge when social actors in an organization confront specific problems in their situation. The concept of teaching perspectives is rather similar to what Strauss conceptualizes as an operational philosophy (Strauss, 1964).

H. Becker *et al.* (1961) in their study of medical students, suggest that when people find themselves in an organization facing a common set of problems and where they are in a situation which allows them considerable interaction over time, the participants will develop a group culture, a body of organized perspectives which will support them and aid them in coming to terms with the problems in their situation.

Such an approach, however, assumes too much consensus. It may be the case that a differentiation at the level of teaching ideology will lead to the same objective situation being differentially interpreted. There may well be a social distribution of differentiated perspectives within the same context. We wish to make the degree to which this is the case problematic in our own research.

What do we mean by the concept 'teaching perspective'? We will define it as a 'co-ordinated set of ideas, beliefs and actions a person uses in coping with a problematic situation'. A perspective includes both thoughts and actions. It contains a number of elements; some concept of the environment and the problems it creates; ideas about social objects within the environment and the various inanimate features of their resources to hand; a definition of the goals and projects, and what can be expected from the environment; a rationalization for being and acting therein; a specification of the kinds of activities one may or ought to involve oneself in; a set of criteria to evaluate one's own and others' actions; and finally, a set of congruent activities and actions which are employed to deal with the situation.

It can be seen that a teaching ideology is less situationally specific than a teaching perspective, but, of course, there will be interaction between them. We want, however, in the study to socially situate the teachers' perspectives in the larger social context which influences and affects their action and the ideas they have about it.

Formally, the teachers' perspectives will be constituted by their total knowledge of the situation. We do not pretend, however, to characterize the teachers' perspectives in all their infinite complexity, but want to examine specifically certain aspects of their perspectives: namely, first, their characterization of the pupils and their background; second, their orientation to the school and its ethos; and third, their perspective on working in the classroom.

Mrs Carpenter

1   The children and their background

In Mrs Carpenter's view most of her children are 'thick and those who aren't thick are disturbed'. These children were perceived as being generally emotionally insecure, with low intelligence and achievement potential. The notion of insecurity was related to that of deprivation, but the latter is subtly differentiated.

> 'We tar them all with the same brush and it's not really very true . . .
> because there are different, sort of, shades of deprivation . . . in each of
> these families are different shades, and it's wrong for us perhaps to be
> so condemning with so many of them. Still, we do.'

Then, pressed a little further about the meaning and existence of 'different shades of deprivation':

'Yes, yes, I certainly do think there are . . . different, ah . . . well with some children one form of deprivation will have very little effect, whereas on another child the same sort of deprivation will have a lasting effect.'

What is important here, besides the implication of social distance between school staff and parents and the idea that deprivations may have differential effects (some backgrounds being less detrimental than others) is the view that, in general, the children are deprived both materially, but more particularly, emotionally. Furthermore, the responsibility for this situation, and blame lies squarely with the parents themselves. This is one of the background assumptions of her work.

Mrs Carpenter is able to talk guardedly about many of the households having problems such as absent fathers, debts, eviction orders, and the disconnection of the electric power. Besides these major structural problems, often leaving the mother to bear the brunt of the ensuing difficulties, there is the added complication that many of the mothers are incompetent. The teacher has a theory, tentatively held, that much of the trouble, which is manifest in the peculiar behaviour of the children, derives from the mothers relying a great deal upon their own mothers during the early stages of their married lives prior to the second pregnancy. Mrs Carpenter suspects that

'a lot of these women got married because they had to or because they wanted to get away from home . . . it's the only way they could see of getting out of their mother's house. Well, of course, they get married for one reason or the other, only to discover they can't afford rent, so they stick with mother, his mother or her mother, and the only way of getting out of that is by having children, because by having children you get a council flat or house, you see, and very often that's why you've got so many of these younger children. They have one child—straight down the Housing Department, you see—"Oh no, you must have at least two"; so they go home and have another one. Easy, isn't it! You haven't got to wash nappies, Mum's doing it for you. So they have this other child and get this lovely flat and it's taken right out of their hands—they don't know how to cope.'

Here we have, in her terms, a picture of incompetence and irresponsibility with implied suggestions that the situation is exacerbated by state provision of housing for families with two or more children. Much of the deprivation which results is a product of the emotional problems generated in the children by their being taken away from their grandparents when they move to the estate, or when a grandparent dies. The impression given is that the teacher feels that many of the mothers neglect their children (leaving them to find emotional security in a grandparent) by going to work soon after the child is born. When this bond is severed the results are various forms of abnormal behaviour in school such as overdependence upon herself, the teacher, and abnormally long initial settling in periods characterized by crying and screaming.

Towards the end of a long discussion about the children and their homes, the teacher summed the situation up:

'but, you see, all of these, a lot of these children are, sort of, difficult, peculiar, you know, difficult in some way, but you can't honestly state yourself, you know, they're abnormal or disturbed. I mean, I talked to you about Jean and Mary, well, they're not what I would call normal little girls, by any stretch of the imagination, but there's nothing I could put my finger on to say they're abnormal. They're just different.'

This represents a summary of her background perspectives on this point. The teacher sees these children as at best merely 'different' from her idea of normal children, so that at this minimal level there is a conception of the norm for these children being outside that life style with which she identifies. At worst, the children were seriously disturbed and psychiatric problems.

The parents' treatment of the children differs from the teacher's own notions as to how they should be handled in certain specific respects. For instance, the parents, in her view, hit the children frequently. They talk to or 'at' them in imperatives rather than 'communicate' with them, as the teachers try to do in school. She indicated that a symptom of the physical control of the parents was that children often flinch when she turns to them suddenly or quickly:

'They hit, they do hit their children a terrific amount really . . . when you talk to the children about it, quite a lot of them get smacked, you know, regularly, some of them physically cringe, so I'm sure that it goes on.'

The parents are also over-concerned with their children's physical welfare. Two aspects of this were specifically indicated. Many of the children become too involved in keeping their clothing clean for fear of their mothers' chastisement:

'I've never had so many complaints about paint on clothes and these sorts of things, you know, and children really emotionally involved with getting their clothes dirty . . . if they fall over and dirty the backs of their socks, or something, they are emotionally upset about it. Really obsessed about this cleanliness.'

The other aspect is the children's health, but Mrs Carpenter indicates that this is often a kind of excuse for a social occasion, out of the ordinary, possibly to avoid work:

'They're very concerned about their clothes and their physical welfare as well because they're always taking them down to the doctor's. You know, it's a regular treat to nip off down to the doctor's.'

Of the thirty-six children in the class during the period of observation, the teacher was able to identify symptoms of disturbance in various degrees of severity from being 'odd' or 'peculiar' to bordering on 'maladjusted' (and therefore potentially referable to the local authority for child guidance) in at least thirty of them. With most of these the aetiology was rooted in some aspect of the family situation of the particular child. Of her older children all were deemed educationally 'at risk' at a meeting of the staff and the local authority social workers who service the estate. This meant that these children were expected to show signs of education failure and underachievement. The teacher felt that there were only three 'normal children' in the class, two boys and one girl, each a five or young six year old. To the teacher they were normal in terms of social-emotional adjustment, and were achieving up to or beyond her expectations, and were the sort of children who could hold their own in a school in a respectable, achievement oriented, working class or middle class area. However, there were only five children who constituted a real problem to her. They fell most clearly within her categories of being 'disturbed' or 'maladjusted', and on these children she had built up a fairly full mental document.

Finally, the home backgrounds, besides generating problems of social adjustment and emotional instability in the children, were thought of as the source of serious cultural deprivation. Basically, 'our children don't have a pattern to emulate that would be useful to us.' It was thought that the homes tended to offer little by way of encouragement or stimulus for reading and writing, and that there was infrequent use of the public library. The parents were viewed as having low aspirations for the future jobs of their children, particularly when compared with middle class parents. Such factors were seen as accounting for low achievement in the skills of literacy.

In the light of these views how does she see the relationship between the school and the parents? The teacher feels that many of the parents do not understand or appreciate what the school is trying to do, and that in fact many show a great deal of resentment. We have seen from the headmaster's account that there has been a history of conflict with the parents, particularly soon after the school was established on the estate. The parents were opposed to the methods, and this opposition was experienced by the staff as extremely threatening. Many of the parents felt that the children should be more closely directed, they were bored with 'doing nothing' or 'just playing all day'. Some of the older children, who had attended other schools, and to whom these methods were unfamiliar, were disruptive. The parents wanted a clearer syllabus, with concentration on the 'Three Rs'. The school resisted this, and held meetings with the parents, explaining that in these modern times the latest techniques were appropriate. Although Mrs Carpenter felt that relations with the parents had obviously improved, both she and the headmaster still felt that they were far from satisfactory. Nevertheless, their explanations of hostility by the parents towards the school involved a belief in the parents projecting their general instability and distress caused by other factors, onto the school, itself. Thus, talking about a parent who had complained about her child being bored at school, in her (the teacher's) view, the boredom was generated at home:

> 'It was interesting, wasn't it . . . that [the social worker] said that in a lot of cases when they say the children are bored it's not them at all, it's the mothers that are bored.'

The parents were very slowly coming to understand the methods, and although relations were improving slightly Mrs Carpenter felt that the school was not yet strong enough to let the parents attend and participate more closely, or even to demonstrate a typical day to them. The parents were seen as being amazed or at best pleasantly surprised when they visited the school exhibition and found that the children had done writing and number work. It would further be impossible to involve more than the most select few in the school because most of the parents did not know how to behave there:

> 'They're the sort of people who would get all the drawers out and they're not reserved in any way like that, you know, they'd march in

and pull all the drawers out, leaf through and have all the books off the shelf and ask the kids questions—and all these sorts of things, they wouldn't be prepared to just stand and watch. If we could put a glass partition between them and us, you know, do it without the children knowing, then it would be all right, but there are, you know, two or three occasions when they come for interviews, marched to the drawer straight away, to the child's drawer pull all the stuff out, "What's this, what's that, what's the other?" because they've still got, they still think the child's drawer should contain the work, you see. Unfortunately it doesn't. It usually contains some old hanky, and a bit of string, a ball or something like that.'

A few parents might be used as aids to the teacher to undertake routine activities and cleaning up. Anything more, such as the teaching of reading, would be an encroachment into the province of the teacher's professional activities and judgment. In this perspective then it was right that the teachers had sole charge because only they had the appropriate knowledge and skills. This teacher shares the headmaster's view that to allow parents to participate in the 'academic' side of schoolwork, meaning reading, number work and writing, would be positively harmful. As the parents would not know the methods the school had adopted the children would become confused. Where the parents would teach the surface mechanical skills, the teachers at the school were aiming to develop the principles of mathematics, and so on, in these children.

2 The school and its ethos

Given this teacher's attitude towards her pupils and their parents, it is perhaps not surprising that she shares the headmaster's general conception that the school should aim to compensate the children of the estate for their underprivileged home backgrounds. This it should do by providing a stable and supportive environment which can facilitate the genesis of an emotional and cognitive basis for the pupil's development in a changing world. Her attitude to literacy and numeracy resembles that of the head—it is not unimportant but it should not be and cannot be the school's main aim because the children are not stable enough to be able to respond to the teaching of these skills. The school must therefore be concerned with trying to cater for the child's present needs, her whole personality development, and the adverse consequences of the instability of home background.

Again, this teacher shares the headmaster's belief that the nature of the children's needs and the aims of the school dictate an informal and 'open' approach to pedagogy and classroom organization. There should be no rigidity of structure but rather an open environment where children can choose what they want to do in accordance with their needs. The instability and deprivation of the children presents problems to the teacher in this approach to the teaching situation but at the same time provides its own justification. The children can play out their problems in a secure and therapeutic environment without feeling threatened.

We have seen when discussing the headmaster's perspective how there is a basic ambivalence in his position between, on the one hand, a radical child centred view of the role of the teacher who engages in a minimum of interference in her pupils' activities, and, on the other, a realization that some degree of structure and direction is necessary. This teacher tends to identify very strongly with the radical child centred model of teaching in the school ethos. Her approach can be illustrated in her account of the serious doctrinal dispute over the teaching of mathematics which occurred during the earliest period of the teachers' experience at the school. This example can probably be generalized to some extent as symbolizing the whole approach to pedagogy within the school. The then deputy head favoured a more structured approach with a more rigid set of aims *vis-à-vis* mathematics in the form of a publicly available (to the staff) programme of work. Most of the staff including Mrs Carpenter had refused to accept and work this programme. She said she:

> 'would never be able to stick to it. I'd be bound to go off the beam, then it would all be wrong. There's nothing very interesting going on then because there's nothing different . . . you get the same thing year after year . . . I'm sure if we'd had a maths syllabus, you see, after that it would have reading syllabus and all those other things. We would have missed a lot of those things that we do now, which we wouldn't have done if we'd had these other things to work to.'

We can see in both this quotation and later ones a reluctance to impose any formality or what se would see as rigidity of organization on her pupils. Indeed, she seems to adhere quite closely to the 'horticultural' model of children's development. Teacher interference with the child's spontaneous development is disruptive and to be generally avoided.

We will see later how this teacher was regarded as the ideal child centred teacher within the school, a position which relates both to her behaviour in the classroom and to the dynamics of staff relationships.

In these two sections we have presented the important ideas which form the background of knowledge and expectations against which the teacher operates in the classroom. These are ideas at a low level of specificity which she may draw upon when accounting for her own behaviour in certain situations. The political and ideological aspects of her accounting will be explicated below, but now, having summarized these general constructs of the teacher's consciousness, we will turn to her perspective in working in the classroom.

3   Working in the classroom

The previous sections constitute the background in Mrs Carpenter's perspective to her work in the classroom. They provide a reservoir of knowledge and a repertoire of accounts for her classroom work, her substantive practices. We will now provide a detailed description of the teacher's perspective on her classroom work.

The class consists of about thirty-six children on the roll, and was vertically or 'family grouped' with 'rising fives' to 'rising sevens.' The sex distribution was skewed, very slightly, towards a female majority. The teacher's overall view of the classroom situation is that it is extremely fluid and constantly changing, as children, with a wide area in which to be self-directive, pursue a wide range of activities, as they take their interest. She sees her way of accommodating to this situation as being *ad hoc* in her practice, using the minimum of direction and structure in order to be child centred. When asked to attempt to describe the class as a whole she thought this a difficult and unrealistic task in the sense that this was contrary to her general perspective and pedagogy:

'It's only on the odd occasions during the day that I do think of them as
a class . . . but they're a very mixed bag, very mixed, all sorts of
different characters—but I really cannot talk of them as a whole class
because I don't think of them like that.'

Variations on this theme were consistently presented to the observer by the teacher.

Routine working in groups set up by the teacher, or with the class as a whole, for reading, was not seen as a usual or useful technique, 'To some children it would get so boring for them and they would really just treat it as something they had to sit through.' Her perspective on this was linked to another significant aspect of substantive pedagogy, the nature of the children as basic material:

'but it shouldn't be like that you know, especially with children like these who need all the encouragement they can get to achieve very little, some of these children. They've got such . . . the only word is barriers, I call them barriers because that's just what it's like when you're trying to teach them, when you're trying to really get them going, getting them to read.'

Thus we note the linking of the pedagogy with a judgment about the general nature of the children, i.e. that they are difficult to teach in the sense of being relatively impervious to the teacher's conception of normal techniques of presentation of the materials.

The child centredness of her pedagogy, as an *ad hoc*, rather than routine process in her eyes, is related to her conception of the nature and mechanics of children's intellectual development in general. To her it is beyond clear comprehension. For instance, when talking about children learning to read, 'some of them seem to learn miraculously what it's all about.' She gave the example of a child who appeared to evade all her attempts at organizing the early learning processes for reading:

'She sat and she'd scratch and fiddle about with her feet and all sorts of things and talked about other things and laughed and did all devious things to get me off the point . . . and then one day I was with another child looking at a book and she (the former child) was telling this (another) child all right. She could just read. So, very often with some of these children you're never sure how they managed it. It certainly isn't, mm (pause), an organized process.'

Here the teacher immediately expanded on the point which to her logically ensues, i.e. that teaching cannot be clearly planned on the basis of known learning sequences and processes of intellectual development. Thus the question 'What's your plan?' or 'What comes first?' is irrelevant to her pedagogy: 'I mean, well really you can't say because with some children it's some things and with others they never do it . . . never do work according to a pattern at all.'

The teacher, then, sees her activities as being unstructured, *vis-à-vis* imparting knowledge or developing understanding in the children. Her aim is to attempt to understand the present situation of each child's intellectual development, the 'stage each one is at, and work from there, though acknowledging that her own understanding is quite limited. So the main technique is a kind of bombardment using a scattering of methods hoping that she will hit the target of the children's 'needs' and 'interests' fairly frequently. For most of the time the children's intellectual development is private and idiosyncratic, and organized by each child personally.

The structure of the time-space matrix of the classroom reflects this. Thus, though the day is divided into periods punctuated by routine breaks for playtimes and lunchtime, the classroom is organized with the minimum of routine and preplanning on her part. Exceptions to this are a TV viewing twice a week at the same time, which is rarely missed, and storytime on Friday afternoons on the radio. The final 20 to 30 minutes of each day is generally devoted to storytelling or reading by the teacher, while the last five minutes of each morning and a similar period in the afternoon are devoted to clearing away materials used up till then. The major exception to this minimization of routine in the teacher's organization of her own activity was that during the Spring term she started to devote most of her mornings to making herself available to hear the children's reading. This left large stretches of time during which the children are allowed and expected to structure their own activities.

Connected with this, the spatial aspect of the material environment reflects the teacher's conception of the appropriate way to arrange the 'learning situation.' She has organized the classroom into activity areas, though the boundaries are weak. There is a maths table or corner, a sticky table (where coloured adhesive papers are cut and used to make small pictures, collages etc.), a reading or quiet corner where a shelf of books is kept, an area for using large bricks, and a large Meccano construction set, a painting area with several easels, and in the corridor outside the room a Wendy House and area for playing with very large bricks and planks. Besides these, there are various table tops, cupboard tops, and floor spaces with no particular purposes other than those the children choose to adopt for them, for instance, writing, drawing, Lego, jigsaws, word games, unifix, etc. Thus the teacher feels that in the classroom a wide range of materials is offered and that she imposes minimal rules on their use other than those of courtesy and fair play. The teacher, herself, would initiate a new craft interest once or twice a week, such as a large display, collage or something associated with a seasonal theme, at Christmas and Easter. The children were expected to become involved with these according to their own choices, for the most part.

Closely associated with the above ideas on her work is the teacher's acknowledgment that she has no formal curriculum as such. There are no clearly articulated subjects or areas of knowledge apart from reading and preliminary aspects of arithmetic. She rejects the idea of a preplanned set of intellectual pursuits in favour of a curriculum oriented to the interests of each child, thus one which is open ended according to the child's developmental needs. She illustrates this concern with examples of occasions when an unstructured approach has given rise to worthwhile work. For instance, on one occasion she was able to pursue concepts in tessellation with 5 and 6 year olds. This is thought of as hardly ever likely to fall within the confines of a planned curriculum. The teacher's perspectives on the way she works, then, is that she has at most a minimal plan of the activities she is likely to establish during any particular day, and that she had some idea of which children are likely to participate voluntarily, from her previous experience of the children. For the most part, however, the children will be expected to pursue the available activities to develop their own knowledge according to their own interests.

The teacher's view of the children has been illustrated to some extent as well as its links with her ideas about her practice. The quotation cited earlier that in her view they were either thick or disturbed runs through much of her explicit ideology of teaching. The child centred methodology is important in order to avoid presenting these children with a threatening environment, and to counteract the emotional and cultural deprivation experienced in their home environments. During discussions about each of the children the teacher was able to relate instances of abnormality, and disturbance in the majority. She found it interesting and rewarding to talk about the children in terms of their social adjustment and development, and both boring and apparently more difficult to talk about them in terms of their developing cognition.

The important point about classroom organization, then, is that it is constituted by a high degree of choice of activity on the part of the child. There are a great many activities available for selection by the children to 'play' with according to their own 'needs' and 'interests' or those of the group the children have voluntarily formed. The teacher specifically rejects the idea of organizing the children, for instance into groups and then rotating them to make sure that each group spends some time on all the available activities. This would be too formal for her in the sense of imposing too much structure on the children's activities.

The teacher's conception of the curriculum or more relevant, curricula, in the organization of her classroom centres upon children's 'needs' and 'interests'. Thus what children are doing they are doing because they have a 'need' to do it, or it is a thing which 'interests' them. There is, therefore, no set curriculum for each child to follow, and against which children's progress might be measured and compared. 'Needs' tend to mean for the teacher 'emotional needs'. Thus, she will notice, for example, that a particular child spends more time than normal playing in the Wendy House, which is perceived as enabling the child to act out or work through its emotional problems stemming from home. Similarly, manipulative play with substances like sand and water is recognized as therapeutic to the emotional needs of children who spend long periods of time at them. As children only learn well when they are doing something which interests them, they must, to a large extent, choose what is interesting and do it. In the everyday running of the classroom the teacher exhorts the children to find something interesting and/or to be 'busy'.

It is clear in the account so far that there are implications for the teacher's pedagogy at almost every point. Thus 'interests', 'needs', and the particularly important concept, 'readiness', for this teacher, are mentioned by her when she described her pedagogic role. The teacher, as indicated above, is unwilling to impose her will and preconceptions upon the children because this may pose a threat to them and render them unable to derive any educational benefit from her interventions. Thus the teacher has given several accounts of how she has attempted to join in an activity with some children, trying to influence what the children were getting out of it, for instance, by offering the name of a concept they were using, or suggesting they do some extensions, etc., which resulted in the children 'losing interest', packing up the activity, and not being able, a few days later, to remember what she had suggested. To her it would have been better if she had refrained from intervening altogether because they would have learned far more on their own. When taking the initiative with the children, she finds it difficult to communicate with them as indicated by the notion of 'barriers': 'No matter how many times, how many different ways you present it, it never seems to happen, not for a long, long time anyway.'

A major aspect of her role, therefore, as she sees it, is to organize the classroom in the minimal sense of making things available for the children to experience various aspects of their environment as a grounding for conceptual growth at a later age. The main point of life in her classroom in terms of the acquisition of academic knowledge is to 'gain experience'.

Mrs Carpenter sees her job as a kind of 'leading from behind', and 'trying to put things in their way'. This, though a mild form of intervention, is thought of as being consistent with the child centred approach of allowing the child to grow at his own pace and in his own time. Intervention of a more consciously directive type is possible on the basis of knowledge about children, if this knowledge indicates that the child is 'ready', both cognitively and emotionally to proceed to a higher 'stage'. Thus there is an overwhelmingly idiosyncratic element in children's learning which makes her job the clinical one of monitoring each child's development, and on the basis of this knowledge occasionally intervening to help him with a certain problem or introduce him to a new activity. But, for the most part, the child is allowed to get on with his own education according to his own interests and needs in the emotionally reassuring environment of an unthreatening atmosphere.

The teacher's view of the proper relationship with her pupils is to be friendly and informal, though firmness is required when occasional discipline problems arise. She feels she is a successful teacher, organizing a classroom on informal lines, keeping the children happy and eager to attend school, and having as good an academic attainment record as other more formal teachers. However, she feels that she, and the school in general, do not change the children much. Most of the damage to their personalities is done while they are at home, which is much longer than the time they spend in school, particularly as they do not come to school until they are almost five.

In summary, planning and routine, in so far as they occur, are regarded within her perspective as minimal. Thus the teacher will plan a particular 'creative' activity such as the making of a collage, or a large model by the children, which requires the assembly of materials and thinking out the major steps involved. However, one activity, reading, has been organized on a more clearly routine basis, and it is the only one for which records are kept, other than in the teacher's memory.

From the above description of the classroom and her role in it, as the teacher sees it, we have the impression of an environment with minimal control being exercised by the teacher over the pupils. This may be regarded as a superficial or 'surface' account in the sense that there may be other 'underlying' social realities not accounted for. The 'deep structure' of the situation which this perspective and vocabulary may be unable to comprehend, confront or make problematic, may be one of quite considerable direction and control over pupils in their acquisition of knowledge. It may be found that, though to the teacher there is an unpatterned distribution of knowledge amongst the children, because each child is essentially an idiosyncratic phenomenon, there is a pattern and structure to it and that the teacher is a key element in it, despite the generally passive self-image of the teacher's perspective. However, we will proceed to a consideration of this issue in our subsequent analysis of the three classrooms under consideration. In the meantime we will now offer a description of the perspectives of our second teacher, Mrs Lyons, who is the school's Deputy Headmistress.

Mrs Lyons

1   The children and their background

Our second teacher's perspectives on her pupils and their parents closely resemble those of the former teacher we have already examined.

Mrs Lyons see her pupils as the products of largely unstable and uncultured backgrounds, with parents who are, in various combinations, irresponsible, incompetent, illiterate, 'clueless', uninterested and unappreciative of education, and who, as a result fail to prepare their children adequately for the experiences they will be offered in school. The parents, especially the mothers, tend to be spoken of very disparagingly. The mothers are perceived as generally immature and unable to cope, having too many young children either by accident or design whilst they are still too young. The teacher declares that many mothers go to work to help pay off rent arrears and electricity bills incurred through bad management. She castigates them for creating latchkey children and for frittering away their conscience money on toys and unsuitable clothes (hot pants, etc.) in an attempt to relieve 'their guilt' at neglecting them.

Alternatively, if they do not go out to work, bad management leads them to build up hire purchase debts through the purchase of consumer goods which they frequently do not need and cannot afford. Indeed, the teacher considers many of the homes unsuitable, disorganized and unstable, with the father often out of work, or working excessively, or the family unit broken and the child exposed to a succession of 'uncles' or 'fancy men', the child often not knowing who his real father is. Moreover, even where there is a conventional family unit with both parents present, the teacher believes that many of the children suffer from a lack of or a surfeit of affection; that is, the mother is said either to 'hate' the child in which case she has most probably farmed him out from an early age 'to nurseries or child-minders' or she smothers him with love. Where the latter occurs, when the mother 'waits on him hand and foot' and 'walks around after him', the teacher considers this a form of self-indulgence detrimental to the child. The teacher, thus, has to train the child to do what the parent ideally should have done but has failed to do. It would involve the parents in too much trouble to teach the child to use a knife and fork, for example, or to dress himself, put away his possessions, and so on.

This lack of consideration which the teacher feels the parents show towards her is illustrated again where the mother sends the child to school 'obviously sick' either because she doesn't want to take time off work (in which case the teacher may be asked to see that the child's medicine is taken) or because 'she can't be bothered to go to the doctor'.

This combination of adverse family conditions means that the teacher is confronted with a group of pupils whom she regards as typical products of abnormal backgrounds; that is to say, her pupils are seen as mainly problem pupils, maladjusted, disturbed and insecure, and it is they who set the tone of the classroom and provide her with the legitimation for the particular way in which she defines her task in the classroom. When asked which pupils she thought were well adjusted, as opposed to maladjusted, this teacher could only mention immediately two pupils. Within the next twenty-four hours, after some reflection, she added a further five to her list of adjusted pupils out of a total of thirty-eight. The other 80 per cent of her pupils she regarded as suffering from various degrees and kinds of maladjustment caused by the pathology of their home backgrounds. Nevertheless, although regarding them as maladjusted and, therefore, in some sense abnormal, she also seemed to regard them as typical products of a council estate—comparing these pupils with the 'nice' pupils she had taught at her previous school who lived on the Bluebell Estate.

What indices did she use for their general social and emotional disturbance? This teacher interpreted many isolated or typical instances of behaviour as evidence of the validity of her deprivation model. She defined the children as more aggressive than ordinary children—their frequent resort to drawing houses as indicative of some emotional need for a secure home life. She saw them as finding it difficult to play together, to form friendships or share toys and equipment in the classroom. They would be over anxious to read, revealing excessive pressurization from home, overfussy if they dirtied their clothes. A great variety of indicators provided 'evidence' for the framework with which she interpreted the actions and behaviour of her pupils. Thus a new child clutching a duster ('a comforter, the only furry thing she could find') is seen by this teacher as evidence of a basic psychological insecurity. Similarly what the school secretary considered as 'quite understandable' crying, 'She was covered in mud and it must have been an alarming experience', was seen by Mrs Lyons as 'positively neurotic', an indication of the child's insecurity.

This teacher, thus, judges the pupils' background in terms of the adverse effects she sees it has on her pupils' emotional and social development. Perhaps even more detrimental, however, for the child, is the failure to provide stimulating cognitive experiences which would benefit the children's intellectual development. Mrs Lyons concedes that some of them may well have the same IQ as their 'normal' or 'well adjusted' counterparts, but believes that few will be able to 'compete' or 'overcome their handicaps and make something of themselves'. Their background has given them so many liabilities which will hold them back. Their being 'at risk' results in a very poor educational prognosis. Even those pupils whom the teacher admitted were bright 'for these children', but not in terms of normal criteria, could not be expected to get very far. This view of the majority of children as being 'at risk' is one shared by the headmaster and the majority of the staff, and receives confirmation from the social workers who have close and regular contact with the school, providing feedback and support for the teachers' view of the homes and the standards of the local community.

It appears that Mrs Lyons has a highly reified view of her pupils and their background and seems to base some very rigid characterizations of the pupils and their families on what appeared to the observer to be often very flimsy evidence and contact. Moreover her very stereotyped views of the parents might suggest a high degree of social distance between her and them. Nevertheless, it must not be thought that in her interaction with the parents that this teacher communicates to them her generally negative attitude. Indeed observations of her in conversation with parents showed that she was always courteous and charming. She seemed eminently diplomatic, appeared to treat the parents' concerns seriously and made constructive suggestions as to how they could help their children. Moreover, when the parents were interviewed it was quite clear that most of them thought very highly of the teacher and were pleased that their children were in her class. We need, therefore, to distinguish between social distance between parent and teacher at two levels. In the case of this teacher, whilst the parents did not appear to experience social distance from the teacher and found her helpful, forthright and direct, nevertheless, the teacher herself, at the level of her ideology, preserves a high degree of social distance and would not want to identify with them. How, therefore, does the teacher see the relationship between herself and the parents, especially as regards the educational consequences of her own and the parents' activities?

Mrs Lyons regards herself as not simply *in loco parentis* but as acting over and above the parents. Her forcibly expressed views which, as we have observed, are largely negative, reveal a very clear image of what the teacher feels the parents ought to be doing, and particularly in what respects they are failing.

The parents' main responsibility is to produce 'school trained children' whom the teachers can then take and work upon. The educational enterprise is not a co-operative enterprise where parents and teachers perform the same tasks to a lesser or greater extent, but an enterprise where there is a clear and sharp division of labour. Ideally, parents should concentrate on socialization, leaving the task of educating to the professionals. It is only when the family fails to live up to its responsibilities that the teacher's task becomes one not simply of socialization but of resocialization, or attempting to compensate for the errors or deficiencies of previous upbringing which undoubtedly will affect the child's later ability to be educated. In this context it is precisely the failure of these parents to school train the child which is the key to the way she interprets her role.

What does she mean by school trained? The child should be encouraged to be independent. He shouldn't follow her around like a dog all day. He should be clean and suitably dressed, but not over obsessive about cleanliness or appear in a different outfit every day. He shouldn't talk in a high voice or a loud one (loudness is a sign of aggression). Ideally he should have a sense of humour and be able to relate easily to her and others, respond to her directions and anticipate her requirements, but he shouldn't be soft.

Naturally some of these aspects of school training are not such as could easily be communicated to the parents. With this teacher, however, we were fortunate in being able to observe how the respective responsibilities of parents and teachers were communicated to the parents because in her capacity as deputy head she outlined the parents' role to a group of mothers of new children in the following terms, 'It is your job to talk to them, take them out to museums and places of interest'. Here the teacher was trying to suggest that the parents should expose the child to educationally stimulating experiences. Then, 'If your child wants to read to you, by all means listen to him but don't pressurize or buy the same books he uses at school' as this encourages parrot fashion reading [i.e. memorization 'reading' without comprehension] and on no account should you try to teach the child yourself, (a) because it's a skilled job, (b) because you risk confusing him with the wrong methods, and (c) because 'this may bore the child and make him unwilling to work at school'. The parents' 'job' is to 'provide a secure home, take an interest in him' including attending parents' meetings, etc., 'support school activities, plays and concerts' and so on, and to generally present a positive image of the school: 'never criticize the school in front of your child'. Parents should never forget that 'above all, your child is you . . . he is formed by the time he is five, by the time we get him'.

Mrs Lyons has fairly clear notions about what the parents should and shouldn't do at home in their attempts to 'help' the children educationally. They shouldn't teach the child the alphabet 'C A T never taught a soul to read'. They shouldn't make them do sums, but they can teach them to count, to tell the time, the names of colours, to hold pens and recognize shapes and patterns. They should be talked to, asked questions, made to think and have their questions answered and not brushed aside. They shouldn't encroach on the teacher's role or 'make a convenience' of school. Above all 'you've got to trust us, leave everything to us', and allow the teacher to be the best judge of what is in the child's interests. She complained: 'they're always complaining that their children aren't making any progress but what do they expect, they're illiterate themselves'. Thus there is the implication that the parents' own educational failure deprives them of any right to have opinions and criticize what they might regard as the failures of the teachers. Indeed, the teacher projects an image of the teacher as infallible with respect to decisions about the child's educational career. She informs the parents that she knows 'what stage each child is at, what he most needs', and that teachers have good reasons for doing the things that they do and if subsequently there should be any changes there will be valid reasons for that too. This public projection of infallibility is interesting when appraised alongside the concession to the observer and to other teacher colleagues of the difficulty of knowing what and how and when the child is learning, presumably with consequent ambiguity for the role of the teacher *vis-à-vis* the taught. Again, teacher infallibility is ironic when seen in the context of the almost universal tendency to blame the home for the child's failings but not necessarily his successes.

The teacher feels that explicit advice is necessary for the parents but she does recognize that the poor environment, a high-rise estate with 'lots of concrete, no trees and grass, nowhere to play' and unsettled uprooting encountered by the families is 'as hard for the parents as for the children'. She also feels that most of the criticism which comes from the parents in the direction of the school is often due to a presentation problem, i.e. the abusive mother is 'really worried about the other child who is ill in hospital'. Thus the school acts as a safety valve onto which the mother's inadequacy and anxiety is projected.

We have thus a fairly clear picture of the demarcation of roles which the teacher wants to preserve between herself and the parents. Nevertheless, it should be clear from what has already been suggested that the teacher's general view of the parents is that they are too incompetent/clueless/lazy or disturbed themselves to fulfil the parental role satisfactorily. Only with a few parents does the teacher feel there is adequate support and co-operation. It is for this reason that she is strongly of the opinion that the parents should be kept at bay. She seems reluctant to support the head's view that perhaps the time has come for a closer relationship to be established between the school and the homes. She feels that the parents just would not be able to understand what the school is aiming for and would not comprehend what the teachers are trying to do. For example, she thinks that if more written information were given to the parents this would only lead to more confusion. A parent, on being told that a certain child was 'quite good' would then want to know why the child wasn't 'good' or 'very good'. If they were allowed into the school more often they would be noisy, and would be unable to act responsibly, they would start to criticize and cause trouble. Only a few parents could be trusted and these are already being allowed to help—making clothes for the school play, helping with the fancy dress, running outings and so on. A further extension of parental involvement just would not seem practicable at this stage . . .

Moreover, even with the 'good' parents, this teacher feels that their role is essentially limited. During a long discussion in the staffroom when the headmaster had been raising the question of allowing the parents to help with reading by listening to the children read and asking questions about books they might be allowed to take home, this teacher was very much opposed to the idea: 'even with the good ones, I'd rather use them for sewing and threading needles', she said. When asked by the school secretary 'What is so difficult about listening to children read?', she said 'They'd do it all wrong, they'd teach the children sounds . . . the books would get torn', thus revealing no desire to share any 'professional' activities with parents. If only they would do their job efficiently it would liberate her to proceed with hers. This is a useful point at which to open our description of her viewpoint upon the ethos of the school.

2   The school and its ethos

In a very broad sense Mrs Lyons identified with the school ethos as it is projected by the head. We have observed how she shares his evaluation of the children and their backgrounds and the problems this presents to the school as an educational institution. She sees herself as a committed child centred teacher, professional in her approach with no doubts as to her ability to put into operation a pedagogical programme which satisfies child centred criteria and is appropriate to the particular needs of these children. But compared with the former teacher who responded to some of the ambivalencies in the headmaster's position by taking up what we have called a radical child centred stance towards pedagogy, this teacher was more inclined to develop what, in the context of the ethos of this school, could be seen as a pedagogy closer to the formal and traditional approach. She rejects complete informality and permissiveness which she thinks would tend to produce chaos and be unsystematic. As a result she affirms the need for discipline 'the children need and like discipline', and with some of the children, from time to time, she thinks it is necessary to be extremely firm in order to prevent them getting out of control.

Compared with the other teachers we have looked at closely, she is more directive at least in the sense that in the ongoing verbalization between herself and her pupils in the classroom there is an ideal model continually being presented of what the children ought to be doing. This should not be interpreted as if she is operating a rigid formalized classroom where minimum work requirements are placed on all the pupils which she then systematically sees are carried out. Indeed, as in the other classrooms the pupils are allowed a great deal of freedom and she regards her role as one of 'leading from behind'. Nevertheless, she is not in favour of licence and has been heard to say on several occasions to the odd child whom she thinks is wasting time and ought to be doing something more productive, given his age and state of readiness, 'If you can't choose properly, I'll choose for you'. She acknowledges the need for firm control from the top and is in favour of facilitating controlled participation from the pupils rather than leaving them very much to their own devices.

Nevertheless, she regards herself and is regarded by others as a child centred teacher. She admitted that in her former school the approach to pedagogy was 'formal' and traditional and did not correspond to what she sees are her own child centred views. She moved to this school specifically because of her general sympathy with the headmaster's whole approach to education and pedagogy. This teacher's child centredness, however, is more an approach to the child rather than a dogmatic commitment to completely informal methods which knowledge of this type of child might conclude were inappropriate. In this connection she comments on the fact that even the headmaster when he is forced to take a class due, perhaps, to staff absences, reverts to more formal methods of teaching—organizing the pupils into groups, teaching the class as a whole, being very directive and so on, however he may talk about pedagogy in the abstract.

Nevertheless, in spite of her feeling some points of disagreement with the head, these differences are not articulated verbally in public debate between them nor do they become a basis for any noticeable conflict.

The headmaster frequently expressed full confidence in her and obviously regarded her as a teacher who fitted his conception of one satisfying his criteria of an ideal teacher. She agreed with the general approach of the school both as a therapeutic institution which would enable the children to resolve their needs engendered by their unsatisfactory and unstable home backgrounds, and on the ground of practicality since 'these children' were considered not capable of fitting in to a formal context, not 'bright enough to conform' and not stable enough to cope. She was regarded by the other staff as someone obviously committed to the school ethos and as a public relations officer who was fluent and self-confident enough to represent the school's view to outsiders whether parents, social workers or visitors.

In addition, although the headmaster, as we have seen, appeared sometimes to be genuinely self-doubting about the basis of what they were doing, and the efficiency of these methods for this type of child, Mrs Lyons never seemed to doubt her general approach and appeared very secure in the knowledge that she was doing the best possible job in rather unpromising circumstances. This leads us to a description of this teacher's perspective on the classroom and her role therein.

3   Working in the classroom

Given such unpromising material the teacher defines her role as one of providing a secure and enjoyable environment in which the child can learn to mix with other children and become receptive to learning. The school must provide an outlet for the children to express those misdirected and infantile urges which are the result of the pathological aspects of their previous experiences as well as provide a context in which to compensate as far as possible for the poverty of their intellectual and cultural deprivation. But these aims can only be achieved if the teacher effectively establishes a firm and clear framework within which classroom activity can occur. It is the teacher's job to provide the rules and the discipline which she regards as essential for the child's needs to be satisfied and to enable him to learn to socialize and attain autonomy. Consequently, she seeks in her practice to establish an articulated framework where the limits and consequences of behaviour and the expectations laid on them are clear to all.

The observer noticed that in this classroom, rules about how to behave towards other children, how to deal appropriately with the equipment, what attitudes and sentiments to express towards the teacher and the various activities, assumed considerable significance in the social structure of the classroom and the initiation of the child into this articulated rule structure was central to the understanding of the teacher's role. For example, her pupils have to learn to sit when drinking their milk, to wear navy pants for PE, not to run/shout/fight, wear long trousers or boots, not to bring toy cars or trucks into the classroom, touch the curtains, talk in assembly, or 'play teachers off against each other'. They must learn to treat books with respect, not to waste paper, wear aprons for glue, water and paint work, to keep their clothes clean, put crayons in a tin, keep jigsaws separate, remember that all pictures must have a title and name on, and so on. The type of behaviour expected becomes more exacting as the child gets older. The children have to learn to discriminate when it is necessary to seek permission to undertake an activity, for example, painting, feeding the rabbits, playing with the big bricks and when it is up to them to help themselves. They have to cue in to her frame of reference and learn to anticipate her requirements and become 'responsive' to teaching.

Thus in what we have already described as the ongoing verbalization between Mrs Lyons and her pupils, a clearer picture of the framework and rules and norms was being communicated. In addition with the frequent reiterations of the teacher: 'I've got my beady eye on you' it would be difficult for a child not to realize how important it was to try to please the teacher by doing what she wanted.

To initiate her pupils into the standards of conduct and behaviour expected, the teacher operates with a judicious mixture of positive and negative, the promise of rewards and the threat of punishment conveyed through facial gestures, verbal exhortations and example. As a reward the child might be given an errand to run, allowed to give out the milk, help the teacher count the dinner money (if he is numerate) take his work into assembly for display (this will depend on the standard, for the teacher's status is involved here), feed the rabbits or play in the Wendy House. Perhaps the most prized favour for which the children vie is being allowed to stay in and tidy 'Miss's' desk instead of being sent out to play.

As far as punishments are concerned, these may only be threatened or actually implemented depending on the child and the actual circumstances, and range from a demand for an apology and rectification of the misdeed through to having to do work set as an imposition, to the ultimate smack or report to the headmaster. Such rewards and punishment, however, can only be understood in terms of the social structure of the classroom, having a purely symbolic significance which relate to the teacher's attitudes and ideologies, her educational and pedagogic aims. Moreover, Mrs Lyons often involves the other children in the reward and punishment process. The child who has misbehaved does not simply earn the disapprobation of the teacher but also loses esteem in the eyes of his peers, through public ridicule or sarcasm, or isolation from the social group. Conversely, for exceptional endeavour, the whole class may be brought in to clap and approve, the child enhancing his status through the public celebration of his activities.

This process of inducting the child into this elaborate framework of rules and rituals, which seems to assume such a central feature in the teacher's manner of relating to her pupils in the classroom is to be understood in relationship to what we have already said about Mrs Lyons' definition of the characteristics of the school trained child. Without these characteristics, the child is unable to derive much benefit from the opportunities the school provides, and it is towards the ideal of the school trained child that the teacher attempts to move the children. Given her generally pessimistic attitude towards the children it is, perhaps, understandable that she finds it necessary to put such stress on what we could loosely call 'socialization'. This assumes a greater importance in her work than it might were she dealing with 'normal' children. 'These children' regard her as a source of security, she feels, and it is vitally important for her to provide 'the security of rules they badly need'. It should not be thought, however, that the teacher is satisfied with the way she has to interpret her role in the classroom. Were she dealing with 'normal' children, she would be able to proceed with the real 'professional' activities of teaching. Indeed, she thinks that many of the things she has to do are demeaning and should have been done by sensible parents, but, given the nature of her pupils and their generally bad training, circumstances compel her to engage in 'school training'.

For Mrs Lyons, a progressively organized classroom is not synonymous with 'permissiveness' in discipline. Indeed, at all times in the classroom she gave the appearance of being in control. The teacher herself feels that the organization of the classroom activity has a crucial effect on the children's well being.

How does she go about organizing the children? As in the other classrooms there is no adherence to a formal syllabus and the teacher again operates on an integrated day. Few of the features traditionally associated with a formal school are present. There were no tables arranged in rows, no regular tests or incentive stars and a good deal of free movement within the classroom was permitted. Generally, the atmosphere is relaxed and informal, and there is a great deal of flexibility with regard to what the pupils do and when they do it.

In the morning the teacher gathers the children together and explains what she wants them to do that day (she may even ask for suggestions) and the children are allowed to choose when they will perform their tasks. Thus, compared with Mrs Carpenter's perspective, the area of choice open to the children is more closely prescribed and there seem to be minimal work requirements placed on the pupils which is not evident in the other classrooms observed. 'Work' may be undertaken during a period specified as free, or children may play during a work period, provided the teacher believes that the work has been completed or will be subsequently. She warns those children she thinks likely to shirk their work, which might be a few specific children whose 'behaviour problems' have rendered them more visible to her, that 'if you can't choose properly I'll choose for you', which would seem to add a qualification to her faith in each child's ability to learn in his own way.

Nevertheless, despite the unsuitable and unstable home environment and the limited social and cultural experiences of the child, the teacher does emphasize the importance of giving the child freedom. For the teacher believes that the child 'knows what he needs' and she has faith in his ability to teach himself, when he is ready, although she contends that the children as a whole have limited appreciation and are unsophisticated, thereby greatly reducing the possibility of any high educational achievement on their part.

Apart from placing certain work requirements on her pupils, the teacher declares her reluctance to intervene unduly in the children's activities. She is 'loath to impose' her will believing that 'children teach themselves'. When presented with a learning situation such considerations mean that the teacher refrains from very close supervision of the child's activities, such as continually correcting a child's spelling mistakes and, in public, maintains that almost any activity can be pregnant for learning; and that children will only do what they are 'ready' for.

She aims, as we have seen, to prepare the child for learning, though not to act as a nurse maid, to make the child school trained, yet she frequently maintains that she cannot teach until her pupils are ready. Nevertheless, it is she who decides when the child is 'ready' and what criteria she will use to justify 'moving the child' to the next stage when he has reached the appropriate level. For example, with respect to 'readiness for reading' she argued 'medical evidence has shown that their eyes cannot focus properly much before five', and would use such things as his ability to complete patterns symmetrically, to persevere and concentrate, his competence in drawing an identifiable figure rather than merely scribbling, his ability to recognize letters, as indicators of the child's readiness.

The use of the concept of readiness to justify teacher intervention is, of course, intimately related to a notion of developmental stages. This process of movement through stages is not explicated further in the teacher's perspective and it was noticed by the observer that the teacher did not closely specify what the stages were and their operational indicators beyond reference to such generalities referred to when giving examples of her notion of 'readiness for reading'. Nevertheless, the pupils did not on the whole seem to present a series of puzzles to the teacher regarding their intellectual growth and the stages they were at. She seemed to 'know' where they were at, and what they needed, and appeared very rapidly to arrive at judgments regarding their cognitive and emotional qualities and their requirements. This self-confidence may be a reflection of her being more highly qualified than the other staff. She has an advanced diploma in psychology, regards herself as an expert and is so regarded by others.

It cannot be stressed enough, however, that until the child has acquired the right 'attitude' to school, that is, not until he has learnt not to rush about and to address the teacher in modulated tones, and possess all the other qualities of the school trained child, is he considered 'ready to learn to read, write and do number work'. He must be adequately socialized before real 'work' can begin.

The teacher expresses the view that play, and allowing the children freedom in play is of considerable importance for socialization. She agrees that 'play had considerable therapeutic value for these children'. It is vital for their education, they can learn through play. Nevertheless, her attitude towards play is ambiguous. Although to the parents she will argue that 'all play has a potential for learning' on the same occasion she may argue 'they may think they are playing all day but this play is not really play'. She seems to distinguish between mere play and time-wasting play. She thinks dressing up, for example, is 'silly'; sand and water play is all right but only for younger children; and will frequently remind the children that 'you don't come to school to play all day'. Nevertheless, all these 'non-work' activities she will tolerate, especially with younger children or those whose emotional problems need some outlet in therapeutic pastimes of this kind. She seems, however, to have a clear distinction between work and play, and work seems to be definitely associated with a productivity ethic. She will tell the children to 'settle down', 'make something nice', 'find yourselves something to do'. This notion of producing something seems to be very important in her perspective on classroom activity. Indeed, there seems to be a strong emphasis placed on the importance of material productivity both in relationship to the categorization and assessment of her pupils, and in terms of the way in which she intervenes in, and organizes, the pupils' activities.

It could be argued that getting her pupils to produce things assumes a great importance among Mrs Lyons' educational aims. Although she argues that she will be content if her pupils acquire a good grasp of the basic reading, writing and number work skills by the time they leave her, it seems that only a general grounding is all that is looked for. She has no specific standards beyond that. In the meantime, so long as the pupils carry out their minimum work requirements, she will be satisfied if the classroom gives the appearance of a high level of material productivity, if the pupils make something nice and thereby give evidence that work is being performed and, by definition, development taking place. Nevertheless, with respect to specific individual pupils, clearer aims are apparent. This is noticeable in the differential way in which she checks up on what the pupils are doing. As we have seen there is no 'across the board' checking up that the pupils have done the work set but with some pupils there seems to be a closer supervision which might relate to the way in which the teacher has a more definite set of expectations *vis-à-vis* their practice in the classroom.

We have made some comments about the teacher's views on the value of choice in the child's education. It was seen how the teacher believes that children should be allowed choice, first because they know what they need and second because the exercise of choice develops self-discipline and the child's critical capabilities. In practice, however, the amount of choice allowed depends heavily on the teacher's assessment of the individual child's readiness—and her own educational aims. That is to say, although she argues that children know what they need, nevertheless, if the child's choices seem to conflict with her assessment of what he needs, or her diagnosis of approved behaviour, then she will intervene in his activities and direct him positively towards something else. It would seem as if the child only has the freedom to follow his needs if the teacher has no prior expectation of him. This is particularly likely if the child is new or if the child for various reasons is rather inconspicuous and not salient in the teacher's frame of reference. She will say to one child 'it is not a case of what you want to do' and 'you don't come to school to do as you like' with the implication that choice is only permitted in so far as it coincides with the teacher's conceptions of what ought to be happening. Similarly although play and choice is given therapeutic legitimation—if a child takes advantage of the opportunities granted by this therapeutic environment and indulges in activities which the teacher regards as providing outlets for immature or pathological tendencies, he is likely to be re-directed elsewhere. Mrs Lyons does not see this as contradictory, and would be capable of providing realistic justifications as to why complete permissiveness or a universal operation of the free choice principle would not be appropriate.

What sort of pedagogic role does the teacher play in the classroom? We have seen how she attempts to provide a framework in which the children can become organized and be productive. Of course, some degree of planning for this is essential. The teacher claims to do about an hour a day in preparation and, certainly, before school, during the lunch breaks and after school she was to be observed regularly organizing materials, and making other preparations for the sessions to come later. Her planning was particularly apparent when associated with certain long term projects, like the preparation involved for the open evening, the school play or the Wednesday Assembly when the classes took it in turns to 'put something on' for the whole school. With respect to these occasions, the teacher appeared to have a clear idea of what the finished product would be like, whether it involved the way the classroom would be decorated, or a play or sketch be performed, and the pupils were organized specifically around the production of the appropriate products or activities. On a more day-to-day basis, however, less pre-thought out plans were in evidence. A great deal seemed to be developed from several regular schools televised programmes. This lack of pre-planning is legitimized by an informal, child centred teacher who would argue the impossibility of working a whole programme out beforehand, because of the idiosyncratic nature of children's interests and development which necessitates decisions being made on the spot appropriate to the child's needs. Indeed, this teacher rarely was observed to be at a loss for ideas about what the children should do, and even for those activities which she had worked out beforehand, she would be prepared to change direction or come up with a compromise plan if it did not seem to suit the children's interest or capture their involvement.

Nevertheless, observations in the classroom made it quite clear that the teacher was of crucial importance in organizing what the children were doing and she tended to spend by far the greater part of her time on activities which she had organized and with pupils she had selected.

Although, as we have seen, the teacher places minimum work requirements on every child, once they have made 'a start' and she has provided a framework in which all pupils are actively involved in doing things—her own time and energies are not shared out equally among all her pupils. This is quite explicitly recognized by the teacher herself. There are, in the class, too many difficult children for her to spend as much time and energy as they need; the size of the class and the poor material with which she has to deal, that is, those who have to be controlled firmly, those she finds it difficult to relate to, those she can't stand or 'has to avoid' prevent her from sharing out her attentions equally. In spite of the concern for the child's individual personality, the teacher has a responsibility for the class as a social entity. The needs of the one have to give way to the demands of the group. And, within the group, those whom the teacher considers most able to benefit, the brightest, receive the extra attention, not those most in need, for them there would be little pay off and the results gained would be few compared with the energy expended. Even were she to spend a lot of time with them, the pay off would probably be minimal. Given that the pupils generally have such a poor prognosis, the teacher believes that her extra attention and efforts should go to the brightest, those who may be able to make something of themselves, or those she might be able to make as good as 'normal' children with a little attention. This differential allocation of the teacher's time and energies is justified in terms of the economic results. Mrs Lyons, therefore, tends to spend her time with those children she defined as 'ready' or 'all there', as pleasant personalities who are in a position to move on to a higher stage and thus more capable of benefiting from her attention. They tend to be older children, mostly girls, who can show that they are more responsive to learning, better trained for school, and have greater manual dexterity to be able to participate in the types of activities the teacher engages in with these groups of teacher selected pupils.

We should conclude by stressing the confidence with which this teacher went about her job in the classroom. She did not appear to feel under any undue pressure or constraint internally within the school from the headmaster and other teachers, and although she was aware of the parents' potential criticism or hostility this only affected the way she presented what she was doing rather than led to any alteration at the level of practice. For example, she would ensure that the children did not take examples of their written work to show their parents, unless it had been carefully vetted beforehand. As a result the children frequently only took art work home which reinforced some parents' suspicions that their children played all day. Nevertheless, it illustrates the extent to which the teacher felt obliged to 'manage' her self-presentation as teacher to the parent. For example, after discussing a child's progress in reading with a parent, the teacher confided in the observer the child 'had taught herself—but I couldn't tell her mother that', showing the obvious influence of the parents experienced by the teacher at least in so far as she presented herself to them. But, within the context of the classroom, her sense of professional autonomy and self-confidence *vis-à-vis* both the other teachers and the parents was higher than with the other two teachers we are discussing. She recognizes that she has greater experience than the other teachers, she can easily 'see' difficulties and come to terms with them in a way which she does not regard as incompatible with the basic tenets of her child centred perspective. Nevertheless, this should not be taken to suggest that what she does in her classroom is entirely the result of her own spontaneously developed perspective on the situation. She is as much part of a situation with its own internal logic and constraints as any other social actor. The ramifications of that situation and its constraints will be taken up again later.

We will now move to our third teacher, Mrs Buchanan, and describe her perspective using the same broad analytic categories as used above.

Mrs Buchanan

1   The children and their background

In contrast to the other two teachers Mrs Buchanan had a very different view of the children with whom she had to deal. Instead of seeing them as deprived, maladjusted or disturbed, she sees them in the main as merely normal children who happen to come from working class backgrounds: 'I just think they are ordinary children. I don't think they are any different from the type of children I taught before.' She is disinclined to think of them as problem children:

'Maybe it's just me but I don't think there are as many problems as is made out. I think the home background of these children must count a lot and must be a problem but it's not a problem as far as they (the children) are concerned. They accept such a lot, I think. They don't go around saying what a shame I'm a working class child, you know, I'm deprived of books and I've got a mother who beats me. It doesn't make any difference. I mean, he accepts that his father beats him, or his mother beats him, it doesn't make any difference to him . . . . If it were a problem I think I would hear about it. I think the main problem in school, or the most difficult thing to do is to understand them and for us to accept that they have accepted their home background—and for us to accept them as individuals. I don't think they want sympathy because they've accepted it. I don't think it's anything strange to them at all.'

Here we have illustrated Mrs Buchanan's recognition that the children come from backgrounds which are very different from those of middle class pupils, backgrounds which encompass different attitudes, values and styles of behaviour from those which she or her colleagues might share. Nevertheless, having recognized the cultural differences, she is reluctant to proceed to negatively evaluate these children as being disturbed or lacking in some way. To her they are just ordinary children:

'To be quite truthful I wouldn't say I've got any who appear to be disturbed, and yet, you know, from the background of some I surprise myself by saying that I don't think there are any with particular behaviour problems and I've none that are so introverted that it's peculiar, and none that are so aggressive that it's peculiar. No, they just seem to be, well, very ordinary children who are naughty when they are naughty and good when they are good. They don't seem peculiar to me at all.'

Nevertheless she does not regard their background as educationally irrelevant. She believes that, in general, the parents are not very interested in their children's education, and do not really provide the right kind of supportive environment. She thinks they only seem to care about whether their children are being cheeky at school. ('Does he cheek you?' is a frequent parental query), and she feels that the parents give their children a completely false conception of what goes on in school. This presents her with problems in trying to educate them. For example, some children are told to expect the cane. 'Well, if they tell them *that* about school, you're fighting a losing battle right from the start.' But she doesn't think that their background is the only relevant factor. 'I think far too much is explained by background—and dismissed by it, too.' She thinks that some of her pupils are far brighter than many think. She sees intelligence as the product of both environment and heredity, but thinks that she's got a fair distribution of bright children in her class.

'Even in a middle class area you'll get some children who, despite their background, will be just plain thick, but with middle class children at home everything is different, isn't it? There's more emphasis on school attainment, encouragement and books . . . whereas with these children a lot of them are just not interested in books, except to rip them.'

In general, however, although she articulates a view of the parents as pleasant but not educationally very interested, the parents and their backgrounds do not appear to be very salient in her ideology, especially at the beginning of the period of observation. She did not seem very knowledgeable or interested in this aspect of her pupils' lives and seemed self-consciously aware of the dangers of premature labelling of pupils by virtue of information which the school might have about the child's family or home. She expresses a desire to orientate herself in an individual way—liking the pupils, wanting 'to treat them as individuals, getting to know them'. Moreover, she also admitted that she preferred teaching this type of pupil. She found them less 'cocksure', more spontaneous, lively and full of fun and humour, admitting that she probably responded to them with a warmth that was related to her own origins in a similar working class community.

It is important to note that the difference between Mrs Buchanan and the others lies not so much in her factual characterization of the life styles, with 'fathers out of jobs and mothers sleeping around and battering their kids' but in the evaluation of its significance. Instead of seeing such a life style as inevitably producing pathological psychological traits in these children, she expresses a relativistic approach to the idea of normality. Her pupils are, for her, perfectly normal products of an environment which they accept as normal and 'which doesn't bother them' and the teachers should recognize that and not pride themselves that they're 'doing a grand job because they're in that school and, you know, what a good thing they're doing for these children ... that's completely wrong.'

This lack of relevance of the family situation comes out again in the same interview:

'You can like the children and accept them for what they are and not for what their family is and parents are. I mean, their mothers can be sleeping around with all the different men in the city for all I care; you know, as long as the child is getting on at school and getting on with me, I don't mind. Not that it would make any difference if I did mind (laughter).'

There is, however, an ambivalence in her ideology because, as time goes on when she talked to the observer about individual children in much more detail, the explanation for a child's failure in school increasingly came to be interpreted in terms of some difficulties or problems that the child was experiencing at home. Almost, by definition, if the child was seen as underachieving, this would be explained in terms of 'something going on at home'. We will return to this later.

We have already noticed how this teacher is rather unconcerned about her relationship with the pupils' parents. She is aware that the school has experienced in its history difficult relationships with the parents and 'knows' about the petition they drew up about the methods and the legacy of bitterness that it left with the staff. She herself, however, felt she had good relationships with her pupils' parents. She thinks they have minimal interest in their children's education but has not come across any who have said to her that the school's 'bloody hopeless' and 'the kids are only playing all the time'. She feels that grumbling talk sometimes goes on at the school gate and that some who are dissatisfied tend to blame the school and its methods because it's so different from their own expectations and 'they don't really understand whats going on', so they blame the unfamiliar. But she feels that there is a tendency to overgeneralize about the parents' hostility and to say 'oh, everybody's complaining', when in fact it's only one or two. In general, Mrs Buchanan seems quite satisfied with the amount of contact she has with them. They come along to the meetings and interviews and seem quite impressed. There is however a level of social distance between herself and the parents which she wants to preserve. When the children first start school she tries to accentuate this distance—doesn't want to hear all about the child from the parent but wants to make up her own mind. Moreover, she would be against involving the parents more because they might start to tell her what to do with this or that child, and she defines that as the teacher's responsibility. In any case, she thinks that the parents mainly have little idea both about what goes on in school and what their own children are like. There are pupils whom the parents say are 'absolute terrors' at home but are very good at school and vice versa.

Mrs Buchanan feels that the parents are not capable of participating in a fruitful partnership with the school and that the teacher must try to educate the children in spite of rather than in co-operation with the parents. Nevertheless, when children are underachieving, it is increasingly to the parents that she is inclined to look for the explanation.

Given that her view of the pupils and their background differs to some extent from those of Mrs Carpenter and Mrs Lyons, it might be expected that her attitude towards the school ethos might differ similarly. It is to this that we now turn.

2   The school and its ethos

In contrast to our other two teachers Mrs Buchanan does not share the dominant view of the school and its ethos as it is articulated by the headmaster. She sees the headmaster as representing a tradition in educational thought and practice with which she cannot completely identify. On the one hand, she doubts the efficiency of its methods with this kind of pupil and, on the other, she seems to question the basic standpoint which she sees the other staff as holding. We have already seen how she has a very different view of the pupils and their background compared with the head and the two other teachers. It is not surprising, therefore, that she should question the therapeutic notion of the school's role which she sees the others as having. For her, the important function of the teacher is to get through to the individual child, to identify with them and appreciate them as individuals, and although the other teachers may also want to do this, she disagrees with what she sees as the tendency to treat all the pupils as deprived and maladjusted products of a disturbed family background:

'It's a bit of a sore point with me, actually because I think most of the rest of the staff, not all of them certainly but I think most of the rest of the staff tend to teach families rather than individuals. If they've had one problem child from a family then the rest of that family that come to school are immediately labelled as problems, which I don't accept at all.'

She goes on to say that she thinks

'they like the children, but they like them at arm's length, whereas you know, they're children to me, and I won't go all soppy and say I love them, but I certainly like them a lot, you know, I like to get on with them.'

Mrs Buchanan is also somewhat out on a limb as far as the school's methods are concerned. There are two main elements in her view of the methods. One is that she feels the methods are just not suitable for the type of children the school has to deal with. The other, and perhaps the most important reason, is that she feels a lack of self confidence about her own ability to operate the methods:

'I think it can work but it would work better in a more middle class type area. It sounds terrible but I think that with children who are conscious of getting on it can work better . . . . To be a good integrated day-type teacher, you've got to be very well organized and very, very efficient and if you're not, then you know . . . I think that's why I'm criticizing it. I think I've got a conscience myself.'

She paints a picture of how the methods would work in an ideal situation:

'In an ideal situation you'd have them all so keen and interested that they'd get on and just come to you for book references and this and that and the other (laughter) but here, they don't seem to get involved in anything, not for any length of time anyway. They've got a very short span of concentration, they've got no perseverance at all. You've got to be standing over them, all the time, pushing them.'

If she had a free hand she would be far more directive. She would have them all sitting down at certain times of the day making them do reading, writing and number work, but she is conscious of her lack of power to do that. This teacher thinks that she would be disapproved of if she did that and is reluctant to publicly express her lack of sympathy with, and her personal feelings of inadequacy to operate, these very informal methods. 'Perhaps I'm just a traditionalist and put a lot on attainment, you know, rather than social training.'

Mrs Buchanan was reluctant to revert to a situation where the teacher is telling the children what to do all day; what she wants is a compromise where there is both some freedom and some compulsion.

It should, by now, be obvious that Mrs Buchanan is out of step with the official ideology of the school. She does not see herself, however, as completely isolated. She thinks that one or two of the other teachers are also more sympathetic to some elements of formality and may surreptitiously be more directive in their teaching. However, she believes that, at least in public, it is important not to voice one's desire for greater directiveness, since this would run counter to the ethics of the official ideology.

An ambiguity in the headmaster's thinking is discerned. She feels that he's not really decided on exactly what he wants.

> 'I think there are different goals in Mapledene . . . a lot of emphasis is put on relationships, you know, whether a child can make good social relationships, whereas in a formal school all the emphasis is put on attainment.'

But then, when talking of the head, she says,

> 'I don't think he's quite sure of what he wants the school to be himself yet. That's just an impression, I couldn't offer any grounds for it at all. But it's an impression I get that he's not quite sure of what he wants the school to be or what he wants. He knows he wants the free methods, but then, you know, I think he expects the same results as if he's got a very formal school where you've trained right from the word go . . . which he doesn't get, I wouldn't think.'

We have, thus a situation where this teacher is not in complete sympathy with the school ethos, feeling herself somewhat out on a limb, not daring publicly to express the difficulties she is having, nor feeling that much advice and assistance would be forthcoming were she to ask for it, because it might reflect badly on her competence as a teacher. In addition, she has a somewhat different notion about what the aims of education ought to be. She would rank raising the level of attainment high in her hierarchy of education goals believing that these pupils are more capable than many of the staff think—and measures her own competence as a teacher in terms of her ability to transmit basic skills. Although, like the other staff, she sees the social and emotional aspects of the teacher's role as important, she rates these as important conditions for the achievement of academic goals, rather than as substitutes for it. In this respect she may be a deviant in terms of the dominant ethos, and this deviance is related to the different way in which she looks at the pupils. Whereas the other two teachers have a view of the typical child as maladjusted and disturbed and hence of low educability, the main task being a therapeutic one to create a context where the children can work through their problems and needs and at least develop more integrated personalities, even if they are never likely to be successes educationally, she sees her task as one of trying to ensure that the pupils develop academically to the level of their capabilities, the range of their capabilities being as high as would be found in any school. Aspects of these differences are reflected in her perspective on the classroom, particularly in some of the difficulties she recognizes in her practice there.

3   Working in the classroom

We have seen how Mrs Buchanan has a different view of the children and their parents compared with the other teachers, and that her attitude towards the school and its ethos is, to a certain extent, critical. We now turn to her understanding of the classroom situation to consider how she manages to make sense of the classroom experience, how she manages to negotiate a role which will enable her to approximate to her own notion of what a good teacher should be doing, and how she resolves the difficulties which the situation presents.

In our discussion of her perspective we suggested that Mrs Buchanan's attitude towards the methods which the school prescribes for the pupils is critical. It is not that she disapproves of the methods *per se* but she regards them as inappropriate for the type of child with whom she has to deal. Nevertheless she does not see herself as in a position to adopt different methods from those prescribed, so it is not surprising that she should find her situation in the classroom as essentially problematic.

The problematic nature of the classroom relates to her view of the pupils as in the main nice, lively, spontaneous children who differ from other children only in the sense that their environment is not conducive to their being interested in and committed to what she regards as education. Nevertheless, she is constrained to use the free methods, allowing children to choose what they want to do, and not being forced to read and write if they don't want to. As a result, she finds the classroom experience fraught with difficulties. She sees that the children are wandering around a lot, never seeming to get involved in the activities, lacking the interest and concentration to persevere with anything, especially those activities which she regards as important:

'They move around so quickly, you can't really notice what they are doing or who they are playing with because they just move around quickly from one thing to another. They just keep going round . . . .

They've got a very short span of concentration, they've no
perseverance at all. If anything goes wrong then that's it. They just
can't be bothered at all. They just don't seem to be interested in
anything except playing.'

She also finds that the classroom is noisy:

'Another problem with this integrated day is noise because I'm sure the
children can't work with the amount of noise here. The trouble is
you've got people dashing around with guns made of lego—you know,
engine noises going off all over the place, and it must be awfully
difficult. I can't concentrate in that sort of situation and I'm sure the
children can't.'

The combination of children moving around, noise, and the pupils not
really getting interested in any of the activities, presents Mrs Buchanan
with discipline problems. She admits that she had had more discipline
problems than with any class she has encountered before. Part of it she
explains by her lack of experience with very young children, but she also
blames the lack of a formal approach: 'In a formal situation I was so used
to saying be quiet and it would be quiet but here you have to keep on for
about 5 or 10 minutes to get anywhere near what you want.'
All these difficulties are complicated by the teachers' lack of time to
deal with so many children. She often laments the fact that if she had
more time and fewer children she would be able to do more:

'I haven't got the time to keep following them up and making them sit
down and read to me . . . . I would have to sit down with him for half an
hour to get through to him, and I just haven't the time . . . . I suppose
it's a question of having sufficient time in the day. It's a long day for the
kids, but you could do with the day being twice as long, and new
children too take up so much of your time. And there are some children
who could do with so much more of your time . . . . You need to chat a
lot to these children, just need to chat a bit more. They come at the
most inconvenient times. You haven't got the time to listen, but they
need to do, otherwise they wouldn't come up and talk to you. You've
got insufficient time all round—that's the basic problem.'

In the light of these difficulties which she encounters, how does she try
to act in the classroom? Basically, what she tries to do is to provide a
context in which the children can gradually learn to settle down and
become involved and interested in the activities. She seems to hold some

sort of naturalistic concept about the process of setting down. With respect to the new children in the class, there is a marked lack of any directive intervention in their activities. She tends to leave them to find their own feet in the classroom, giving them little explicit instructions about what they should or should not do and perhaps allowing them more leeway in their behaviour than she would expect from other children. In the case, for example, of two children whom she admitted 'drive her crackers' she argued,

'you can't really shout at them, she's still very young yet, she's just got to settle down . . . . They tend to get away with a bit more than anyone else which I don't like, but unless I let them run round a bit and go wild, then they'll never settle down.'

Her attitude to her own *laissez-faire* approach is almost therapeutic in its justification. It is as if she feels that after a few weeks in the classroom the pupils will play out their problems and then become more adjusted to the situation, in accordance with certain natural developments. She finds it difficult to explain why some children settle down more easily than others—it's because of some natural attributes that they possess which will come out sooner or later. For example, when talking about a particular child she said 'There's been quite a change in him. I never thought he would settle . . . . It's not been by any effort or influence on my part. He was fairly wild—I didn't really stop him.' Interviewer: 'When he was difficult—did you have any special policies towards him?' Teacher: 'Not really, he's just naturally settled down. I don't really know why.'

This notion of the teacher playing a passive role in the settling down process does not characterize her view of the teaching process generally in the classroom. She recognizes that the proficient teacher must be very active as an organizer in the situation. If the teacher is not organized then it will be impossible to achieve her own objectives. Indeed, this teacher, when expressing doubt and concern about her own competence and performance in the classroom explained it in terms of her own failings to adequately organize the situation, to get the most out of the pupils. She feels that good organization doesn't come naturally, and she would have been grateful for more help and assistance from the other more experienced teachers, but had been left to flounder at first and gradually learn from her own experience, and mistakes.

What does she mean by good organization? Good organization seems to mean being aware of what she can expect her children to be able to do—and organizing work to suit them—having enough activities set out for the children so that they get involved in something and don't just wander around aimlessly. With good organization the pupils know what they should be doing or not doing. They experience a sense of structure. Without organization, in the classroom, the whole situation becomes chaotic:

'At first children were wandering around all day and not occupying themselves. I would turn round and see them just not doing anything. It was my organization that was wrong. I didn't have enough activities set out for them . . . . The methods are more difficult, you've got to be a marvellous teacher in that sort of situation. You've got to be very organized.'

How does she set out to achieve good organization? Initially the teacher will have some idea of what she wants to do that day. This might involve preparing something to go on the walls for display, or preparing something for the school assembly. It could mean getting the pupils started on some sort of project. She might decide that that day she wants all the six year olds to do some writing or all the seven year olds to do some number work. She doesn't think, however, that it is possible to have very definite and precise plans fully worked out beforehand. The plan has to be flexible and often, even though she has a plan, it does not mean that she will stick to it, regardless of whether the children seem interested or bored. Nor is it possible to plan for each child—just a general plan, a flexible plan is called for, capable of being altered or abandoned in the face of the actual process of events.

Given a general plan, the teacher then tries to get the children involved. At the beginning of every morning and afternoon session she gathers the pupils together in the quiet corner to organize their activities. She tries to get the pupils to commit themselves to doing things, asking them whether they would like to do this or that, subtly trying to shape their activities towards the things she wants them to do. But circumstances, again, do not permit that every child expresses his choices or makes a definite public commitment that he is going to do a certain activity. Every planning session leaves quite a sizeable majority who do not seem to have been organized or to have organized themselves into any definitive task. After she has asked several times, 'Who would like to do . . .?' there is always a group of children left who have not volunteered for anything and to whom Mrs Buchanan responds with the typical comment: 'The rest of you, walk out into the classroom quietly and find yourself something to do.'

Having planned the session, the teacher will then proceed to 'do the rounds'. By this she means that she moves from group to group, child to child, getting them organized, seeing that they are involved in something, suggesting ways in which they might develop further an activity, singling out some children to do some reading, getting all the six year olds to do some writing, and so on.

Mrs Buchanan attaches great importance to this activity of 'doing the rounds'. She feels that most of the children she has to deal with are just not able to get on by themselves without her pushing or encouraging them. She explains that she is trying to get them to the point where they will no longer need her close attention all the time, when they can work by themselves, with interest and self-confidence. The basic ideal behind the methods, she feels, is that they should get on alone—but this is only an ideal which cannot be achieved at the present moment, particularly with this kind of child. In the meantime, they need her help, but whilst she is helping one group of children, there may be others who are wandering around aimlessly, who are unable to get on until she responds to their clamours for assistance. However, with such a large class and with children who have different needs and problems, she must just try and get round to see as many children as possible:

> 'The best policy I can pursue is to sit with them, and hope that they'll work . . . you know . . . get them writing by themselves, with me sat down with them—you know, and in the end I hope I'll be able to go away and they'll get on with it by themselves . . . . You start six off with something—then they can get on on their own—then you move around to another group. Each day you try to do the rounds, you try to have some kind of contact with each child—you might be dealing with different sections of the class . . . but you have to do the rounds.'

But the teacher appreciates that even 'doing the rounds' still is unsatisfactory from the point of view of some children:

> 'You can spend an awful lot of time with slow kinds who need to be pushed. I just rely on grabbing one whom I know needs help and trying to get him sat down with a pencil—but it's sometimes so difficult to get through to them—and in the meantime, everybody else wants help.'

Her immediate practical aim is to get the children working on their own for, as she says,

'unless they can work on their own, the children are in difficulties.

In an ideal situation you'd have them all so keen and interested that they'd get on and just come to you for book references and this and that and the other.'

This notion of the self-teaching child is one which relates to her activities in the classroom and her conception of her own difficulties. It is as if she has to develop such a notion, given her lack of self-confidence as a teacher, and her realization that pressures of time and resources militate against giving enough attention to each child, especially those whom she acknowledges she has difficulty in getting through to. As she puts it herself,

'You see, the very young ones I could dismiss and say, oh, they never do anything, but they could, for all I know, have got out the unifix blocks and counted up to ten. They are learning through this. They are doing by themselves.'

Again when talking about the difficulties of organization she said,

'I was dashing from one group to another, getting them to do reading and writing and number work because that's what I thought they ought to be doing—I tried to do that, but I was wrong. It doesn't really matter if they don't do number work every day. They might have picked up some unifix blocks and done something by themselves . . . I try to get them to get on with things by themselves—which is the idea of these methods.'

'Get on with what you are doing', 'find yourself something to do' are frequently uttered directives in the classroom. It becomes problematic, however, how the teacher sees the different activities in the classroom and what sort of role she takes up *vis-à-vis* these different activities. Although the children are encouraged to get on with things on their own, the teacher does not view the outcome of their choices neutrally. Different activities have different significances for her, in terms of what they denote about the child who chooses them and in terms of the role she plays towards that child.

We have seen how she puts a great deal of stress on the acquisition of the basic skills of literacy and numeracy. We have also suggested that if she had a free hand she would develop a more formal, that is, in her terms, more directive approach to these activities in the curriculum. Moreover her lack of sympathy towards the emphasis laid on freedom and a wide range of choice relates to her judgment about such a pedagogy being inappropriate for 'these children', given their lack of interest in education due to their home environment. It is not surprising, therefore, that she should differentiate clearly between what she regards as work and play. She relates play and work to a notion of stages. Play is what younger children want to do naturally. Work, on the other hand, is something that older children ought to do but frequently avoid. 'The younger ones are very little problem—they just play mainly, you know', or, 'he has fallen back to the playing stage'. Again:

'The younger ones are supposed to be brought up by the older ones, you know, to see the older ones working—but I find it works very much the opposite way; that the older ones see the younger ones playing and go and play. It's the middle ones who suffer because they are young enough to play yet old enough to work.'

How does the teacher differentiate between work and play? She seems to operate with a commonsense definition of play. Play is something which children naturally want to do, something which provides more intrinsic satisfaction for the child—something which younger children can more legitimately be allowed to do than older children. This is not to suggest that, in the teacher's term, play has no useful function for the child in the classroom. When children are playing they may at the same time be learning something which the teacher regards as important—a child playing with bricks may be teaching himself to count or learning the basic principles of addition and subtraction—but this need not necessarily be the case. But perhaps, more importantly, it had a therapeutic value. It helps children get rid of their inhibitions and aggressions. It's a process whereby they can let off steam and gradually learn to settle down. Other things being equal, the teacher should not interfere with play.

Work on the other hand is hard, it requires effort. Children, especially these children, don't naturally incline towards work. Generally they won't do it unless they are made to. They don't find it intrinsically satisfying, at least in the early stages when they get very little satisfaction from the end product, and yet it is important because society demands it. If these children are going to grow up into all round human beings, able to function in a complex society, able to get jobs, able to survive without being 'conned' they must become involved in work—and this means, at this stage of the educational ladder, learning to read and write and be numerate. She admits, though, that number work is of far less utilitarian value than reading and writing. As an adult one can get by, being able to do simple counting, subtraction and multiplication, but being able to read and write proficiently is of fundamental significance and the *sine qua non* of everything else.

This work/play distinction continually reappears in her perspective and is basic to the way she conducts herself in the classroom. She admits to only being directive with the children as regards work, and would be much more directive if she had a completely free hand. This is not to suggest that she is against children being given freedom—only that they should have freedom after they have done what the teacher thinks is important. The work idea also explains the different roles she takes up *vis-à-vis* the different activities. She regards herself as a teacher when she is interacting with a child about work—in her common sense understanding, when she is helping with writing, reading or number work. However, when she interacts with a child who has been playing, she described her role as one simply of being an admirer: someone who will respond with approval and encouragement to whatever the child has produced as a result of a play activity, a model, a picture, a sand castle; who will make him return to that activity, to give him the satisfaction that he's done something. She would not dream of interfering. In reply to the question 'Are there some things in which you regard your role as a teacher as crucial, and others not?' She said,

> 'When they're painting or drawing, etc., you play a crucial role in admiring what they've done, encouraging them to do it again . . . the number of times a child will bring up something to show you, so long as you say, oh that's nice, or that's good, the child will always go back and do it again, whereas with reading and writing, you're a teacher then.'

And it is this notion of teaching which is central when she is 'doing the rounds'. So long as the children are not being disruptive and are playing quietly and with interest, she tends to leave them alone. In the meantime she moves around from group to group, now helping a few with their reading or writing, now explaining the principles of addition or subtracting with some others, now encouraging a child to find out how to spell a word by looking through the flash cards or pointing it out to him on the wall. In the meantime she will compliment a child on a painting he's doing, warn another that he's banging the bricks too loudly and so on and so on.

Thus the teacher's perspective on her practice is related to the structure of time/space relationships in the classroom. To the observer an impression of a minimum degree of routine and formality is presented, such routine as is observable being related to the teacher's attempts to get the pupils involved as often as possible with the activities which she sees relates to the acquisition of literacy and numeracy skills. The classroom is organized in an open and flexible manner, very much as the former classrooms, with the children being permitted a high degree of choice among a wide range of possible activities. Allowing the pupils choice, as we have seen, is far more a function of how the teacher feels her role is being prescribed by those who present the school ethos to the individual teacher, especially one, such as herself, a probationer, who lacks experience rather than to her own practical judgments as to the efficiency of this approach to pedagogy for the kinds of pupils she feels she has to deal with. Nevertheless, in spite of the differences in her perspective there is little in the appearance and mode of organization in the classroom which would immediately lead one to suppose that this teacher is a deviant in terms of her attitudes to education and pedagogy.

The classroom has all the appearance of an informal, child centred, fluid setting where children are allowed to choose activities in accordance with their emotional and intellectual needs.

Conclusion

In this chapter we have characterized the major dimensions of the three teachers' perspectives which are of relevance to our substantive concerns. We do not claim to have explored these perspectives in all their idiosyncracy and uniqueness. Such a project would be impossible. Even in the most intensive we-relationship, to use Schutz's term (Schutz, 1960), knowledge of the other is mediated through typifications.

Our intention has been to present a fair and faithful, if idealized, conception of the teachers' world views on various issues as they relate to their work situation. So far, the project has involved a relatively descriptive enterprise. In the following chapters, however, our attention turns to a more analytical level of enquiry. The project is to situate aspects of the teachers' perspectives in a broader context in relation to such issues as the social structuring of pupils' identities, staff relationships and parent/teacher involvement. It is to the first of these themes that we now turn.

6

Social stratification in the classroom: an ideal type

The analysis of social stratification in the classroom provides an interesting opportunity to examine the usefulness of a social phenomenological perspective. We have observed in our summary of the three teachers' perspectives some significant contrasts between them in their view of the pupils and their background, the school and its ethos and their own practice in the classroom. Following from this the phenomenologist would expect to find significant variations in the stratification processes at work in each of these classrooms. In this chapter, however, our intention will be to try to show how elements of their situation and the teachers' perspectives together produce what could be regarded as essentially similar formal properties of the stratification system in all three settings. The analysis will suggest that certain key elements are present in each. This will be explained in terms of common features in the material and social environment of the teachers which cannot merely be intended away in consciousness, and which structure the activities of each and produce similar patterns in the social structuring of pupil identities. We will then proceed in the next chapter to sketch out what seem to be important variations between the three classrooms arguing that within certain constant parameters there is scope for the specific consciousness and practice of the teacher to make limited differences. Thus we are not claiming that the careers of individual pupils would be identical regardless to which classroom they happen to enter, but instead wish to concentrate upon the overall similarities, reducible we argue, to constant parameters contingent on each of their social contexts. There is no absolutist reduction here. These parameters are not metaphysical absolutes, but are themselves historical products of social structural formations. In the same way that Durkheim in his discussion of suicide avoided extrapolating from the regularities he discovered at the social level to the explanation of particular cases of suicide, so we are trying to develop a perspective on levels of social differentiation within the classroom which reveal a facticity other than that which can be explained amid the intersubjective worlds of the actors. As we have argued, however, in chapter 2 we would depart from Durkheim in our understanding of the nature of this facticity, its derivatives, and its relationship to wider structural variables.

The analysis will initially proceed ideal typically. That is to say an attempt has been made to isolate the essential and key features of the stratification system in all three classrooms. A useful entry into the analysis is to note two significant paradoxes. The first paradox is that all three teachers claim that their approach is child centred and oriented to the needs and requirements of individual pupils. All claim to want to get to know their pupils in their idiosyncracy and uniqueness and are aware of the dangers of premature labelling, preferring to retain open minds regarding the potentialities and capabilities of their pupils. Nevertheless, in their substantive practice the quality of intersubjectivity between teacher and pupil varied considerably. Some pupils seemed to have acquired reified identities and were thought of as really 'thick', 'peculiar' or had other stable and hard categorizations applied to them. Thus whereas in the teachers' ideology as educationalists, open mindedness towards all pupils should prevail, in their substantive practice it only seemed to apply to some of them.

The second paradox is related to the first. Whereas all three teachers would claim to be supporters of the egalitarian principle that all pupils are of equal worth, having an equal right to receive an education appropriate to their needs, in practice there was a marked degree of differentiation among the pupils in terms of the amounts and kinds of interaction they had with their teachers. Now the principle of equality does not necessarily commit one to identity of treatment. Nevertheless, it is significant that those pupils whom their teachers regarded as more successful tended to be given far greater attention than the others. The teachers interacted with them more frequently, played closer attention to their activities, subtly structuring and directing their efforts in ways which were noticeably different from the relationship with other pupils less favourably categorized.

Such paradoxes could be seen to be related to certain inner tensions and ambiguities in the teachers' perspectives but they should not be interpreted solely as the products of such processes at the ideological level in the teachers' consciousnesses. Indeed we shall argue that these very ambiguities are in themselves reflections of the structuring of material and social constraints, external to the classroom which impinge upon the teacher and structure her activities. The understanding of stratification in the classroom, whilst it may be related to and affected by the teachers'consciousness, cannot be solely explained by it. In our analysis we shall suggest that the teachers are encapsulated within a context which produced the necessity for some hierarchical differentiation of the pupils in order that the teacher may solve the problems she is confronted with and provide some legitimation for the allocation of her time and energies.

The teacher is faced with an immediate problem of 'what to do' in the classroom which itself is embedded in a wider structure of material and social relationships. In this situation the following are of importance for the teacher's practice: expectations are placed upon her from professional colleagues and superiors, from parents and others regarding the levels of achievements she is to maintain. Similarly she will be required to live up to certain standards of 'good pedagogical practice' set within the wider community of professional colleagues and more crucially by those who are in a position of power over her within the school itself. In addition parents and colleagues will look to her to maintain social order in the classroom. Moreover, her pupils are not merely passive 'objects' but will exert some influence on the teacher. Such constraints on her practice could be regarded as social and are traditionally analysed within a discussion of role theory and the teacher. Role expectations on the teacher may well be incompatible thus creating the potentiality for role conflict. Other constraints are of a more material or physical nature. Of particular importance are such factors as the teacher-pupil ratio. An obvious physical constraint on the teacher relates to the sheer number of pupils with whom she has to deal. Teachers frequently cite overcrowded classrooms as causes of their difficulties but it is significant that the pedagogical implications for the teacher of having large classes have not yet been systematically explored. Other physical constraints[1] relate to such factors as the architecture and layout of the classrooms, the 'materials' therein, and other human and non-human resources at the teachers' disposal.

Within this situation are generated a series of concepts and categories with which she orders the situation and objects in the world of her practice. The categories 'work' for her, they have a pragmatic basis for their existence in that to her, they have an elective affinity with her situation and projects. This is not to suggest that they are completely unstructured nor that she has complete freedom to select her categories. She operates within systems of available and legitimized categories within the community of her colleagues which have an immediacy for her actions in that their expectations relate to sanctions of a more or less stringent nature. The acceptability of these categories will relate also to the teacher's prior experiences, her history and socialization in other contexts of relevance. Clearly the teacher will operate with a stock of knowledge influenced by each of these factors. Given these social and physical constraints, there will be an ongoing attempt to accommodate[2] her stock of knowledge and her projects to the situation and the physical and social opportunities it offers. The outcome of this dialectic will form her behaviour and her consciousness; the one cannot be understood without the other.

Some of the categories with which the teacher orders her experience will be stable, others unstable or transitory or developing dynamically over time. For the observer it is most easy to chart the contours of the social structure of the classroom *vis-à-vis* the teacher's practice where routine can be identified. Such routines refer to the key ongoing and stable practical or substantive categories which relate to activities of relatively high importance to her. In the teacher's perspective there are at this point notions like 'busyness', 'good pupil', 'bright pupil', a 'good day', 'maladjusted child', and so on. We can divide these types of category used by the teacher into categories of situation, categories of activities, and categories of persons. The distinctions are analytic and only arise from our interest in the generation of and consequences for categories of pupils as the main focus of attention, whilst retaining an interest in the context of social action as important for explanation. Such key and stable categories tend to relate also to the unproblematical nature of aspects of the classroom as seen by the teacher.

It is less easy to introduce key diachronic processes into this synchronic structure. The changes in the teachers' perspective and practice are more elusive to chart and understand. In addition, the precise technical relationship between the teachers' categories and the elements of the situation or types of pupil they purport to describe is problematic. With both stable and unstable categories there is a level of ambiguity *vis-à-vis* substantive practice which in later sections we will try to illustrate. Such ambiguity characterizes the teachers' attitudes towards some of their pupils.

We have referred to the paradox that some pupils take on a reified identity and are categorized as abnormal, 'really' peculiar, despite the ideology prescribing open-mindedness. In contrast most are thought of as not 'really' anything other than complex, slightly baffling but normal children within the parameters of the teachers' background expectancies. The key feature associated with the abnormal children was that the teacher's approach manifestly did not work for them. These were children who were 'difficult to get through to', who did not get there by 'leaving out a stage' or 'going round the back way' who 'dribbed and drabbed' or 'wouldn't show an interest' in anything. These children did not get there at all, or when they did it was at the expense of great effort on their and the teacher's part. With these children the teacher had, in consequence, become less openminded, had developed a clearer typification of each child, in Schutz's terms, as more contemporaneous than consocial and a prognosis was in the making both in the teacher's perspective on such a child and in the social structure of the classroom and the school. By this, we mean that the child was becoming clearly distinguishable as a 'problem' to the teacher. In addition and, for the child, more importantly it became increasingly likely that the teacher's colleagues and outside agencies[3] would become involved in the categorization of the child as a 'problem'. Thus for such a child, a career is potentially being generated beyond the classroom context by the involvement of increasingly anonymous agencies as structural features of his fate. As this occurs the teacher may receive feedbacks from the agencies which feed into her present definition of the child and in so doing tend to further reify the categorization she has of him.

On the other hand, there was a majority of pupils in the class to whom the teacher when trying to understand their intellectual accomplishments would give the benefit of the doubt when a failure occurred. Thus when a child was unable apparently to understand a particular point or had slowed down or come to a halt in its progress at reading this was interpreted as a temporary lapse and that if carefully handled the child would soon recover. It was not interpreted as an indication that, within the parameters of her overall conception of normality-for-these-children, this particular child was 'slow', 'dim', 'thick', 'peculiar', etc. So in effect, no adverse prognosis or prophecy of deviance other than a conception that the child is pretty normal, at least 'for these children' is made. Thus to all intents and purposes the current failure of the child is no great problem and is not dealt with in any particular way. The important aspect of the teacher's prognosis in this case is that it is relatively loose and open-ended, just as her behaviour towards the child, when having initially failed to elicit the required response is noncommittal and to a large extent nondirective. At this point the teacher is realizing the child centred vocabulary in her classroom practice from within her own perspective. It is important to note that this approach 'works' for her, and is linked closely or has a logical affinity with the teacher's understanding of how children learn. In this connection, it is interesting that none of the teachers seemed to have very clear understandings of how children acquire or develop knowledge. This could be an example of what P.W. Jackson (1968) refers to as the 'mystery' among teachers of what the learning process might be in young children. Yet for the teachers, this does not appear to be a problem because in their perspective most children achieve normally or normally 'for this sort of child' most of the time and their classroom practice reflects this.

The children who are normal in the teacher's perspective are such because they can be comprehended easily within the structure of the teacher's common sense; especially the ideal 'good pupil' where teacher-pupil intersubjectivity is high. In commonsense understanding the actions of these children are obvious and can be satisfactorily comprehended with minimal reflection. This reading of the situation has similarities with Sudnow's account of 'normal crimes'. However, as we will see below, the main substantive difference lies in the issue of intersubjectivity as a crucial aspect of infant education. We will, at this point, expand on the previously cited discussion by Schutz (1964) of common sense. Schutz notes that in commonsense knowledge other human objects, present in the phenomenal world of the actor, may be placed on a continuum from consociates to contemporaries. Consociates are people whom the actor knows in their unique individuality, while contemporaries are more remote and appropriated in consciousness via typifications. In the we-relationship shared with consociates typicality of the other does not exist, while in the actor's perception of contemporaries it does. A type is generated by taking a set of characteristics formed by 'anonymization', by which is meant that the subjective meaning of immediately experienced individuals is omitted. Schutz's construction is useful but needs to be expanded and fitted into the material context of the teacher's project to provide a more complete explanatory model for understanding the structure of the self-fulfilling prophecy. For Schutz, anonymization appears to arise because of the *ad hoc* invocation of physical remoteness in time and space of the object. In the infant classroom this manifestly is not the case on the scale Schutz would imply is appropriate for his constructs. The teacher and the pupils are contemporaneous and yet a structure similar to Schutz's anonymization arises. Certain children appear in the teacher's perspective of them as closer to the contemporaneous than consociate end of the continuum. These latter arise as phenomena in the teacher's perspective not because they are remote in time and space but because the teacher's commonsense knowledge is no use to her in handling them, given her classroom management problem. Whilst consociates fit easily into the actor's common sense, other children arise as contemporaries because of the ignorance which is part of the structure of the teacher's knowledge *vis-à-vis* her practice with these children. While the consociate is known in a relatively complex and personal but generally unreflective way, certain children emerge as contemporaries because it is impossible to communicate with them. This is not to suggest that the impossibility of communication between the teacher and her pupil would occur, whatever the circumstances. The teacher involved in a one to one relationship with such a child over a long period of time would undoubtedly develop a relationship of high intersubjectivity and consociality. Nevertheless, given the material and social constraints on the teacher in this context the contents of the teacher's consciousness which lead to anonymization between the teacher and certain pupils reflect these constraints. Her consciousness is not the prime independent causal variable. Thus such pupils present themselves as strangers to the teacher's cognitive paradigms and routine practices in this context and this generates problems for the teacher which in her theoretical practice entails the need for non-common sense, reflective theoretical knowledge where the categories are drawn from 'esoteric' or abstract knowledge. This is an initial process in the reification of the child's identity as a social structural process and phenomenon in the classroom. The category tends to be hardened, the fit being more convincing to its user (the teacher) the more the child continues to feed back the appropriate behavioural cues. We may widen the context of this phenomenon and in so doing indicate that the process of hardening in the child's identity is related to the degree to which extra-classroom audiences come to accept this reified definition of the child. Parents, other teachers, social workers, etc., may be brought in and so increase the likelihood of the implementation of structures such as psychiatric testing, special schooling and the wide range of administrative techniques for the processing of 'social problems'. In so doing, pressure is taken off the teacher and her management problem is reduced.

The child who has acquired the identity of 'really peculiar', 'dim', 'difficult' is unlikely to become less problematic to the teacher and so to change in identity the less time he spends interacting with the teacher. The central aspect of the contemporary-consocial continuum lies in the level of communication links or intersubjectivity. The more remote the child is from the teacher's common sense, the less will intersubjectivity be a feature of their relationship and the less individuality a feature of the teacher's perception of the child. It was noticed that in each classroom in the deployment of time-space resources the teacher tended to spend less time interacting with the 'peculiar' children than with the 'normal' ones and, particularly much less time than with those (abnormal for this context) who were good pupils or approaching the conception of the teacher's personal conception of the ideal client. This was as much a product of the pupil's own choice or style of being in the classroom as a function of the teacher operating within the structure of an informal child centred classroom regime (Jackson, 1968; Jackson and Lahaderne, 1967).

It is interesting to note that many of the key categories in the teacher's perspective on her work relate to control rather than learning, teaching or instruction. To explain this it is important to reiterate that each teacher is faced with the practical problem of how to implement in the classroom a child centred philosophy given the nature of the school ethos and the expectation that each teacher will operationalize the key features of that ethos. We have observed how the 'integrated day' and 'freedom of choice' are of crucial significance in the school philosophy. In attempting to put these into practice the teacher is confronted with a major problem of 'what-to-do-with-freely-choosing-children'. It is suggested that the notion of 'child directed learning' is related to the categorization of the pupils via the control problems presented to the teacher in this open fluid context. The bright ones are the 'biddable' easily controllable ones who are on the teacher's wavelength. The dull ones are those who are not motivated to be 'indirectly directed' to the activities the teacher defines as important. Given this very complex problem in the practical implementation of a 'progressive' approach to pedagogy the teacher's practical solution is 'busyness', where children do something they have chosen and are thus engaged in activity without requiring the constant attention which the teacher is unable to give them. To the teacher there is a logical relationship between her notion of busyness, her educational philosophy and her actions. However, there is also a contingent relation in that the situation is objectively given in the sense of the limitation of her time-space resources. Thus the notion of 'busyness' is not merely a second order construct based upon a rather limited aspect of her work as the teacher would see it but indicative of a social structural phenomenon characteristic of control in this type of fluid situation, and as such is a construct which has ramifications latent to the teacher's perspective. Thus the teacher's major working concept, or central technique in her operational philosophy, is her emphasis upon 'be busy' or 'get on, on your own' or 'find yourself something to do'. Such exhortations to the pupils are a frequent occurence. As this becomes acted out by the teacher and by the child, certain types of pupils as social structural position in the classroom are generated as the teacher in her practice solves the problem of 'what to do' in the classroom. The key feature of 'being busy' for the teacher is that in a situation perceived by her of fluidity and constant change in the children's interest and activities, the more they take seriously this command, the greater the area of freedom it allows her and thus the more manageable her task becomes.

'Normal pupils' in this context account for the identity of the majority of the children in the class in this way. They form a 'bedrock of busyness', that is, for the most part, they settle down to follow the routine of self-directed activity within the range offered. They are normal in the sense that they can be accounted for generally within the framework of the teacher's commonsense perceptual structures and rationales. As manageable problems in terms of behaviour and intellectual attainment they fit mundane common sense and require little by way of esoteric understanding. In this way children occupying this social position are invisible to the teacher and can be handled with little reflection.

By contrast, the problem child, the one labelled 'disturbed', 'very maladjusted' or 'peculiar', illustrates a key form of deviance. While the normal child is no threat to the teacher's competence or the underlying social order of the classroom, and can be readily dealt with on a commonsense basis and fits into the classroom routines, this type does not.

The low level of intersubjectivity between the teacher and this type of child makes him extremely problematic to her commonsense perspectives and at a wider level presents a serious threat to the school's accountability to the parents and other interested parties. The teacher is assisted with dealing with such pupils, however, by those elements of the school ethos which support the view that these sorts of children benefit most from this unthreatening atmosphere, as well as through the tendency to employ esoteric or 'scientific knowledge' from psychology or psychiatry which 'explain' the child's deviance in terms of some inner pathology. The teacher is thus enabled to integrate the child into her practice for he can now legitimately be left alone to 'work through his problems' to pursue 'what interests him according to his needs'. This, then reduces the management problem of having to devote too much time to these difficult children and in so doing integrates him and his activities into the 'bedrock of busyness' discussed above. The second respect in which this type of child allows the teacher to integrate her practice operates more at the level of her identity in the structure of staff relations, and further to the school as such. We will take up this issue in a later chapter but for the present we may note that according to the school ethos these children are ideologically the 'ideal clients' in the sense that it is the psychologically abnormal maladjusted child who really needs the child centred approach and classroom situation. The fact that the teacher has been able to handle a child who is 'clearly maladjusted' creates a favourable identity for her, the fact that he is so difficult to deal with completes the circle of the rationale that these methods are needed and should be employed by this school and so reinforces the school's ideal self-image of child centredness.

The third type of pupil is the teacher's ideal client in the sense which the other categories discussed are not. This sort of pupil fits the teacher's ideal for children 'from a good area' or a 'middle class district'. This type is bright and articulate, interested and interesting and would 'get on' in other schools. This type of child most approximates to the teacher's own ideal of what school children should be like.

It is crucial now to understand the operational philosophy of 'busyness' as it relates to the social stratification of pupils in this social structure. One of the central functions of busyness is to free the teacher to handle the ever changing situation in the classroom. The latent function, however, is to free the teacher to be engaged by the articulate, bright, 'pushing' or teacher directed children who tend to take up dispro-portionate amounts of her time and energies. The level of inter-subjectivity between this type of pupil and the teacher is extremely high, and given the egalitarian ideal central to child centredness it is with these children that an egalitarian relationship most clearly develops. While the 'problem' child is a contemporary and anonymous stranger requiring esoteric rationales, this type of child is a relatively consocial companion with whom a joking relationship may develop and who can be expected to carry out tasks successfully and responds to the wide range of subtle cues the teacher emits.

The social stratification that is thus generated operates in the following way. The 'problem' child is in a position of low status which is relatively rigid and binding. His life chances in the classroom, to the extent that he has relatively little contact with the teacher and so is unlikely to alter his identity from that of peculiarity, are severely limited. Being really 'odd' in the teacher's account he has a reified identity to her which is socially structured and reinforced at the classroom level as he has less opportunity to develop contradictory cues and at a wider level, as his identity is accepted by other teachers, parents and social workers. The normal child for this school is in a relatively more fluid position with the chance of moving upward or down the hierarchy of social status to the extent that he or she moves from the low profile position of the normality of adjustment to the routines of busyness.

The élite of the social structure are the few 'bright' children who are able to take most advantage of the 'free day' and 'leading from behind', in that they readily know what it is the teacher wants and can reward the teacher for the time spent with her thus confirming her in her identity as a competent teacher. While the maladjusted or problem child can be used by the teacher as an illustration of the difficulty of her task and the need for this type of approach to pedagogy, so the bright ones can be cited as the operational indicators of the teacher's success, i.e. confident readers, articulate interactors, the child who produces 'interesting', creative work. Thus the structure of pupil stratification illustrates a central paradox of the child centred approach. In practice, though attempting to generate the lowest possible degree of boundary and hierarchy in pupil identities, social stratification does occur. The pressures on the teacher require her to produce certain goods such as competent standards of reading and number work. The generally low level can be accounted for by citing the maladjusted children as examples of the operational problems. The bright ones can be cited as evidence of the successful working of the whole approach. Within this pupil differentiation is generated and justified. The teachers recognize differentiation among their pupils but within the child centred philosophy differentiation does not entail hierarchy. What we are suggesting is that hierarchization, and the differentiation of the material life chances of the children, is being produced within the social structure of the classroom. Neither from the child centred ethos of the school, nor the immediate personal common sense of the teacher embodied in her operational philosophy is it recognized that these phenomena are a part of the social structure of teacher-pupil relations in the classroom. Where it is recognized that some children 'get on' better than others the individualistic and psychological vocabulary is invoked to illustrate the personal problems of the non-achieving child, or the social pathology of their deprived home environment.

The major irony in the situation, however, is that the position of the élite in the classroom depends upon the other pupils' nonconformity to the teacher's personal ideal. Were all her pupils 'interested', keen and teacher directed, the management problem thus presented to the teacher would be insuperable in a context where the school ethos requires informality and pupil choice. It appears that the latent function of allowing pupils choice is that the onus of responsibility for the child's success or failure in the classroom lies with the child. The child determines his own mode of being in the classroom and in so doing the teacher is liberated to perform those activities she defines as important.

The self-fulfilling prophecy

Before proceeding to examine the dimensions of variation between the three classrooms it is appropriate to make some comments deriving from the analysis above regarding the notion of the self-fulfilling prophecy. This idea has come to acquire a central role in certain types of sociological understanding particularly in situationalist deviancy theory (Becker, 1963; Lemert, 1967; Matza, 1969; Sudnow, 1968; Schur, 1971) where labelling and its consequences are investigated. In the sociology of education it is offered as an explanatory device by micro sociologists who are interested in the understanding of educational achievement and failure and the social construction of educability (Rist, 1970; Rosenthal and Jacobson, 1968; Beez, 1970; Nash, 1973). The basic notion, deriving from symbolic interactionist thought on deviance and social control, is that the agent of social control may himself be implicated in the creation of deviance. It has been noticed that such agents have the power, often latent to their own consciousness to set up a situation in which their definition of the actor in their environment as deviant, together with their own behaviour consequent upon his definition leads to an increasing possibility for that actor to feed back cues confirming his own deviance. In the labelling process there is a hidden prophecy by the agent of social control that this deviant will remain a deviant for the normal time-span of the agent's interest. This prophecy will tend to be confirmed as the agent's actions in concert with those of his colleagues structure the deviant's possibilities into a career of deviance rather than normality. This sort of explanation has been offered or implied in the analysis of various types of educational failure and is currently of considerable importance in the sociology of education.

Our own analysis of the social structuring of pupil identities suggests that much work on the self-fulfilling prophecy in educational contexts is too simplistic. The process of classroom social structuring is far more complex than tends to be suggested. We suggest that the notion of the self-fulfilling prophecy is a crude characterization of what is in fact a complex process of attitudinal or consciousness change. It involves an ongoing accommodation to, or transaction in consciousness with, an apparently unavoidable phenomenon encountered by the actor (the teacher) in her practice rather than an initial construction of the identity of, in this case, a pupil, by a teacher. Thus, rather than looking for consciousness at T1 and relating it to outcome at T2 and as such relating prophecy to its fulfilment or not as the case may be, we should look for the conditions for the occurrence of this mechanistic process and for the conditions for the more processional or transactional phenomenon. The mechanistic structure will require certain types of knowledge in the initial stages with strong support for the actor making the initial construction of (pupil) identity and certain sorts of unambiguous responses fitting this construct on the part of the object of the prophecy. Thus we may take the idea of the self-fulfilling prophecy and set it upon a continuum with this mechanistic structure at one end where the meaning of the object is simply and clearly conceptionalized (i.e. where there is little which is problematic about the object) and where the consequences for the object are unproblematically predictable. This, of course, is an ideal construct unlikely ever to occur substantively but it refers usefully to the totality (in a sense similar to Goffman, 1968) of the institutional context of both prophet and object. At the other end of the ideal continuum is where the prophecy and outcome are completely problematic to the prophet. This would refer to a situation where any institutionalized expectations are non-existent, where the self-fulfilling prophecy is non-existent because the consciousness of the actor and the structure of the situation of fulfilment are linked by nothing more than chance.

Our other line of criticism is that when classrooms have been examined and the contexts in which they operate, there has not been developed a perspective which can appreciate both the ongoing processual nature of the creation of the social structure through meaningful interaction among social actors and see social structures as at the same time embodying constraints, giving limitations both recognized and unrecognized on the actors concerned. In our analysis it is not only the fulfilment of the prophecy which becomes an object of attention but also the generation of the prophecy itself. Each aspect of the actor's practice has to be situated in the context of structural constraints upon the prophet, in this case the teacher, in order to understand her consciousness, practices and their consequences. This is particularly pertinent in the case of classroom management where the teacher's actions may have as a consequence, the reinforcing or regeneration of the conditions in which the prophecy becomes a useful technique for managing these conditions. Here the structure would be one of feedback making for synchrony, at a level latent to the teacher's consciousness.

From our analysis it is evident that our approach differs from discussions of the self-fulfilling prophecy in educational contexts which implicitly seem to be putting the onus of 'blame' on the teacher. It is as if it were being suggested that if only the teacher did not rigidly categorize and stereotype some pupils negatively, then the outcome of teacher/pupil interaction would be very different. Such a perspective we would suggest ignores the extent to which teachers are encapsulated within a context where the problems of management and control require some implicit hierarchical differentiation of pupils in order to solve the problem of order and provide some legitimation for the allocation of scarce resources, i.e. the teacher's time and energies.

In addition we have suggested that in the process of the construction of pupil's identities through the differential management of pupils' careers in the commonsense world of the teacher, the pupil plays a highly significant part in his own identity construction.[4] The kind of style-of-being adopted by the child in the classroom is crucially related to his being integrated in varying ways into the teacher's common sense and practice as she tries to solve various management dilemmas. Thus rather than seeing the labelling process as one where the social controller, in this case the teacher, applies some hard label to her pupils, we should instead see it as a far more subtle process where the rigidity or variability of the labels are as much related to the state of social control within the organization, and to the social control implications of varying ways of acting therein as to the rigidity of the social controller's thought processes. Therefore in our analysis we have tried to show how the meaning of the child as an object of the teacher's attention is influenced by the ongoing social structure in which she works which partly she creates and which partly creates her. The social structure throws up problems and allows her, given her projects and the field of constraints, only certain solutions or structures of opportunity to solve them. This process is dynamic and open-ended but points to the way in which social structure, meanings and behaviour, are related to each other.

7

Social stratification in the classroom: dimensions of variability

So far we have explained the emergence of a system of social stratification among the pupils by exploring the crucial interrelationship between, on the one hand, the teacher's consciousness, and on the other the structure of material and social constraints. It has been suggested that these latter present the teacher with management problems the solving of which leads to a stratification of pupils' identities and opportunities. This may serve to widen and accentuate the initial differences between them, producing consequences latent to the teacher's perspective but which are explained and legitimized in terms consistent with that perspective.

Our analysis has pointed to the way in which pupils vary in terms of the social control implications of the roles they adopt in the classroom, these being related to the hierarchical nature of the categories the teacher applies to them and of the likelihood of acquiring a reified or open-ended identity. In addition we have explored the way in which these are related to the amounts and types of interaction which take place between pupil and teacher. We have also suggested that there is a degree of negotiability between teacher and pupil and that certain pupils have more power than others over the teacher and can manoeuvre themselves into a favourable career position.

In short the thesis so far developed suggests an absence of arbitrariness in the development of the social structuring of pupil identities such that given the logic of the situation and the constraints it imposes on the teacher, certain features of the stratification system are bound to occur. In all classrooms, moreover, the teacher is crucial in these processes not simply because she is a reality definer, but because there is a sense in which she can be regarded as a scarce resource in that she possesses and can transmit the means whereby the careers of her pupils can be facilitated or held back. Here, the particular way in which she distributes her time and energies has implications crucial for this process.

In the previous chapter the intention was to specify as far as possible certain constant parameters of the stratification system in all three classrooms through the construction of an ideal type. We recognize that there are crucial common features, consequent upon the common socio-historical location of all three classrooms, which override elements of idiosyncracy. However, within these structural limits variations can occur. In this chapter we shall sketch out some of the dimensions of variability and suggest ways in which they are socially structured and related to other significant processes which we shall try to identify.

It was suggested above (p.119) that the pupils can be ranked along a contemporary-consociate continuum where at one end they acquire a rigid reified identity and occupy a low status position with limited life chances, whilst at the other they share a high level of intersubjectivity with the teacher, where the categorizations of them are more open-ended, subtle and complex, and where they have considerably more power in gaining access to the teacher. The first significant way in which the classrooms vary is in the likelihood of the children acquiring a reified identity and the possibility of the child having room to negotiate a satisfactory relationship with the teacher, where intersubjectivity and a high level and intensity of interaction is a feature of their relationship.

This in its turn is related to the second dimension of variability which concerns the degree of fluidity within the classroom and the possibility for the child to be socially mobile within the main layers of the stratification system we have identified. The greater the teacher's proneness to the employed reified categories, the less the child has possibilities for negotiating his own identity in the classroom, the more the child's position in the stratification system will be stable with a closure on opportunities to transform his social structural position.

Third, the potentialities for deviance within the classroom will vary from teacher to teacher. In our ideal typical scheme we suggested that the deviant child is the child whose mode of being in the classroom cannot be integrated into the teacher's common sense and practice and who presents the teacher with management problems in the maintenance of social order. It is suggested that the more elaborate the system of norms and rules which define acceptable pupil behaviour, the greater the possibility for pupils to transgress these institutionalized expectations and thus acquire a deviant status.

The fourth dimension of variability relates to what could be called the range of the stratification system or the distance between the lower and upper levels. In the same way that potentialities for deviance are related to the degree of elaboration of the system of norms and rules within the classroom so the range of the stratification system is associated with the degree of teacher surveillance and teacher directiveness over the pupils. The more the teacher's substantive practice approximates to an ideal *laissez-faire* fluid regime the greater the distance between the pupils of low and high status in terms of such indicators as academic competence and behaviour.

This discussion of the dimensions of variability in the stratification systems of the three classrooms reinforces the proposition that the teacher's consciousness and practice are crucial mediating factors in the classroom context influencing the social structuring of pupils' careers. It is suggested that the variations can be accounted for by invoking the teacher's own interpretations of the school ethos and the realization of their perspectives in their substantive practice. This in its turn relates to the other extra-classroom influences which will be elaborated in the next chapter where the teachers' consciousness and practice will be discussed in terms of their respective positions in the system of staff relationships within the school. For the moment, however, we are only concerned with the effect of the teacher's consciousness and substantive practice in determining the specific content of stratification within the classroom.

In our discussion of the teachers' perspectives it will be remembered that Mrs Carpenter and Mrs Buchanan held dissimilar conceptions of their pupils and attitudes towards the school ethos but somewhat similar notions about their substantive practice in the classroom. Similarly whilst there seemed to be convergence at the level of basic assumptions about the pupils and the school ethos between Mrs Carpenter and Mrs Lyons, their perspectives on their substantive practice diverged.

In trying to differentiate the stratification systems in the three classrooms it seems appropriate to draw a distinction between Mrs Lyons's classroom on the one hand, and the other two on the other. Of necessity this will involve a closer examination of the stratifying processes in Mrs Lyons's classroom compared with those in the other two classrooms. This is thought justifiable because in this chapter we are concerned with variations and it is Mrs Lyons's classroom which most epitomizes the levels of variation which occur. By discussing the teacher furthest along one end of a continuum it is possible to draw out the relevant dimensions of variability. In so doing, the subtle qualifications and modifications to our ideal type set out in chapter 6 are rendered possible. Thus in this section we shall attempt to isolate some of the significant ways in which Mrs Lyons's classroom differs from each of her colleagues, before proceeding in the next section to illustrate this analysis in both this and the previous chapter, by discussing specific examples of pupil stratification from each of the three classrooms.

In the first place, both Mrs Carpenter and Mrs Buchanan for different reasons are attempting in their practice to operate a completely informal 'child centred classroom' where the overriding emphasis is on the importance of pupil choice. In Mrs Lyons's classroom however, the commitment to this form of child centredness is less strong.

Although lip service is given to children choosing, their choices are circumscribed by the teacher in a relatively more directive way than occurs in the other two settings. It is important to reiterate 'relatively', for we do not want to characterize Mrs Lyons as a formal and traditional teacher who is out of sympathy with modern trends and tendencies in primary education. Rather we want to stress that it is merely in relationship to the other two teachers considered here in detail, that she is more formal in that minimum goals are presented as ideal targets to which her pupils ought to be aspiring, especially those who are 'ready'. Free choice in this classroom could be taken to mean freedom to decide *when*, rather than *if*, to do certain things the teacher thinks desirable. Again, of course, we should reiterate the qualification previously suggested that the teacher does not closely monitor the children's activities and ensure that her idealized work requirements are completed. The difference between the teachers here is that in Mrs Lyons's classroom a more explicit, general impression is given that the pupils ought to be doing certain things even if in fact they do not, whereas in the others freedom of choice for the pupils is more openly offered.

Second, Mrs Carpenter and Mrs Buchanan seem to be operating a more open and fluid regime where the degree of discretion for pupils to define a role for themselves is high. In Mrs Lyons's classroom, however, there is communicated to the pupils a more elaborate system of norms and rules which define appropriate ways of acting in the classroom, this system of rules and regulations in one sense narrowing the areas of discretion allowed to the pupil but in another sense providing what appears to be a clearer definition of the broad parameters of the good pupil role and the areas where discretion and negotiation are permitted.

Third, and associated with the two previous features, Mrs Lyons's classroom seems to be far more teacher-centred than the other two. This might appear to conflict with our previous discussion where we have stressed that in all classrooms the teacher plays a crucial role in the stratifying process. Nevertheless, we need perhaps to distinguish between, on the one hand, the observer's analytic model which gives significance to the teacher as a distributor of scarce resources, and on the other, the teacher's and pupil's commonsense understanding of the significance of the teacher. What we are suggesting is that in Mrs Lyons's class the pupils themselves related to the teacher as a key figure both as the imparter of significant rewards and punishments and as the key definer of reality. Similarly, the teacher herself saw her role as crucial in moulding the patterns of social interaction in the classroom. For example, in her everyday activities she managed the situation through a complex pattern of teacher-pupil intervention in a manner which the other teachers did not. Her will is paramount, the status differences between teacher and pupil were accentuated and the classroom climate seemed less 'democratic' and 'permissive' than elsewhere. In this way there is a lower salience of consociality in teacher-pupil relationships in Mrs Lyons's class compared with each of the other teachers studied. Generally, a higher level of contemporaneity characterizes the milieu of Mrs Lyons's classroom.

Fourth, and related to this, it would seem that the teacher has a more crucial role to play in the sponsorship of pupils in Mrs Lyons's classroom than in the others. Whereas in the other classrooms, élite pupils were to a certain extent self-selecting this is not so to the same extent in Mrs Lyons's classroom.

In our discussion in the previous chapter we referred to the notion of busyness as both an aspect of the teacher's consciousness linked in with her perspective on classroom management and as having social structural elements connecting it with the maintenance of order within a context of material and social constraints. We explained how 'busyness' operates to free the teacher to deal with the élite pupils in the classroom, those who can capture the teacher's attention, getting into a relationship with her which both provides the teacher with satisfaction and confirmation of her own performance, and has feedback for the child in the sponsorship process. In Mrs Lyons's class, too, the bedrock of busyness is also observable but the élite pupils are not in such a direct sense self-selecting. Here, the teacher's role in sponsoring those pupils she regarded as 'ready' was apparent through the mechanism of her choosing children to work with her by virtue of her assessment of their ability to benefit. Indeed, children who ask to be assisted by the teacher could be readily rejected, as 'pesterers', one who is 'always following me around like a dog' instead of being sponsored. This is not to suggest that the role the child adopted had no relationship to the possibility of it being 'chosen', only that it was very clear that in the first and last analysis it was the teacher who decided who should be moved on rather than the pupil. In the other classrooms the basic prescription was an open-ended 'get busy, find yourself something to do' which thus liberated the teacher to spend time with those children who for whatever reason chose to get busy pleasing the teacher by doing the things which the teacher was pleased with. However, in Mrs Lyons's classroom it was more as if the teacher was saying 'Please me and get yourself school trained, and then I will select you and sponsor you into the élite'. This classroom operated more as a teacher managed bureaucracy than a child centred permissive democracy. Nevertheless, both types of classroom were similar in the sense that the non-conformity of some children to the teacher's 'real' motives was functionally necessary for the furtherance of the élites' position. Given large numbers of pupils, a failure to conform to the ideal pupil role both legitimized the teacher's non-involvement with them for they were not yet 'ready' to benefit, and at the same time, it solves the teacher's problems of how to cope within the constraints of the situation. Thus we see again the relationship between the social structuring of pupils' identity and the management of social control.

Fifth, in the other two classrooms the teachers only seemed to possess hard and reified views of the pupils they found difficult to get through to or with whom it was problematic to establish any relationship at all. Most of the pupils were categorized in a relatively open-ended way and within the fluidity of the classroom had some potentiality for movement. In Mrs Lyons's classroom, however, there seemed to be a greater proneness to operate with relatively clear and rigid typifications of her pupils. We have observed how Mrs Lyons has a somewhat reified view of the pupils as being deprived, disturbed, malajusted, insecure products of pathological backgrounds, as indeed has Mrs Carpenter. Nevertheless the specific application of such a label to a particular child in Mrs Carpenter's classroom depends to a greater extent on whether she can successfully integrate him into the fluid harmony of everyday life in the classroom. In Mrs Lyons's class, however, the pupils seemed less able to break through the hard typification which the teacher holds and become something other than they are likely to be.

This problem is made more difficult because so many of the pupil's attributes and typical styles-of-being are likely to become objects of evaluation and are considered relevant within the teacher background expectancies regarding the characteristics of the ideal pupil. Nevertheless, given the explicitness of the structure of rules and regulations which define appropriate ways of being and acting in the classroom, in one sense it might be easier for the child who is oriented towards pleasing the teacher to acquire a favourable identity. Moreover, the fact that the teacher plays a relatively more active role in the socialization process might suggest that the child has a greater possibility of transforming his identity. This would be the case where the teacher assists him to become school trained, this being the necessary prerequisite for gaining intellectual advancement. However, what appears to be happening is quite the reverse. In this classroom the teacher seems to operate with somewhat inflexible, and reified views of many of the children such that whatever they do in the classroom merely confirms her categorization of them. The degree of reification seems to relate very closely to the teacher's categorization of the home background. A structural feature of Mrs Lyons's position which is most probably directly related to this aspect of her general ideology and operational philosophy is that as deputy head she, along with the headmaster, has had to contend more directly with the general crisis in school-parent relations than the other staff. The ideology of domestic pathology has become more sharply articulated for her as a device for understanding and handling her situation. The more the home background deviates from the ideal, the more likely that the child will develop a hard and unfavourable identity and find it very difficult to break through the barriers to a favourable identity. This is not to suggest that such a breakthrough is impossible, only that it is difficult. Whether the child manages to break through will depend upon the degree to which he can consistently present counterindications over a period of time of the validity of her reified view of how he 'should be'.

However, not all the pupils in Mrs Lyons's classroom acquire a reified and stable identity. This can be illustrated by her use of half open-ended phrases to describe the children. She quite often used the term 'potentially' which would seem to suggest some possibility for the child to go either way. For example, of one child, she said she was 'potentially at risk but bright enough to conform'. Whilst of another, whom she sometimes admitted was bright, at other times she said his brightness was only skin deep. Of another she said 'she's potentially with it', although her previously expressed attitudes seemed to suggest that she thought the child 'hopeless'.

The observer found it extremely difficult to attempt to explain in some cases how or why a child had changed his identity in the teacher's eyes. Where rapid changes in categorizations did occur, they generally seemed to be from the negative to the positive, and can be partially explained by the fact that identity changes seemed to occur with new pupils. A child who initially was defined as 'hopeless, a real problem' could, a few weeks later, be described as 'lovely', 'gorgeous'. Similarly, another whom the teacher confessed she couldn't stand, had a few weeks later, similarly been redefined. Nevertheless, there were indications that once a child had been in the classroom for several weeks he would have acquired a definite 'form' which tended to be fairly stable.

Finally, whereas in the other two classrooms the élite pupils did not seem to be age related, nor indeed did age seem to be a significant organizing category, in Mrs Lyons's classroom the teacher interacted more frequently with older children and the élite pupils tended to come from a nucleus of the older pupils who were sufficiently responsive to the teacher to become defined as 'ready' for intellectual advance. This does not mean that all older pupils would be part of the élite group, only that among both élite and non-élite, the older one was, the more likely that one would receive more attention.

Mrs Lyons's mode of interacting with older children would of course be differentiated according to her categorizations of them, but in this classroom even negatively defined older children would receive a proportion of her attention simply because they were older and by virtue of their age alone they are expected to be doing more than younger children. As we have seen, Mrs Lyons operated with certain underlying assumptions of the minimum standard of competence in literacy and numeracy which her top infants should acquire before they left her class, irrespective of how she defined them. Therefore, the older children did tend to get more attention from the teacher with respect to these basic skills. The younger children were less likely to receive attention unless they had successfully demonstrated that they were 'school trained' and thus could now be sponsored for cognitive advance.

In the light of this discussion of significant differences between the classroooms it remains now to summarize what the implications of these might be for the social stratification systems in each situation. First, it is likely that a higher proportion of the pupils in Mrs Lyons's classroom would acquire low status, rigid, and deviant identities both because of her proneness to think in reified typifications and because of the more elaborate system of rules and norms which itself creates a greater potentiality for deviance.

Second, it is likely that the potentiality for social mobility for the pupils is more limited both because of the difficulty of breaking out of their identities and because the teacher is more active in selection and sponsorship than elsewhere. Third, given that the teacher has perhaps higher minimum standards of what all children should be able to do by certain ages and operates closer control over the pupils' activities than in the other classrooms, we suggest that from our own observations the range of stratification seemed to be narrower. The 'less able' pupils seemed to be performing at a higher level than those similarly defined in the other classes. This might point to the greater opportunities for pupils negatively defined in Mrs Lyons's class to transform their identities when they moved up to a higher class.

Chapter 8 will present examples of the points made in the previous two chapters in the form of case studies of the social positions of selected children in each of the three classes.

8

The social structuring of pupils' identities: some examples

In this chapter will be presented a series of examples of the social status of particular children in each of the three classrooms in order to provide substantive exemplification of many of the aspects of the formal accounts in chapters 6 and 7. These examples, drawn from our field work, illustrate the way in which various pupils were categorized and socially processed in the teacher's working contexts of the classroom. Our accounts go beyond the straight description of the teacher's consciousness of their pupils and are based upon our own emerging analysis.

Mrs Carpenter's classroom

1   Michael

The first child, Michael, is an infant whose general persona to the teacher is that of a problem in many areas of significant activity in the classroom. He is a child categorized as 'most peculiar' or 'really odd', who, when he first entered the school seemed to show little interest in the activities she expected of children.

> 'Nothing I said would make any difference, you know, he wouldn't . . .
> he didn't want to write or anything, he wasn't very interested in that.
> He wasn't very interested in joining in with a reading group—he wasn't
> very interested in the story. He just wanted to go on his own sweet
> way . . . he just dribbed and drabbed about . . . you know, he never had
> a true friend. But he's ever so willing to join in if you organize a little
> group—and he'll join in and he'll be, you know, quite an important

member of that group—but he doesn't *need* to . . . I can't make up my mind why he is so peculiar.'

The teacher then discussed the child's mother in somewhat disparaging terms as 'silly', 'daft', 'not very organized'. The child remained throughout the period of observation within this category of 'peculiar'.

It is not enough, when we attempt to explain the generation of these categories, to suggest that the teacher was projecting the properties sketched out in her words above. Objectively the teacher was unable to communicate with the child which immediately raised problems for her in her classroom practice. She had to solve the problem of what to do (behaviour) *vis-à-vis* the child, and the related one of how to explain the child to herself and significant others interested in her accounts. In the above quotation the teacher specifically mentions reading and writing and listening to the story as things the child was uninterested in, while, he, in her view wanted to 'go his own sweet way', but seemed lacking in positive direction ('dribbed and drabbed'). These aspects of the child and their relationship indicates (a) that certain activities in the classroom are deemed more valuable, are 'work' to the teacher, than others: (b) the child was unwilling to engage in these; but that (c) we know from observation and interviews with the teacher she was unwilling to impose sanctions to ensure that children did these important (work) activities. This is part of the connotation of 'need'. She would not 'force' or 'make' the child do the activities he seemed unwilling to do, even where his achievement was poor, compared with other children, because to do so would violate the integrity of the child. So the problem of how to behave towards Michael is solved by initially appealing to the optimism implied in the notion of 'needs' (i.e. that the child will come round, communication with him will improve when he 'needs' to) when he is 'ready'. These terms, with their many connotations, are part of the school ethos. This endorses both her behaviour of avoiding the child and a fully *laissez-faire* attitude towards him for long periods. But because the child has continued not to communicate with her, and to be difficult to motivate, in comparison with other children, he is deemed 'peculiar'. Further, explanation for this peculiarity is sought by the teacher in the extra classroom, extra school environment, i.e. the home, and is given neo-psychiatric connotations. This receives endorsement from significant others, particularly the headmaster, whom she quotes as perceiving the mother as 'silly' and inadequate; here, then, the teacher can appeal to the available socially approved vocabulary to endorse her explanation.

It was mentioned that this child had taken on a stable meaning of 'peculiar' to the teacher. With this categorization the child was unproblematic to the teacher and as such the typification of this child's behaviour had hardened or become 'reified'. To the teacher there was little tension in the meaning of the child. This hardening of his social meaning needs to be related to the wide social structure of the classroom and the possibilities it offers for actions on the part of both teacher and children. As we have noted, the regime is *laissez-faire*, and the teacher particularly presents it as such to the children. At the beginning of each day, and often before sessions within the day the children are urged to 'choose for themselves'. Nevertheless, as we indicated above the teacher does operate with a notion of hierarchy with regard to the available activities, (work-play dichotomy). However in the distribution of the opportunity to work, and therefore of acquiring this, more valued, knowledge, the teacher adopts a policy of 'leading from behind'. She aims to influence the direction of children's efforts via expressive and exhortative means, i.e. indirectly. This child is extremely difficult to 'lead from behind', because communication between them is difficult, but while he is not able to motivate himself consistently and forcefully in the teacher's terms, he is able to be 'busy' in the sense of doing something most of the time. Particularly important is that he is seldom in trouble with the teacher, seldom breaches the prohibitive norms of the classroom. Now given that the teacher has only limited time-space resources available, and that the structure of the classroom is of fluid group formation and breakdown around several activities, it is possible for certain children to become lost from the teacher's attention for long periods, so long as they are generally 'busy' and keep out of mischief. It occurs in this instance and with it a circular process of reinforcement in the teacher's concept of the child and the social structuring of his activities within those of the classroom as a whole. It becomes easier, and more real to the teacher that the child was 'peculiar', and to leave him to his own devices. So that given the great demand on her time by other, more insistent, forceful and communicative children less attention and effort at developing bridges of communication between the peculiar child and the teacher occurred. The child was not brought out from his 'withdrawn' state and so remained 'peculiar'.

2   Karen

Next we will illustrate the social position of a child whose identity changes in the classroom practice of the teacher. While the former child's identity had crystallized into a pessimistic prognosis from which the social structure of the classroom left little opportunity for escape, Karen's took a somewhat different turn as we observe her initiation in the school. The child took up a position which reflected the fluidity of unproblematic common sense in the teacher's perspective which leads to relative pupil invisibility as the teacher generates workable routines.

As with the previous case, it is important to note the ambiguity in the teacher's perspective in the difference between work and play in her substantive classroom practice, and the idea at the more general level of her 'theoretical practice' that 'work is play'. The main problem of what to do *vis-à-vis* Michael, was that the low level of intersubjectivity or communication made it difficult for the teacher to motivate the child successfully 'from behind', particularly with reading, an area where she was especially accountable (see below, p. 178). At the general level of her perspective the teacher indicates that work and play in the classroom are indistinguishable, and that the knowledge which is constituted by each classroom activity cannot be hierarchized. However in the classroom, the teacher operates with the substantive practice based on the idea that time wasting occurs when a child spends too long on a self-chosen activity which is beneath its intellectual capabilities. This is a rationale for her active intervention and moving the child to a 'serious' activity. Thus a bright child may be moved from playing with crayons and sticky paper to 'starting on the balance'.

It is crucial for a child to be defined as bright for it to receive this sort of attention from the teacher. The other important factor implied above is the assumption that teacher directed 'work' is threatening to all but secure, bright children. At this point judgments as to intellectual ability and emotional equilibrium become substantively fused in the teacher's praxis.

As the children enter the class, the teacher attempts to develop working categories for her relationships with them. These categories have implications for their likely success, failure, difficulties, and so on. There may be some 'form' on the child or its family background which will influence the initial stance of the teacher towards him. In this case Karen had 'form'. She had an older brother in the school who had proved troublesome, and there was friction between the parents and the school. From information supplied by the social workers concerning discord between the child's parents, the family background fitted the normal 'problem family' category of the school ethos on its clients. This fit with the model of domestic insecurity, explained the older sibling's problems, and made for a poor prognosis for Karen. However such background expectancies of poor performance are not necessarily involved without symptoms being found, in the child's observed classroom appearance and behaviour. Thus we are now looking for the teacher's construction of the child's 'motivational type' but leaving problematic the extent to which the child was predefined in the sense that whatever it did would be slotted into a preconceived interpretation. Karen's behaviour did fit the preconceptions. She was defined as being 'noisy' and 'raucous' and as the teacher pointed out to the observer, was likely to be a problem: 'I can see we're going to have trouble with that . . .' In the initial stages, then, Karen is defined as troublesome, in particular as being ill-mannered, especially when interacting inappropriately with the teacher. The observer noted how she tended to push in and shout or make her requests to the teacher in a loud voice. As the teacher observed, the child did not say 'excuse me Mrs —', she did not know how to approach people. Thus, it is mainly on the grounds of poor etiquette that the teacher has transformed the background expectation into a practical observation and an attitude to the child.

It is suggested that Karen was unable to interact adequately with the teacher because she did not know the appropriate rules for child/adult interaction as defined by the teacher. This in turn led to a mode of interaction in which the teacher expressed her dislike of the child's uncouth assertiveness so that she tended to interact less with the teacher. If we recall the structure of classroom interaction, little contact with the teacher is not a 'problem' to her so long as it reflects 'busyness'. The child, then, was able to 'get on and do things'. However it is upon the basis of what she did that a further transformation of her identity occurred, though reflecting in part the poor initial prognosis, given the way the child's identity was integrated with the home background diagnosis. While self-chosen activity is part of the busyness norm, the child's choice of activity has implications for the teacher's definition of her. Thus if the child has chosen to participate with the teacher in what she was doing, and also presented herself in the appropriate manner, the definition of the child may have been different. As it happens, Karen chose to play rather often in the Wendy House at what the teacher interpreted to be various role playing 'domestic' activities. While her 'manners' improved *vis-à-vis* the teacher, i.e. the teacher noted that the child learned to wait her turn when there were several children waiting for the teacher's attention, and to say 'excuse me', etc., she was noted by the teacher and observer as not interacting with the teacher as much as other intake children. She became defined as not 'needing' the teacher so much and compulsive in her use of the Wendy House as a place to be assertive and act out her problems. When it was noted that Karen frequently opted for this activity, she fell into the teacher's category of a dull child who 'needs this sort of activity'. Thus the teacher was able to draw parallels between her and other children, who similarly were 'dull', 'slow', 'plodding', in so far as intellectual achievements were concerned, but who to the observer had learned to please the teacher by being behaviourally conformist, 'no trouble' children. In this way the teacher formed a very complex judgment having cognitive and psychiatric dimensions which made for a further spiralling in terms of the way the child's behaviour could only confirm the definition. Thus getting little satisfaction from interaction with the teacher, compared with other of her companions, she chose another way of pleasing the teacher, 'doing something', 'being busy', and at the same time realizing her own requirements in terms of having few pressures upon her. Thus she took seriously, at face value, the teacher's exhortation to 'choose for yourself', 'there's plenty to do'.

This in turn made it increasingly impossible for Karen to demonstrate to the teacher as often as other children, her possible intellectual capacity. The children with whom the teacher was able to communicate, without her identifying them as ill-mannered or deviant in other ways, were getting more feed-back as to her motives, and learning to differentiate types of activities. This was the case because those activities in which the teacher often participated had higher status and received more teacher-donated rewards for them. Also these children had more practice in displaying positive cues to the teacher of 'brightness'. Thus another child, 'flamboyant and outgoing', and who 'seems to need me', who was helpful to the teacher, was not only defined as 'nice' but also 'bright' and fitted positive models with which the teacher operated as provided by older children.

This example constitutes aspects of the 'normal pupil' as a social structural position in the classroom. The child was initially expected to show symptoms of (normal) deviance and the teacher treated it as naughty and ill-mannered. When it settled into a 'busy' role the teacher invoked neo-psychiatric categories and rationales for its avoidance of her and poor intellectual start. As with most of the class, Karen became manageable, she was no longer a behaviour problem and thus freed the teacher to deal with the constant flow of demands made of her. The solution Karen had adopted to her identification by the teacher as 'loud' and 'naughty', was to withdraw from interaction with the teacher, to be shy and reticent in her company, and to spend most of her time playing at an activity which fitted with the teacher's reality test for 'insecurity' and 'dullness'. It is suggested that these categories and the related social position, though by no means reified, if compared with the case of Michael, place Karen in a somewhat restricted context. Certainly this is the case when compared with our next example in terms of opportunities to develop teacher endorsed knowledge.

3 Sylvia

In contrast, we will now attempt to analyse a teacher-pupil relationship where the meaning of the child to the teacher is less stable, but again where social structural influences are important. In this relationship one of the ambiguities in the teacher's practice and perception of her task touched on above, the *laissez-faire* 'leading from behind', plays a role in understanding how a child moves from a position of 'ideal pupil' to being 'naughty', and a serious behaviour problem involving an emotional response in the teacher and physical sanctions imposed on the child.

Sylvia was offered by the teacher as an example, during the early part of the period of observation, of what a young pupil, new to the infant school should be like:

> 'who likes to spend rather a lot of time with me, you know; if they could, they would be with me all the time and always doing the activities (by this she is referring to the activities she sets up, small projects of art and craft work, etc.). The sort of children you like to have doing things with you because they want to.'

When asked if Sylvia had settled down quickly in this sort of classroom, it was confirmed. Further she was 'always asking questions, a bit like a fairy, you know, to talk to. Lots of little bits to tell me. "What I did . . . what I didn't do" (the teacher is quoting the child here). As I say, asking all the questions all the time.' It is clear from these quotations that this child is perceived in a completely different way from the previous children. Sylvia was thought of as achieving well up to standard, and was one of the brighter children in the class. She was thought of as being the sort of child to expect in a 'normal' and 'respectable' district. Thus she is unusual in the predominantly 'rough' working class district. The child's behaviour, as spelt out above, confirmed the teacher's practice. It was rewarding the teacher with amusement and interest and fitted the structure of the provision of activities set up by the teacher. In this *laissez-faire* environment, this child was one of those who was not difficult to 'lead from behind', indeed she was eager to have the teacher's attention, was bright and amusing, in ways which the previous children were not. In the case of Karen the teacher–pupil relationship was tenuous, and relatively unproblematic, if compared with Michael, while with Sylvia, it was much more intimate, complex and egalitarian. In Schutz terminology it was relatively 'consocial'.

At this point we may look for social structural clues to the breakdown of this relationship, in which Sylvia became, in the teacher's terms 'disobedient and unbearably naughty' towards the end of the period of observation. Given this *laissez-faire* environment, but yet one in which the teacher was the centre of power and rewards, in fact, in many ways the 'hidden hand' behind this liberal system, which most of the children recognized, to have the teacher's ready attention afforded high status in the embryonic culture of the children, and particularly amongst the group of (mainly) girls, who positively sought it. It was observed that Sylvia consistently forced the teacher into a double bind by doing right and wrong at the same time, especially at the end of sessions when it was time to clear up. She would exploit the ambiguities in the rules in order to assert her status amongst the children as one who can command the teacher's attention. Thus at the end of clearing up sessions she would meticulously work at it, but generally be the last to sit down in the 'quiet corner, and, given the recognized norms, be late. This then was a mild way of testing the teacher's affection for her and so objectifying her social status. As time went on the child escalated this to direct disobedience which resulted in a slap. The point of this brief analysis is that we are attributing an active role to the infant (5½-6 years) child in the social structure of the classroom, and the teacher–pupil relationship. In this *laissez-faire* set up, Sylvia is able to perceive (though not articulate verbally) a status system amongst her peers (there is generally informal sexual segregation) as constituted by the nature of the teacher–pupil relationship. If we compare her with the case of Michael, he was also an active agent in the social structure, though to the teacher he appeared limited and passive. But crucially, in a sense, the child chose his activities, which happened not to coincide with those the teacher appreciated and to the extent that the teacher was limited in her ability to enter and manipulate his perceptual world and values, she had no leverage for communication and thus to influence his choices in the way she would like. It is important to note that Michael though somewhat isolated, was able to hold his own in the company of his male peers. He communicated with them well enough to play, etc.

Sylvia's style-of-being in the classroom is encouraged (a) by the constant invitation to the children to do what they are interested in, i.e. to be inner directed, and (b) by the teacher giving her so much of her limited attention, which is the opposite side of the coin of inner direction for Sylvia and her peers. In Sylvia's case inner direction only becomes real in the sense that the teacher rewards her with praise and attention for her self-directed efforts. In fact the teacher generally directs quite closely, though indirectly, such children's activities.

Mrs Lyons's classroom

4   Peter

Our next example is a child, Peter, who had been at school for a month when the observation period commenced. It was immediately apparent to the observer that he was seen as a difficult problem child by the teacher. He was small and shrimp like, with a speech impairment, and poor eyesight. He related with great difficulty both to the teacher and to the other pupils. The child's oddness was explained by his 'impoverished' home. The mother was separated from the father and Peter was an only child. The mother had 'doted on the child', 'babied' him and 'has not really got the first idea'. The teacher thought she recognized the mother as having gone to the same school as her—but she came from a 'scruffy' street and was a typical 'lower class type', 'sitting on the windows: low mentality'. As she explained, 'I think he (Peter) suffers from having a peculiar mother which obviously (laughing) makes him very peculiar'.

The child lacked all the ingredients of a school trained child: he could not dress himself properly; was unable to use a knife and fork, he had a 'dreadful vocabulary', he came from a verbally deprived background. He could only understand and respond to the simplest of her instructions; he seemed to suffer from bad muscular co-ordination in PE, had no concept of number, could not tell his colours, seemed to resist most attempts to make him do anything. He played 'silly' with the other children.

The teacher saw the mother regularly. She had tried to get the mother to stop 'babying' him, to get herself out to a job and give herself some other thing to interest her. As Mrs Lyons explained to the observer, she would find it difficult to decide whether Peter's trouble was his thickness or his immaturity until she had 'broken him from Mummy'. She noticed how 'regressed' he was after each weekend he had spent at home but thought it was a bit of each. She said he was 'emotionally peculiar as well; I've never seen him cry' and she found it odd that he didn't cry when his mother left him at school or when she reprimanded him and that 'his reading does not seem to have any emotional connotation for him', she said: 'For a child who is virtually six, he is, well, he would be good for a three year old really', she had 'never known a child like him'.

The teacher expected that he would be a slow learner. She said 'if he's as bad as this in a year's time, I'll get the education psychologist to have a look at him'. This will enable the 'expert' to pronounce on the validity of her assessment of him as decidedly peculiar, certainly not normal.

It is quite obvious that he presented a problem to the teacher. He was difficult to motivate. He could not obey simple instructions. She found him impossible both to get through to, and to establish a relationship with; his speech was difficult to understand and he frequently said 'can't' or 'won't' to all her suggestions. Occasionally she said to him 'It's not a question of what you want—do this or that', and then he might try to do it but there were few positive achievements for his efforts.

Similarly any interaction with him on her part was not rewarded by speedy results. He didn't seem to be very interested in number work and reading. Nevertheless the observer did notice how after the teacher had appeared to be making an effort with him over number work and flash cards the teacher commented that he was improving slightly, showing a bit more interest. The teacher's explanation for this was that Peter could see how the younger pupils were surpassing him and 'wanted to catch up' although it could equally have been due to the fact that whereas the child was usually left very much to his own devices compared with other children of the same age, he had come in for some unusual attention, as a result, perhaps, of the stay in hospital which had caused his absence from school for some time.

This child illustrates well the position of one who had acquired a hard and negative identity. The 'knowledge' which the teacher had of his home background accords with the teacher's reified notions of the typical background of her pupils. Moreover, his whole mode of coping with the classroom confirmed her background expectancies instead of providing contra-indications of his abnormality which over time might have enabled him to break through the boundaries of the reified typification she had of him. Whatever he did, he provided her with confirmation of the validity of this typification. Moreover, her own way of interacting with him served to reinforce the child's inability to present himself as other than peculiar, but she had little alternative in the situation. His 'peculiarity' was especially visible to the teacher particularly when she received a new intake of younger pupils against whom Peter compared very unfavourably.

Nevertheless, there were some signs that some transformation in his identity might occur. The teacher related how his mother was beginning to help him with his reading but she was not 'pushing' him. It is interesting that even though Mrs Lyons thought her a poor mother, that the teacher allowed and indeed even encouraged her, to help him at home. Perhaps, as a result, the teacher noticed that he was beginning to show interest in various activities, starting to respond more to simple instructions and relating a little more easily to the other children. It was too early to ascertain whether in the long run a gradual transformation into 'normal' pupil would be possible. He would have a long way to go, nevertheless, since, as we have seen, being unprepared for school was regarded by Mrs Lyons as an indication of a lack of readiness for intellectual advance. Whilst he was being socialized into a school trained child, others already in that state would be increasing the gap between him and them with reference to the acquisition of the skills of literacy and numeracy.

It is also important to point out that others also were involved in the categorization of the child as peculiar. The child's own mother who regularly saw the teacher about the child, told the researcher that she could see she had over-mothered him and 'babied' him, even though she confessed to a feeling of relief when the teacher had told her that there were others who were more peculiar than hers in the class. It is significant to note how the teacher interacted with Peter's mother. Whilst to the observer she had very little positive to say about her, to the mother herself she appeared helpful, concerned and interested and was prepared to spend a lot of her time patiently talking over Peter's difficulties, giving advice and reassurance. This 'helpfulness' and 'interest' was typical of her interactions generally with parents. Indeed, this teacher was well thought of by most of the parents we interviewed who were pleased that their children were in her class and found her helpful and constructive. It is significant that, in spite of her generally negative evaluations of the parents which were publicly communicated within the confines of the staffroom, she could successfully present herself as 'constructive' and helpful in face-to-face interaction. This aspect of self-presentation we will take up again in a later chapter, but this time in relationship to the successful parent.

Mrs Lyons also communicated to her colleagues the troubles she had with Peter. This involvement of significant others in the prophecy acts in a way to structure and limit the opportunity for the child to move out of this deviant category. He acquires 'form' with others who increasingly perceive him and interpret his activities, interacting with him in ways which confirm him in his identity.

5   Daniel

Our next example, Daniel, is a more difficult and complex one. In the former case the child was inarticulate, lacking in self-confidence, physically gauche and, compared with other pupils, immature. Daniel, however, was quite different. Nevertheless in one respect they were similar, that is, they were only children living with their mothers who were divorced. This child, however, as the social workers related, had an 'intelligent and ambitious mother' who had a good job, was financially secure and was keen for Daniel to do well at school. He had been at nursery school since he was three and a half and had been to baby minders from an early age.

After a couple of days at school it was apparent that he was another problem child, even though Daniel himself said this school 'is the nicest I've been to'. He was certainly not peculiar in the sense that Peter was. He appeared self-confident, was verbally very articulate, did not seem frightened to relate to adults. Nevertheless, the teacher found him 'abnormal'. What indicators did she use to define him as abnormal? It was noticed that he kicked other children, that normal children cried when reprimanded whereas this one didn't, that he was 'too clean'; he corrected the other children for dropping their 'h's, and he had a loud voice. He seemed to get involved in quarrels with other pupils and was frequently singled out by the teacher for 'causing trouble'.

After he had only been in school for three weeks, at a meeting with the school social workers, the headmaster argued that the child was 'very emotionally disturbed' and should be marked 'at risk'. There had already been some suggestions made to the mother that the child was in need of child guidance treatment which the mother had at first refused but the social worker thought she might eventually 'co-operate'. The social worker who had met Daniel had thought him a 'handsome child' but agreed that 'he is a very tense little boy and does all the things at school which he daren't do at home'. The consensus of opinion was that his 'problem' obviously related to his father whom the mother is always running down in front of the child: 'He must obviously feel he is going the same way.' The same comment was made about Peter. At a later stage the teacher alleged that his troubles stem from being 'too clever': he is able to blame himself for his bad background, 'because he is like his father, he will turn out badly and he realizes this'. She also remarked that he was 'too clever for his own good'.

Now it is important at this stage to raise the question of the direction of the causal sequence involved with the crystallization of this child's negative identity. Is it that the child's behaviour which he exhibits at school is such that it presents the teacher with management problems and there is, therefore, some search for non-threatening (to the teacher's self-conceptions as competent) explanations which result in his 'bad background' being cited as the explanatory factor? Alternatively, does the knowledge of the child's background activate the teacher's typifications about the likely consequences of such a background such that his behaviour is interpreted in a way which validates her expectations? Whereas in the former case it was not difficult to see why the child was defined as pecular, with this child it was more problematic. Moreover, much of his aggressive self-assertive behaviour could have been interpreted as a direct reaction to the kinds of comments and denigrations he was receiving from the teacher. It was as if a battle of wills had sprung up between them at a very early stage, putting the child into a double bind from which it was difficult to extricate himself. When, for example, he had retrieved a car he had brought to school which the teacher had confiscated, he was told he could have it back if he were good. At the end of the afternoon when he had been unusually good, a fact which Mrs Lyons herself acknowledged, he asked for it back but was told that he couldn't as he had been naughty. At this the child went into a rage, cried and said he would kick her and tell his mother. Whereupon the teacher was annoyed and the child went off grizzling. Nevertheless, the episode had provided the teacher again with evidence of his maladjustment which confirmed her view of him. Similar examples of the incompatibility of their wills and the ensuing cycle of behaviour which mutually confirmed each's concept of the other could be quoted. This is not to suggest that the teacher never complimented him or in any way rewarded him for his activities, but that on some occasions when this happened they were often accompanied by qualifications: 'That's good . . . I don't know what's come over you . . . That's very nice—for you.'

Daniel's case has been quoted because he is a good example of a child who was finding it very difficult to 'break through' the reified typification towards being defined as a normal child. This is odd because in many ways he could be regarded as from her point of view well trained for school. He could count, he knew his colours, he could draw, manipulate Lego, was verbally fluent and appeared self-confident. He could eat properly, dress himself, etc. The key to his difficulties lay in the interrelationship between, on the one hand, the 'hardness' of the teacher's typifications regarding the likely consequences of the child's 'pathological' background and, on the other, the child's unbiddableness. He was not sufficiently deferent to the teacher's authority. He would not conform in the sense that he would not allow the teacher to feel that he accorded her the legitimacy which goes with her position. He would not take her word, but wanted reasons. This child's position was an essentially ironic one because from many points of view the teacher's standards of good behaviour were shared by the child. Much of his interactions with other pupils were coloured by the way in which the child reprimanded the other children because their behaviour deviated from the ideal norm. They snatch things and don't say please and thank you. It is this, perhaps, which is precisely the child's problem; he usurps the teacher's function. He is a perfectionist and attempts to intervene where other pupils do not live up to his own high standards. The results of his intervention, however, backfired on him and led to him expressing his aggression against an apparent sense of injustice going on. An additional problem for him was that since before coming to the school he had already made a good start on 'real learning', he perhaps found the classroom boring, there may not be enough opportunities for him to find things to interest him, and Mrs Lyons did not always appear to stretch him intellectually, presumably because of her view that children with personality problems need a therapeutic resolution of these before they could be considered to be 'ready' to advance. For the child's part, however, it was noticed that he appeared to be modifying his behaviour so as to avoid doing what would incur her displeasure. Whether over time he could do this sufficiently to present himself as other than he 'must' be, remained problematic. Certainly by the end of the observation period he had not managed yet to achieve the status of being 'normal'.

6   Linda

Our next example is of a child who managed to break through an initially adverse typification and is *en route* to becoming a successful pupil. Linda started school at the same time as the child discussed above. The teacher described the mother as 'not cultured' and communicates the view that the family background is not conducive to great success. The mother, for example, did not complete the child's medical form so she missed seeing the doctor, and she had 'pushed the child onto an older brother' to bring to school after the first day—both were taken to be indications of general neglect. However, the school social workers were not able to provide any additional 'information' about the family so no more reliable picture could be gained. Moreover the teacher had seen little of the child's mother in the early period of the observation.

The teacher formed a bad impression of the child during the first few days at school. She was said to be odd with a loud voice, a 'flighty child who wouldn't settle to anything'. Another teacher observed that her behaviour was 'very bizarre'. The basis for these judgments was not very clear. It appears that the teacher found her irritating because she was too noisy, moving around a great deal 'you keep swopping, that's your trouble'. Mrs Lyons commented to the observer that she was 'one of those who needed sitting on'. It appeared that the child's difficulty was that she had no idea of the sort of behaviour expected of her. For example, she washed her hands in the water trough. For this she was severely rebuked 'don't you ever let me see you do that again—it's very naughty'. The teacher thought her 'insecure'. She holds onto a duster which the teacher describes as her 'bit of comfort' and sucks her thumb.

Three weeks later, however, the picture had changed. The child was now a success story. The headmaster was heard to remark that he thought her a real problem child when she first came but she 'conforms now reasonably' and the teacher also said she was 'potentially odd but bright enough to conform'. This 'bright enough to conform' comment relates back to our previous discussion of Daniel, who although 'bright enough' and sharing her standards of good behaviour, yet usurps her authority and sets himself up as the teacher *vis-à-vis* his pupil peers. Daniel's case can be compared to that of Linda who, it was noticed, was being described a little later by the teacher as 'gorgeous', 'lovely'. Increasingly as time went on, the child managed to become defined in a favourable light, whereas for Daniel no comparable changes occurred.

What happened to explain Linda's transformation? The teacher denied any responsibility for the change. 'Linda did it all herself—she transformed herself.' Such a view is, of course, in line with the child centred faith in the spontaneous development of the child itself. The teacher denied that she had given the child 'special' treatment.

Nevertheless, the observer noting the teacher's avowal that the child needed 'sitting on' remarked that the child received more than usual instruction in the type of behaviour expected. Unlike some other new children, she was being singled out for individual instruction, for example in learning to say 'please' to Mrs Lyons, 'excuse me'. She was clearly being told how to behave. Moreover, in spite of her 'bizarre' behaviour she soon appeared to have sufficient powers of concentration to pursue a task through to the end, she 'knew her colours' and could count and seemed to understand the teacher's instructions and comply with them. Furthermore, she was able to gear into the teacher's system of relevancies very quickly. For example, she was the first new child to start participating in flash card work, at first only as an observer, but she had managed to perceive that doing flash card work was the route to getting a reading book; thus she cues into the correct sequential routes and is sufficiently interested to embark on them.

Essentially the child is a 'doer' even though 'flighty', she got through more in her first day than the average child in a week. Whilst other children paint one picture, Linda does five; she appears self-possessed and independent. In this sense she won't be a 'pesterer or a fusser'. She can get on by herself—and does. She knows what she wants and after some initial *faux pas* perceives how to get it in such a way that she won't displease the teacher. She also amused the teacher through her funny expressions, 'watcha doing mate?' and began to impress the teacher with her lively independence. She learned to clear up well—after an initial period when she expected to have things done for her.

It seems that the key to the child's transformed identity lies in the fact that the teacher did differentiate her treatment towards this child in a way which brought about a closer approximation to the ideal pupil. The fact that the teacher 'sat' on her, which took the form of constant stricturing in the correct behaviour expected, meant that this child whom the teacher marked out as more deviant than some of the other new inmates had potentially a better opportunity to learn the underlying structure of rules and regulations on which success depends. Moreover, the child herself did not pose a threat to the teacher's authority, unlike Daniel. She may have been difficult, in the sense that she was always rushing around, wouldn't settle, but seemed to be sufficiently teacher oriented to respond to reprimands and modify her behaviour accordingly. Additionally, even though the teacher alleged that Linda had transformed herself, it is important to note that on the third day at school this child was being pointed out to Peter thus: 'This little girl has only been in school a day and she's very good'. The child had obviously been capable of good behaviour from the beginning, it had merely been lost sight of.

Now although the teacher in the early period alleged that the child 'won't be brilliant—won't learn quickly' because the mother is 'not cultured', it appears that by the end of the observation period the child was well on the way to becoming a successful pupil for 'these children'. She was beginning to get more involved in serious instruction in reading and writing in a way which differed from the other pupils who started school at the same time.

We should remember that Mrs Lyons spent more of her time with chosen groups of top infants and with a few sponsored younger pupils from the middle infants. Since this child was only a bottom infant who generally tended to be left very much to their own devices, it is not so easy to regard her as part of the élite of the classroom. Nevertheless, given a continuation of the type of relationship she was developing with the teacher we would argue that the breakthrough to a successful identity had been reached. Her main handicap seemed to be that the teacher still seemed to think negatively of the child's background. The child's desire for milk was interpreted as due to the fact that she had no breakfast, her absence from school on several occasions was 'because the family had overslept' and when the mother didn't come rushing up to the school to complain about Linda's more than usually paint marked clothes, this was seen as 'most odd', a sign of a mother 'pushing the child off'. Linda's capacity for getting her clothes filthy and paint marked was outstanding which made her mother's lack of complaints even more surprising. Nevertheless, from other possible examples we could quote, were she to complain, this also would possibly have been categorized as indicative of over-anxiety or unnecessary fussing. The line to be taken by a well meaning parent was difficult and threat-ridden on either side. It is problematic whether it is possible to become a successful child in this classroom if one suffers from the handicap of a 'bad' home. We have seen how Mrs Lyons typifies the pupils generally as coming from pathological environments, and that even with her best pupils, she cannot hope for very much, i.e. her best are not like good middle class pupils—they are the best 'for these children' but their background is such that none of them will go far. With this child, however, the failure of the mother (it is the mothers whom the teachers regard as particularly educationally relevant) to present herself as somebody keen, interested, ambitious and 'cultured' might in the long run, were she to stay in this classroom, be dysfunctional. On the other hand, the fact that the school did not seem to have any really hard 'data' on the family and that the elder brother was defined as making good progress, may have meant that if the child continued to do well, the view which Mrs Lyons held of the family might be revised and reinterpreted. With Daniel, on the other hand, it was as if the reliable knowledge which the teacher had of his background condemned the child willy nilly to an unfavourable career, for such a background could only be productive of a highly disturbed child.

7   *Mary*

The final example to be discussed is that of a child who could be regarded as closer to the teacher's conception of the ideal pupil than any we have considered so far. Mary comes from a good home, a 'cultured home' as the teacher puts it. Her mother is 'one of the best mothers even though she can't spell'. The teacher thinks favourably of her intellectual ability. She observes how the child makes efforts to do things on her own and believes that she 'will go a long way'. Her reading is good for her age, a fact which the teacher explains as being due to the child having taught herself to read by asking the other children. The teacher maintains that she didn't teach her, but then she regards the process of learning to read as a little mysterious, in any case.

The observer noticed that Mary frequently was given certain rewards and privileges: she is allowed to assist the teacher in various tasks which require responsibility and care, or which are valued by the pupils for the status which accrues to their performance. Most pupils do these 'helping' activities at various times but this child is exceptional for the frequency with which she does them, and for the high amount of contact she has with the teacher. She also brings useful items of equipment from home which can be used for art work. Although she is only a middle infant, she receives as much attention from the teacher as the girl top infants, so much so that for some time the observer assumed she was a top infant, until the teacher pointed out that this was not so. It did become apparent though, that there were some children who were really top infants but where the teacher did not seem to have registered the fact.

It is important to note this because it shows that this child's sponsorship was a function of her inherent potential, not of her age. Less able top infants would be included in some activities simply by virtue of their age if the teacher was conscious that they were top infants, because certain standards of reading and writing were expected of that age group. They would not usually, however, be selected to participate in teacher initiated theme art work which was characterized by far greater teacher contact, and where Mrs Lyons had a more egalitarian consociate relationship with those pupils she had chosen to assist her. Mary, however, had become part of the group of pupils who were often singled out. She also read far more frequently to the teacher and the welfare assistant, and in the lunch hour as well, and was often to be seen 'working with the teacher' whereas others of her age were more likely to be left to their own devices.

Mary gave all the appearances of being a pleasant happy co-operative child, one who conforms closely to the teacher's concept of being school trained. The fact that she is 'no trouble' will mean that the teacher will indulge her requests to read without this being taken to be symptomatic of having pressurizing parents who are unprepared to wait for readiness to emerge.

Mrs Buchanan's classroom

8   Glen

Glen is a child who occupies a very low position in the social structure of the classroom and who increasingly begins to acquire a hard identity of being peculiar. At the start of the period of observation, the child had been in school for several weeks. He was physically slight, delicate and sensitive looking and seemed to find it very difficult to establish relationships either with other children or with the teacher. On several occasions at the start of the observation period he was noticed crying as a result of some comment made to him by another child or being roughly treated, pushed and jostled as the pupils went about their classroom activities. The teacher related that he was 'a bit of a wingerer. He cries a lot, he winges and whines. He moans a lot ... I think this is what annoys the other children—he just mooches about really.' In the classroom he never seemed to get involved in anything for any length of time. He was always hovering about, always on the outside of various working groups, wandering from place to place as if he was trying to find a stable niche somewhere where the other children would include him in their activities—but they rejected him, pushing him out of the way, and he lacked the self-confidence to assert himself. The teacher found him a problem:

> 'He wouldn't attempt anything. He just didn't seem to be interested in anything. He wouldn't speak to anybody. He does anything under sufferance. He won't draw much because he's not very good, he rarely paints a picture, or plays with the Lego, he just wanders around. He's got no friends. He's tried to make friends with Geoff and Malcolm but they just wander off. He doesn't talk much to me. I don't think he likes me very much. If you try to talk to him he just looks straight through

you. . . . If you try to get an answer out of him—well, it can take you all
your time to get an answer out of him.'

She obviously found it difficult to develop any rapport with this child.
When she tried to communicate with him she got little response or
feedback. He just stared at her, looking frightened or just wandered off.
When she tried to organize the pupils at the beginning of the sessions he
was always one of the residual category of pupils who had failed to
respond to any of her suggestions about what they should do. When he
was told to find himself something to do, along with the other members of
the group, he would wander in the classroom with an aimlessness about
him rarely ending up spending more than a moment or two at anything.

Nevertheless his quietness and unobtrusiveness were such as to facilitate
his increasing anonymity in the classroom. He was not a problem to her
for he was no threat to the social order of the classroom. He was never
seen to be transgressing any of the prohibitive norms. His inactivity was
not accompanied by socially disruptive behaviour. But his inability to
make his presence felt either with respect to other children or, more
importantly, to the teacher meant that increasingly he was entering a
career in the classroom which would lead to a hardening of his identity
and a closing of opportunities to escape from a lowly position. Because he
never initiated any interactions with the teacher, nor responded to any
generalized suggestions to involve himself in activities which might have
alerted the teacher's attention, he was able to avoid any interaction with
the teacher for days on end. We have suggested that some degree of
interaction with the teacher is a necessary if not sufficient condition for
educational advance. That Mrs Buchanan could complain at the end of the
session 'considering he's been at school for nearly a year I would have
thought that he would have shown an interest in writing or number work,
which he just won't attempt' was as much a function of the very few
opportunities he had had to acquire or demonstrate any competence in
these areas as of any inherent deficiencies on his part. Nevertheless, the
teacher seemed to have arrived at a judgment that he was stupid: 'He's
very soft, he's dopey, is Glen. He'll always be a bit slow.' But these
designations of the child as stupid were accompanied at the same time by
a recognition that her inability to establish a relationship with him would
disadvantage him *vis-à-vis* other pupils. She admitted that

'He's very peculiar . . . he's a funny little boy. One needs to be able to
establish a relationship with him. I just can't get through to him and I
haven't got the time so he won't get on as far as a child I can get through
to.'

Given the constraints of time and resources, however, this child who presented such a problem to the teacher was increasingly acquiring a hard identity. 'He's a drip . . . He's got no personality . . . he's very much a nonentity is Glen . . .' and the child himself gave the teacher few cues to lead the teacher to redefine her view of him.

In this connection, the observer noticed several occasions where the child had brought up to the teacher some writing that he had done but he was unable to gain her attention. Some degree of forcefulness was necessary to divert her away from whatever she was doing, but this child seemed to lack the confidence and the means of interposing himself between the teacher and her current object of attention. Had he been able to do so, he would quite probably have gained some approving reinforcement for his efforts or some more specific direction as to how he should occupy himself. This child illustrates a casualty of the competition for teacher's attention which operates among the pupils. But this competition among the pupils was not something latent to the teacher's consciousness. What was latent, perhaps is the extent to which the demands of the maintenance of social order in the classroom were ultimately related to the social structuring of the pupils' identities.

This can be illustrated by seeing how the categories which the teacher employs to assess achievement in relationship to the pupils perceived abilities are interrelated with the roles which the pupils play and the consequent problems presented to her in trying to manage the infant classroom. We have suggested that dull stupid children are those whom the teacher finds it difficult to motivate or interest. Moreover motivation and interest in the activities which the teacher approves of are necessary conditions of becoming defined as a successful pupil.

The case of Glen admirably illustrates the position of one whose lack of intersubjectivity with the teacher and failure to be motivated by the teacher earns him the designation of stupid.

Nevertheless, even with this child she did admit that 'he surprised me the other day because we were going through some words and he knew quite a lot of them so he must have been listening somewhere on the line.'

However, though at one level she defined her problem with Glen as due to a lack of time to relate adequately to all the pupils with whom she had to deal, at another level the teacher seemed to be legitimizing her low level of contact with him by, first, appealing to the inherent pathology in Glen himself, but, second, by suggesting that the child didn't like her. Indeed there were quite a few examples of pupils who had minimal contact with the teacher and whom she declared did not like her.

This example again illustrates the importance of the style that the child adopts in the classroom for a favourable career. The child has to be able to initiate and sustain interaction with her to be able to facilitate his transition to a more favourable position in the classroom where interaction and inter-subjectivity between the pupil and the teacher is high. In our example, the child's inability to establish a relationship with the teacher deprived him of the structured opportunity to get into a position where he would demonstrate to the teacher that he was not so stupid as he appeared. Nevertheless it is interesting that his reified identity was not the result of any extra classroom 'form' that the teacher had on him. The teacher thought the mother 'very nice really' and the child was always 'nicely turned out'. His pathology was not explained or legitimized by any inherent pathological characteristics he possessed as a result of his home background, but rather due to his whole mode of being in the classroom and his inability to fit into the teacher's conceptions of how 'normal' pupils should react to the classroom experience.

9   Robert

It is proposed now to turn to consider another child, Robert, who is similarly part of the bedrock of busyness but who differs in a number of respects from the previous example. At the same time this child well illustrates some significant differences as well as similarities in the stratification processes in this classroom which relates to the teacher perspective towards informal methods of pedagogy.

In general terms, it was suggested that in each classroom one could rank children along a continuum which has as its extremes the peculiar child and the ideal pupil, with the normal children in between. Along this continuum children could be varyingly differentiated in terms of the frequency and quality of contact with the teacher, the degree of intersubjectivity between pupil and teacher and the chances of being defined as dull or bright. It was suggested that the ranking of each pupil along these various dimensions to a great extent overlapped and coincided. Thus the bright child would also be the child who was on a successful career path, taking up a large proportion of the teacher's time, receiving more subtle cues as to the teacher's intentions and closer direction over his activities and so on.

Now in Mrs Buchanan's class although some of these phenomena are found, others are absent. This is particularly the case with regard to being defined as bright. In this classroom, amid the bedrock of busyness were several children whom the teacher defined as 'really bright'. Nevertheless they formed part of the bedrock of busyness because of their failure to become involved in activities which the teacher approved of and the fact that they did not seek out the teacher and make demands on her time.

Our second child Robert is particularly interesting because, whereas with Glen the teacher found it almost impossible to 'get through to' him and intersubjectivity was low, with Robert the relationship was characterized by a high level of intersubjectivity, rapport was excellent and the teacher claimed to 'know' the child in some complexity. Moreover the teacher had a very warm relationship with him: 'I think he's super. He has a marvellous sense of humour. I really get on well with him', she reported. This was interesting because to some of the other teachers Robert had acquired a reified identity as a problem child. This can partly be explained by the fact that Robert had 'form' in the sense that most teachers defined him as being a member of a problem family. He was one of four children living with his mother, and his parents were separated. In addition the school had had trouble with the mother over the older children. One of his elder brothers was still in the school and although universally recognized as very bright, was also a problem—naughty and defiant with respect to school rules especially those which concerned clothes. He often came to school with long trousers on, whereas these were forbidden. There had obviously been considerable 'trouble' from the mother in the past and she was well known as a 'bad parent', not supporting the school or providing the sort of background of which the headmaster approved. Mrs Smith frequently was the subject of criticism in the staffroom. She was thought to send the children to school dirty and unkempt. Her house was full of children whom she was minding. 'She's paid £3.10 for each of those children and look what we get for looking after 35' and she was known to complain frequently about the school.

Now Robert had all the family characteristics which might have led him to become a 'problem' child to the teacher and develop a reified identity—being maladjusted, insecure, etc. Nevertheless this teacher, whom we have already seen acknowledges that she tries to treat the children, not as members of problem families, but as individuals, not wanting to label them as problem children before she has seen what they are like, got on very well with him. Moreover she found him very bright, perhaps more so than any other pupil in the class. She describes him as 'well adjusted for his age, both mentally and physically, he's very verbally advanced, he gets it from his brothers and sisters—he converses easily with anybody' and on other occasions she said, 'He's so far ahead of the other children anyway.' To the observer he certainly appeared very self-confident and was always saying witty things to the teacher and to other pupils. He was thought to ask 'intelligent' questions and always knew the answers to any puzzles or problems the teacher posed. Nevertheless Mrs Buchanan thought of him as an under-achiever. He was not doing as well as she would have wished. Whilst he was known to be very good at number work and was the only child to have a number book of his own to work with, far more of his time would be spent playing about, out of the teacher's sight. The other children tended to find him a nuisance. He would make fun of them, play jokes on them, disrupt their games. He would usually avoid having to do any writing and rarely settled down at anything for long. The teacher recognized that the other children didn't like him but explained this by the fact that he tended to be a bit of a bully and a show off, but this was explicable in terms of his being so much brighter than they. Nevertheless his under-achievement concerned her. Robert's failure to concern himself with the three Rs was, however, not explained in terms of a social pathology model, involving neopsychiatric categories at the beginning of the period of observation. The case of Robert was cited by Mrs Buchanan as an illustration of the failure of the informal approach to teaching and pedagogy. Had the teacher felt able to use a more directive approach with him she was sure he would do better and become the successful pupil that his 'obvious' brightness warranted. She was not in any way puzzled by his actions in the classroom. His whole behaviour and orientation to the classroom was perfectly understandable and fitted into the fluidity of unproblematic common sense of the teacher. He conformed to her stereotype of a normal bright alert child, whose family background did not lead him to be naturally interested in matters educational. No moral categories were used against him. Rather the inappropriateness of the 'free approach', and her own inability to organize the context to motivate the pupils, was seen as responsible for his under-achievement. Meanwhile Robert's behaviour in the classroom was considered naughty but the result of high spirits but since her whole approach to discipline tended to be fairly free, except when serious breaches of the underlying code of behaviour occurred, Robert continued in this way. In addition, he was particularly capable of carrying out his naughtiness in areas which avoided the teacher's scrutiny or in a way which did not quite lead the other children to call the teacher's attention to him. From the child's point of view, he did not seem to be oriented towards the teacher any more than anyone else as a source of self-confirmation in his projects. Whilst relating easily with her, conversing with her, having jokes with her, he was very much 'doing his own thing' choosing to please himself but not appearing sufficiently oriented to the teacher to please her by doing the things that she defined as important for his educational advance. Nevertheless, it is questionable whether it was apparent to the child that what the teacher really wanted was not what appeared to be demanded. In one sense the child received plenty of cues from the teacher that he was a good fellow. She would laugh at his jokes, respond confirmingly to his responses to her questions, and it was not difficult for the observer to notice that she felt very warmly towards him. She found him a delightful, likeable child.

Robert forms part of the bedrock of busyness, that structural basis which provides her with sociological psychological and temporal space to operate. He made few demands on her time. She rarely 'made' him do anything and in that sense, in spite of his designation as being bright, he fails to acquire the identity of a successful pupil. He admirably illustrates the crucial role of the child seeking out the teacher and becoming oriented to teacher's 'real' wishes as opposed to what she seems to permit which is the free pursuit of the child's own interest.

Before turning to our next example it is perhaps important to mention some indication of transformations in Robert's identity which seemed to be occurring towards the end of the observation period. It was noted that the teacher herself underwent some significant changes in her perspective as the year went by. Whereas at the beginning the methods and her own inability to carry them out adequately were seen by her as the major cause of under-achievement, towards the end her views shifted somewhat and the child himself and his family increasingly became invoked in the explanation. We will take up the question of the reasons for these changes in a later chapter. With the bright under-achievers, initially, their cultural differences meant that they would not naturally be oriented to the three Rs but no moral categorizations were used, but as time went on, increasingly, the teacher began to castigate such pupils as lazy. With the 'average' under-achievers some emotional deficiencies caused by family pathologies began to be invoked. With Robert the teacher began to think of him as lazy. She said of him 'he's really lazy. If I want to hear him read I have to go and grab him and set him down, he just won't come voluntarily.' Again, of another child, who with Robert had been classed as one of the children who are 'far brighter than they think', she complained

'She's lazy, she just can't be bothered to do anything. She's lazy in herself, in her person. If she takes her cardigan off and drops it on the floor, there it stays . . . I haven't got the time to keep following her up and making her sit down and read to me, she'll get out of it if she can.'

Nevertheless, in spite of Robert's alleged laziness, some good things were happening to him. He began to make friends with one of the pupils whom the teacher defined as both very bright and achieving well. This child was in the top layer of the stratification hierarchy. She appeared motivated and interested, and though on the outside of the little clique of successful children which will be discussed in connection with the next example, she had access to the teacher and had considerable guidance and direction from her. As a result of this friendship he was observed to be making more requests for the teacher's assistance. The teacher was also aware of this. She related

'He can't get the intellectual satisfaction he needs without reading, but he's started to show interest in that now. He never did before . . . He comes up and asks me to hear him which he never did before. That's a good sign I suppose; that's to do with Elizabeth. He wants to catch up but she's way ahead. They do each other good.'

The observation period ended very soon after this statement so it was not possible to see whether Robert managed to move from the bedrock of busyness into the élite of successful children.

This emerging transformation in his identity, however, illustrates the fluidity of the bedrock of busyness and the importance in this classroom of the style that the pupil adopts in moving upwards or downwards in the stratification hierarchy.

10   Sharon

We now turn to the third layer of the stratification system and consider the case of a child, Sharon, who is one of a small group of six children who form the core of the élite. This group, although undergoing some internal changes in the pattern of social relationships over time, was one of the most stable social units throughout the period of observation. The group was characterized by their close relationship with the teacher, the high proportion of the teacher's attention they managed to acquire, and their favourable categorization as interested, keen children whose progress the teacher was pleased with and who confirmed her in her identity. The group included several children whom the teacher initially defined as only average in intelligence but were all seen as getting on well, trying hard, even at the beginning of the observation when, as we have seen, Mrs Buchanan was generally dissatisfied with her pupils' performance.

Sharon is a good example of the teacher's notion of the ideal pupil, the child 'who would do well whoever the teacher'. She oriented significantly towards Mrs Buchanan but not in a way which the teacher defined as over-demanding. She would come into school each morning and amuse the teacher with bright conversation relating the various happenings at home and at the same time showing as much interest in the teacher's life as discretion allowed. She would frequently volunteer to help the teacher at the sorting out sessions when the pupil's 'chose' their activities for the day, and would always be one of those who 'wanted to do reading or writing or number work', when the teacher asked them to state their preferences. Moreover, she would persevere with these activities. She seemed to the observer to have a long span of concentration and would work at something until it was completed. For example, at one point the teacher had tried to get the pupils involved in doing special interest books where they would make a little book of writing and drawings on some theme that interested them. This child persisted more than any other with this activity and was often to be seen working on her book without being prompted for a long time after all the other pupils had apparently lost interest. Moreover she would seek the teacher out for assistance when she needed help and approach her with tact and discretion in the sense that she wouldn't pester the teacher but would choose the appropriate moment. She would also regularly ask the teacher to help her with her reading unlike other pupils whom the teacher needed to chase up: 'She's very pleasant and keen is Sharon.'

Mrs Buchanan obviously liked her. She related how the mother had told her how difficult Sharon was at home, but how she found her a model pupil. She was thought of as bright—'She's bright—definitely bright . . . she's probably the brightest of my middle infants—with Elizabeth' and the child herself was continually feeding back evidence of her brightness through the kinds of work she produced and her ease of verbal communication. It should be noticed that all the members of this élite group, of which Sharon was perhaps the centre, were girls. There were two boys in this upper layer of the structure but they tended to be relatively isolated compared with the girls.

In our discussion of Robert we mentioned how some transformations in the child's identity occurred as a result of changes in the structure of his activities. It is interesting to note a similar but reverse process at work here in the last few weeks of the observation. It was again too early to say whether this transformation might have involved her movement down into the bedrock of busyness.

The child was noticed over a few weeks to have been having less contact with the teacher and initiating fewer interactions with her asking for assistance and guidance. Indeed she and her friend, who had been similarly located in the élite group were tending to isolate themselves more from the group as a working unit and spend long periods of time drawing in a corner with their chairs facing away from the centre of activity.

The teacher also noticed this, and appeared puzzled. Whereas, when she seemed to be performing well, Sharon fitted into the commonsense, unreflected upon, categories of the teacher rendering her capable of being handled with little selfconsciousness, a deterioration in her productivity rendered her more problematic to the teacher. However, from the observer's point of view the child was behaving in a very similar way to many other pupils in the classroom who did not appear to pose problems of interpretation to the teacher. It is, however, precisely the fact that this child had shared a high level of consociality with the teacher that her behaviour called forth the need for special explanations. Mrs Buchanan said

> 'Just recently I've noticed that she's looking very miserable and morose. I've been meaning to ask her . . . I don't know whether anything has happened at home . . . I know she's got a father and mother . . . the family seems OK. Somebody said that Sharon was upset because she was going to go away. The thought occurs to me, perhaps it's because the guinea pig has died . . . I don't know what's come over her . . . she used to be so chatty . . . she'll still come and talk to me but she's not nearly so chatty.'

In this conversation she also mentioned the fact that the child had become really spiteful: 'Lately she's becoming very spiteful . . . she'll fight with Barbara or anybody else who comes near; they are always fighting each other.' It is important to notice here that the teacher immediately turns to some problem connected with the home background as a possible area where the explanation for the child's falling back can be sought. When she cannot think of anything, she becomes more puzzled. Similarly, with Barbara, the other child mentioned, the teacher explains her deterioration in terms of the fact that her grandmother had died and that this must be the problem: 'There must be something going on at home.'

This growing tendency to seek for explanations of under-achievement in terms of home background ties in with those shifts in her ideology we mentioned before.

Whilst discussing this élite child we want to emphasize that there is no necessary relationship between being defined as bright and being considered a successful pupil, one who was responding well to the classroom situation. Nevertheless, showing 'interest' and 'motivation', wanting to do reading and writing, and seeking out the teacher, were important attributes of those children who transformed themselves from being defined as of merely average intelligence but very keen, trying hard, interested, to being defined as bright. Such transformations in their mode of categorization can be partially explained in terms of the rewards and pay offs for the child which accrued to them as they interacted closely with the teacher and received guidance from her in those areas of work which she tended to spend most of her time assisting.

Whilst not all bright pupils are successful pupils in the sense that they are achieving up to their potential, all successful pupils, whether bright or average or even dull have the chance of becoming or remaining bright simply by virtue of the feedback effects from the quantity and quality of the relationships they develop with the teacher.

Conclusion

During the course of illustrating the formal considerations from our field work experiences, various categories drawn from that constellation of ideas which comprise the dominant child centred ethos of the school have been used.

In the next chapter attention will be focused upon this vocabulary and its sociological significance as an accounting device (Scott and Lyman, 1968) in two analytically and empirically distinct contexts. The role of the child centred vocabulary will be explored, first, in relationship to the context of intra-classroom practice, teacher-pupil relationships and the social stratification of pupils and, second, to the extra-classroom practice of colleague relationships in the internal political structure of the school.

9

The child centred ethos as
an accounting system

In this chapter we will look more closely at certain aspects of the accounting procedures of the teachers, trying to situate aspects of the vocabulary, particularly the 'child centred' vocabulary, both in the classroom and in the wider context of staff relations. We will be particularly concerned to explore the social construction of the teachers' autonomy *vis-à-vis* the headmaster and the parents in so far as this relates to the child centred vocabulary and accounting system. In doing this we will be attempting to understand the degree of the teachers' discretion in the classroom by relating it to these extra classroom structural influences on the teachers' practice. Before doing so, however, we shall try to show, using several illustrations, how the vocabulary itself is very loose, containing many inner ambiguities and lacunae. It does not necessarily provide for the teachers clear explanations or legitimations which can bridge the gap between their substantive practice on the one hand and their educational aims on the other. Nevertheless, and at the same time, our discussion will suggest the crucial importance of aspects of the vocabulary not so much for providing clear operational accounts and unambiguous meanings but for the maintenance of social control and commitment to the underlying political structure of staff relationships. We will then try to illustrate in a 'vocabulary of motives' framework, (Mills, 1963) the rhetorical (Spencer, 1970) and presentational aspects of accounting procedures. Nevertheless, our approach differs from that of the authors mentioned. Accounts need to be situated *vis-à-vis* not merely the conscious level of ideas of other actors to whom accounts are being rendered but also the material context of action and the possibilities and opportunities this presents. This will become clear in our analysis.

Our first illustration will be taken from several discussions with Mrs Carpenter, who, as we have seen, characterizes the school ethos as being concerned to implement 'radical', 'new' and more appropriate methods of infant education. Our evidence will suggest, however, that the teacher is confused about her practical role in relationship to the education of the children.

While superficially Mrs Carpenter has a rational and appropriate vocabulary drawn from the 'progressive' tradition, when probed it is confused and offers an inadequate account to the observer and herself of what she does. This does not mean to say that her actions are not deliberate and meaningful in her practical work, only that the vocabulary available to her, that is, the appropriate one for this community, is inadequate. What we are highlighting is the distinction between the commonsense internal and habitual procedures of accounting to self whilst engaging in the practical activity of supervising a class of infants, and the accounting to others using objective categories, i.e. categories which are available to others and which imply, but do not necessarily realize, a commonly held set of assumptions. We find that the teacher when probed is unable to bridge the gap between her behaviour and the appropriate modes of explanation.

The illustrative evidence is taken mainly from an interview with Mrs Carpenter about her work, in the context of her description of a 'doctrinal struggle' which occurred in the school during the year before the period of observation commenced. We have referred to this before, in chapter 5. From this teacher's account, the then deputy head had tried to introduce a more formal set up, particularly in the teaching of mathematics. Mrs Carpenter and most of the other staff, had opposed this, including Mrs Lyons who succeeded the deputy head. In Mrs Carpenter's account of why she had rejected a formal maths syllabus, she admitted she would be unable to operate in that way. It would have been too restrictive and uninteresting, involving annual repetition and would have opened the door for the introduction of other formal syllabi. All this contradicted the educational perspectives or doctrines she had adopted.

Mrs Carpenter remarked that this formal approach would have meant that 'we would have missed a lot of things which we do now'. When asked what sort of things would have been curtailed, and what difference it would have made, she differentiated her own practice from the situation:

'When you've got a set plan . . . everything in its place . . . you taught length immediately after you taught so and so, and it was taught, you

know, it was not a matter of children learning really, not in the way
that we'd been thinking that they should be learning.'

She gave an illustration of what she would regard as appropriate
teacher-child educational interaction, involving informal conversation
about a topic, which might entail the child's going beyond the stages set
for the formal syllabus. She spoke about very young children working
with the concept of parallels and tessellation. However, the teacher
remarked that 'You can't just float in and float out again, there are limits',
i.e. there has to be some structure to the process of learning and teaching.
The interview proceeded as follows:

Interviewer   How do you mean?

Teacher   I mean we all, well, I have a little plan but I don't really . . . I
just sort of, mmm, try and work out what stages each child is at and
take it from there.

Interviewer   How do you do this? How does one notice what stage a
child is at?

Teacher   Oh we don't really know, you can only say the stage he isn't at
really, because you know when a child doesn't know but you don't
really know when he knows. Do you see what I mean? You can usually
tell when they don't know (long pause). (There was a distraction in the
interview at this point.) What was I talking about?

Interviewer   Certain stages, knowing when they know—

Teacher   —and when they don't know. But even so, you still don't know
when they really don't (pause) you can't really say they don't know,
can you? . . . That's why really that plan they wanted wouldn't have
worked. I wouldn't have been able to stick to it, because you just don't
. . . you know when they don't know, you don't know when they
know.

Interviewer   How do you know when they don't know?

Teacher   How do I know when they don't know? (pause) Well, no, it's
not so much that you don't know. I know when they're not ready to
know, perhaps that's a better way of putting it. You see it's all readiness
really, when you're with little children, because you can't really
(pause) they all do it at different stages and different times. The only
thing you can do is just sort of provide as many different sorts of things
so they've got every opportunity to go as far as they can—now I can't
really, sort of (pause) I don't quite know how to put it (pause) again it's
concentration, and if they're not really, sort of, ready, or going to

understand something they're doing, then their concentration will go straight away, that's one of the first things. I mean, one day we were talking about—it doesn't always work out, because you see we had two sticks and they were playing with these sticks, and they'd be putting them at angles, and then putting them, you know, beside each other, and I just went . . . along with them and poked my nose in and said 'Those two lines run the same you know, they run near each other but they're always the same'. I said, you know they were talking to me quite happily about this. Then I said something stupid, absolutely stupid, 'Of course, you know they're called parallel lines'. Bonk! . . . not interested! As soon as I said 'parallel lines'. They would probably have learned a lot more about parallel lines if I hadn't gone and poked my nose in and added my little bit of superior knowledge. You know I'd said to them . . . I'd introduced something that was obviously not, you see, I'd tried to give them the name of something, but it wasn't really what was important to them at that stage obviously; I mean, just the fact that it was parallel lines doesn't make any difference . . . they might be called 'snooty lines', if I'd gone and said they were snooty lines it would have meant the same, because they weren't really, they were still sort of, thinking about them in a sort of subconscious way, they weren't abstracting from the experience.

We will first treat this as an account which has certain strategies for overcoming communication problems specifically associated with this child centred perspective. The central difficulty for a teacher (attempting to operate a child centred approach) is knowing when to intervene and how to intervene in order to structure the children's environment for learning the things she feels are important. Thus having rejected the 'traditional' solution that the children's work should be rigidly paced and timed, classified and framed, how is the teacher to be active in the children's learning? It is realized by Mrs Carpenter that these children generally do not just learn on their own, even though she can give examples of this, but on the other hand, her understanding of the child centred philosophy implies to her that children gain a great deal by being left to work alone. In the above text this is the meaning of 'now they should be learning'. As we will see when discussing the problem of teacher autonomy, this ambiguity is unresolved and important for the structure of the staff relations, as it reflects constraints impinging upon the position of the headmaster. However, at this point we notice that words such as 'readiness', 'stages', 'need', are key sensitizers, in rendering meaningful accounts to colleagues. The model rationale says that in order to know what to do with a child to aid his intellectual development and thus not to allow him to waste all his time playing, one has to know what 'stage' he is at. This will legitimize intervention on the teacher's part, without this leading to closed, preplanned, formal teacher-pupil interaction. The phrase, 'knowing what stage he is at', evokes the image of the teacher as being centred in her work by an intimate knowledge of the child (which implicitly she recognizes that she does not have).

In conversation with teachers who operate the child centred model, this type of account is rendered, but the operational meanings are left as commonsense, assumed, and in need of no explicit account. Thus to explain our actions in terms of a child being at a certain stage makes for what the researcher feels is superficial communication. What is being confirmed is the speaker's commitment to a loose amalgam of philosophical, psychological and sociological assumptions which are not articulated, and the receiver, by not asking for a further account and thus not making the speaker's meaning problematic, is expressing his own commitment to, and integration with, the rest of the assumed community. This type of act of communication will represent a ritual of commitment and will be rhetorical rather than express intricate meanings about how a child learns or the teacher operates. To proceed to the latter, we will analyse the above account further.

In the interview the idea of 'stages' was made problematic by the interviewer, in an attempt to get the teacher to articulate its operational aspects. However, the response was an extremely confused and at times clearly contradictory discussion of her own consciousness of children's learning. Thus there were phrases like 'we don't know what stage they're at—only the stage they're not at'. The teacher was initially unable to describe any operational indicators, the implications of which will be taken up below. What occurred, though, was the invoking of another concept, 'readiness'.

Mrs Carpenter describes herself as 'knowing when they're not ready to know'. We might fill in this account by linking it to the notion of 'stages'. What the researcher infers is being said is that 'children can only learn when they're ready', or when at the right 'stage'. In discussion with her colleagues, this would be unproblematic, she would not be called upon to further justify this account when applied to her activity, *vis-à-vis* a child's learning. In such accounts the speaker is credited with knowledge of what it means for a child to be at a 'stage' and to be 'ready' for further progress. When called upon to render a further account of this to the interviewer, the teacher becomes confused and is engaged for a while in an implicitly circular discussion in which 'stages' and 'readiness' are being defined in terms of each other. However, the discussion moves to the specification of something approaching the teacher's own indicators of 'stages' and 'readiness' when she talks about 'concentration' and 'interest'. Again this is part of the common sense of her classroom practice and the community of her colleagues. Mrs Carpenter states that one must provide all sorts of material to give the children the opportunity to 'go as far as they can'. Here then, reaffirming the child centredness of the enterprise, she proceeds to justify her lack of intervention by the fact that children are unable to 'concentrate' upon what they are not ready to learn, and by inference she is justified in intervening to keep the children 'interested' and concentrating. This is the nearest we get to an operational account of her work, its reality tests and thus of the link between notions like 'stages' and 'readiness' and what she actually does. This can be linked to the teacher's situated perception of the educability of each child. If we recall the previous discussion of types of children, Mrs Carpenter's reality tests for notions like readiness and concentration, interest and needs, are most highly developed and sensitive for the children she is most clearly able to communicate with. Where there is a high degree of intersubjectivity, the bright children are identified and where there is a low level of intersubjectivity, the 'really peculiar' type of child is perceived.

The researcher is assuming that the confusion in the account rendered by the teacher indicates that such accounts are rarely called for, they are part of the community's common sense. They reflect the vocabulary of the community in its 'educationalist' (Keddie, 1971) discourse. This vocabulary is constituted by a series of concepts whose meanings are interdependent, but not explicitly articulated as such Its function is to integrate the community by enabling mutually agreed definitions of the situation to be made without probing below this veneer to bring out the possible operational differences which exist in the teachers' modes of action in the classroom.

A further interesting aspect of the account was the way in which the teacher expressed problems about knowing where the child 'was at', i.e. 'that one doesn't know when the child knows' was meant as a justification for the rejection of the teacher's conception of a formal approach. In the teacher's account, a set syllabus is not useful because she is unable to know what the children know and do not know. The point is that knowledge of the child is probably the central theme of a child centred approach to education. It attempts to direct the teacher according to a thorough knowledge of the child. The teacher has here noticed that such knowledge, on reflection, is extremely hard to come by, but does not see this as problematic for the child centred approach, only for the formal approach. This reflects an important account implicit in the actions of the teacher, and tacitly assumes that because she does not know where the children are at, because this is impossible, she should allow them to develop according to *their* interests, and what interests *them* is what they are *doing* (authors' emphasis). The children are assumed to be 'doing' something useful to their development so long as they are 'busy'. Thus we are able to find a rhetorical link between the child centred vocabulary of motives and the solution to the operational problem of knowing how to handle the fluid classroom situation by the device of 'busyness'. There is a tension running through the accounts covering the degree of activity or initiative she should take in structuring the children's learning. All children have a socially imposed need to be literate and numerate and very few children, in practice, develop such knowledge autonomously. The operational solution, integrated via the control device of 'busyness', is to develop differential categorizations of the pupils, illustrated above, and the accompanying rationales that bright secure children can be more directly 'pushed' while the dull ones, and particularly the 'peculiar' and 'disturbed' children should be provided with an unthreatening classroom environment. Here the child centred vocabulary links sociologically to the structural phenomenon of children's identity reification in the context of the classroom, on the one hand, and the construction of teacher autonomy *vis-à-vis* others outside the classroom, on the other. This issue will be further examined in the next section.

Before turning to that, however, we propose to discuss another example of the looseness of the vocabulary and its relationship to the solution of the operational problem of what to do in the classroom by considering the case of Mrs Buchanan's attitudes towards 'formal' education. We have observed how Mrs Buchanan characterizes herself as being out of sympathy with the general ethos of the school and the specific prescriptions with regard to the pedagogy she feels constrained to use. Nevertheless, when the observer cross-examined her on various occasions about what she meant by formal education and its operation indicators, our illustrations show a level of vagueness and generality about certain concepts comparable to that which we revealed in our previous example:

'When I say formal, it would be integrated really in as much as they would have a choice of things to do all the time, but I would be in a position to say—you must come and do your writing now.'

In this quotation, for her the criterion of formal education appears to be some sort of compulsion, but in the next sentence something more seems to be involved.

'I suppose formal teaching has its place even in a free situation, though. It's not done so openly or blatantly. If you've got a group round the table trying to do something, then that is a formal situation. No matter how informal the rest of the children are . . . . Any reading, that's a formal situation, one to one, it couldn't be anything else.'

'Informal teaching and freer methods, I suppose one could say would be formal teaching with smaller numbers. Rather than talk to forty you talk to four.' Here the essence of a formal situation appears to be where the teacher is directly communicating with a child or small group of children in a teaching situation. This idea is backed up in the following way:

'Right at the beginning I was accused of having done a lot of formal work—that was listening to children read. How are you expected to hear children read other than with the child sat next to you? . . . A formal one to one relationship—ridiculous!'

But, in the last quotation the idea of compulsion again appears as a defining criterion of formality:

'The only formal work I do with them is a few words or flash cards . . . When I say more formal, I mean that for a short time each morning I would make them do reading and writing first . . . I don't really mean everybody sat behind a desk . . what I would consider a good compromise, would be, to say to half of them, right then . . . you can do your writing now . . . and then the six year olds a little later on—so you'd have work going on all the time instead of giving them a completely free choice.'

Here again, we also have some identification of work with compulsion and formality. But the absence of compulsion seems to be precisely what, for this teacher, characterizes the integrated day.

'I agree with more freedom in the primary school—the last teaching practice I was on the children sat behind their desks all day. They didn't move. They were told exactly when to put pen to paper all day. That I didn't agree with . . . I tried to make that a little more informal'.

Interviewer   What exactly do you mean?
Teacher   A little more integrated, really.

In the same way that in our previous example the idea of 'readiness' and 'stages' were being defined in terms of each other, so informality and the 'integrated' day are inextricably linked with each other and with some notion of absence of constraint. But since neither complete compulsion is advocated by Mrs Buchanan who thinks of herself as more formal, nor complete permissiveness, it would be interesting to know the conditions under which compulsion is or is not required. The teacher when cross-examined about her role in intervening in the children's activities was definitely embarrassed when pushed and retreated into subjectivist justifications:

'Well, I just felt it was right to try to make him . . . I can't say why . . . I just felt it at the time . . . well er . . . you know . . . he's capable and he could do it.'

Interviewer   How can you tell their capabilities?
Teacher   Only by trying them out at different tasks and if they just can't do it then they are not capable of it . . . but if they are halfway there then you know they will be capable of it some time in the future.

Now, these accounts which the teacher gives are clearly inadequate, not simply if measuring them against some norm of scientificity, but also to the teacher herself who when probed will admit that there is a gap between the theory available to her and the operational accounts of her practice. Nevertheless, as with Mrs Carpenter, we should note that Mrs Buchanan was not used to being closely questioned in this way . . . In her everyday practice, her commonsense understandings provide sufficient legitimations for her everyday activity in the classroom.

However, what is interesting about this teacher is that in spite of her privately expressed opposition to some of the key concepts in child centred methodology, informality, free choice and the integrated day for example, like the other teachers she is faced with similar management problems in the classroom and increasingly comes to adopt similar strategies for their solution (we will pursue this point in greater detail below). It is sufficient for our purposes, at this stage, to note that this was especially so with respect to her notions of brightness and dullness. The bright child was increasingly being seen as the child who 'gets on, on his own' who is 'interested and concentrates, who would do well whatever the teacher'. Thus, again, we observe the vocabulary linking the phenomenon of pupil stratification with teacher autonomy, which we will proceed to consider further.

To recapitulate, we are therefore suggesting that there is no direct logical relationship between the child centred vocabulary and the teachers' actions in all their intricate complexity. The vocabulary does not immediately inform or motivate all their actions. Rather, the teachers' actions are directly informed in an *ad hoc* manner by routines, habits and motivations, many of which in the immediacy of classroom work will either be unconscious or only minimally reflexive. What the child centred vocabulary does is to provide a general background of organizational principles and strategies, and as such, is only realized when the teachers are called to account to significant others (e.g. colleagues or researchers) in specific instances. We suggest that the teacher in her daily work does not have categories like 'readiness', 'needs' and 'stages' constantly or even saliently in consciousness, ready to be operationalized when coping with the problem of what-to-do in the classroom. In the immediate flux of this situation, *ad hoc*-ing and the use of tried and tested routines will be undertaken *vis-à-vis* particular children. The child centred vocabulary is linked to motivation and appears at the level of consciousness

(a) when a teacher is called to account to significant others,

(b) in a very general way, as she plans the sorts of activities which might be undertaken in the classroom, and

(c) when problems arise either at the general level of classroom organization, but more particularly when a child is proving difficult to teach or handle.

In each of these three types of instances there is a tendency for the vocabulary to incorporate or articulate with a psychiatric perspective.

The point of our account is to suggest that, if unprobed, the vocabulary may legitimize a wide range of different personal categories used by the teachers in their classroom practice. Thus Mrs Carpenter and Mrs Lyons appear to be speaking the same language but their personal sense about their teaching and certain aspects of the social structure of their classrooms are substantively different especially with regard to teacher directiveness. Mrs Buchanan, on the other hand, showed much less confidence in the use of the vocabulary, especially in the early stages of the research. As time went on, however, she increasingly came to apply it to her class in order to generate socially legitimate explanations for phenomena she observed therein.

The child centred vocabulary and teacher autonomy

In this section we will clarify and exemplify our second major problematic: that is, to locate or situate the teachers' classroom practice in the wider context of extra classroom relationships. Aspects of the social construction of their autonomy *vis-à-vis* the parents and headmaster will be noted, laying particular emphasis upon the role of the child centred vocabulary as an accounting system. We are attempting to understand the degree of the teachers' discretion in the classroom by relating it to such extra classroom influences.

We will begin our analysis by considering the case of Mrs Carpenter. It was noted earlier, in our description of her account of the school ideology, that the ethos entails an attempt to implement radical, new and more appropriate methods of infant education. This involves the parents by invoking their trust, and although they do not understand these methods very clearly, the teachers do. Two points are important here, for the specific practice of the teacher in the classroom. First, within the school ideology, as presented to the parents, is the notion that modern teachers have certain types of objective psychological expertise, and, that this is crucial for their pedagogy. As we have shown before, at a meeting where the headmaster and his deputy attempted to explain their approaches, much stress was laid upon the tests for 'readiness' available to the teacher. Second, it was apparent that the parents' chief concerns are with the traditional skills of reading, writing and numeracy, plus the discipline and control of the children. With these in mind we can construct a pattern of constraints and discretion which structure the teachers' practice.

The notion that modern infant educational technique draws upon a fund of psychological knowledge is an account which, it is tentatively suggested, reflects the wider social position of this occupational group, particularly where teachers work in what are considered by them to be 'rough' working class districts. As with social workers in this type of situation (and it is noteworthy that the school has developed close ties with the social workers servicing the estate) we might see the teachers as 'dirty' workers in Everett Hughes's and Lee Rainwater's (1967) sense. Their job is to 'socialize' the population via 'gentle' or soft psychological technology. Here they are called upon to deal with what, in the political hierarchy of the wider community and culture, are thought of as the personal difficulties of 'problem' areas (Platt, 1969). Associated with this has developed a vocabulary of motives grounded in a theory of personality dynamics, which can be termed neo-psychiatric. This vocabulary operates at several levels. In the child centred methodology, it operates as a rhetoric in the teacher-parent relationship. Thus the children have to be approached from the perspective of their 'needs', 'interest', and 'stages of development' which must be 'from within'. These verbal constructions are presented by the teacher to parents to allay anxieties about what occurs at school in terms of teacher-pupil relations, the tone and atmosphere of the classroom, and certain areas of activity, i.e. generally everything except 'the three Rs'. Parents are contented with the way in which their children settle happily into the school, and although less sure about the apparent informality of the classroom organization, many accept that it is more pleasant for their children than had been their own experience. This is the reality test they are able to apply to this aspect of the implied psychological expertise presented by the teachers to them. At another level this vocabulary, being the vocabulary 'of experts' and 'of scientific research' has added kudos. Parents remark that the headmaster 'believes in this psychology a lot'. The inference is that psychology has scientific integrity. At this level it is coupled with the belief held by many parents that there are 'psychiatric cases' amongst the children, and that both the school and the social workers are dealing with this. If we recall the earlier discussion of the reification of a 'peculiar' pupil identity in Mrs Carpenter's classroom, the case of Michael, we may note that this child was recognized by his parents as somewhat 'peculiar' also. To the extent that this wider audience of parents, and social workers, accept the definition made by the school, the child is set upon a career path likely to be more predictable than that of other children. In considering the context of the neo-psychiatric aspects of the child centred vocabulary, we must note that in the bounded context of the teachers' classroom practice, the identification of one or two 'really peculiar' children rationalizes and reinforces (a) for the teacher herself and several other colleagues imbued with the school ethos, that they are dealing *generally* with difficult children, and (b) the parents' perception of the teachers as, in some sense, psychiatrists possessing the appropriate esoteric knowledge.[1]

This allows the teacher to preserve an area of very high discretion in the classroom *vis-à-vis* general organization, atmosphere and discipline. It is reinforced by the invisibility of classroom activities to the parents. Their tests of the reality of the classroom situation in these respects rely mainly upon children's reports, their own observations on official parents' occasions, brief periods of scrutiny when collecting and delivering children, plus conversations with staff. There is, then, relatively little opportunity to observe and intervene, a situation characteristic of most public organizations and their respective clients. However, there is an area in which closer examination of the children's activities is possible for both parents (and the headmaster), i.e. the 'three Rs'. Here her autonomy is far more problematic for her, and it is here we find the teacher's identification of ambivalence concerning the child centred ethos as it is presented by the headmaster. There was widespread concern amongst the parents that children might be 'playing all day' rather than acquiring the basic skills, as they see them, the traditional skills of literacy and numeracy. Here the teachers are rather more open to parental scrutiny, in that most parents have notions about how well their children can and should read, and what numeracy skills they should have by a certain age. Many parents are keen to help their children, particularly in reading, by buying the books they use at school, or by hearing them read at home, or indeed occasionally teaching them to read before they arrive at school.

The school, including the headmaster, presents to the parents the view that children should be reading 'sometime before they're eight . . . if not you've got trouble'. To many parents this is a complacent attitude, and is one which the headmaster finds most difficult to sustain when confronted with parental criticism. Reading was thus one activity in the classroom where Mrs Carpenter adopted a high level of routine identifiable to herself, and it is only here that any recording of children's activity and achievement seems to be done by the teacher. Reading also dominated the work of one of the welfare assistants. The teacher's area of discretion in this aspect of her work was relatively low. However, the teacher has developed a technique for defending her autonomy here. She has indicated that much of the time devoted to hearing children read has the function of dampening parental criticism. Thus if a parent has expressed concern about her child's progress the teacher will tend to select the child to read to her more frequently, though she may feel that it is doing very little for the child. The main purpose is that the child will reply that it has been doing reading when asked by the parents.

Though the headmaster publicly declares that reading does not dominate the school's priorities, it is clearly extremely important to him. Formal testing and recording progress occurs and there are records available to the local authority. Thus comparisons may be made between schools. The headmaster's position is subject to certain pressures which he cannot ignore. These form a structural context to the construction of teacher autonomy *vis-à-vis* the headmaster.

Mrs Carpenter indicated that she operates in a situation of ambivalent expectation where the headmaster is concerned. On the one hand, he appears to present, particularly in public to audiences such as social workers, visiting researchers and observers, parents and staff in staffroom discussions, the image of being a committed child centred teacher, accepting an informal approach with the minimum of teacher direction of children. On the other hand, he expresses the view that children 'get more out of an activity if there is a teacher there', the implication being that teachers can encourage and develop the children by contributing from their 'infinite knowledge'. The present teacher rejects this view, or is highly critical of it, as a move away from her conception of child centredness. She often remarks that such direction can do more harm than good and that in attempting to deepen the children's knowledge, intervention often detracts from their interest. She feels that the children often resent the teacher's interference. This amounts, in terms of the dynamics of the teacher's autonomy, to another aspect of the ambivalence in the operationalization of the notion of 'readiness' as expressed by the headmaster. The problem with a notion like 'readiness' is that it can rationalize teacher passivity or initiative and activity because, as part of the school ethos, it is unclear as to whether teachers should allow children to 'become ready' to do things, or to 'make them ready' for the next stage of their intellectual development.

The former is embedded in a naive 'horticultural' developmental view of child development, the latter is one which gives far more room for teacher initiative. In the process of staffroom discussion this ambivalence is not pursued and the notion of 'readiness' takes on a rhetorical function of uniting the staff community under an apparently homogeneous conception. Thus when discussing the anomalies of certain children's intellectual development, the headmaster was able to round off the discussion and suppress the ambiguities by declaring 'it's all readiness, isn't it?'. This phenomenon takes on greater significance when we recall that staff discussion in the 'educationist' context takes the form of a debate with an idealized critical audience which is reactionary in its approach to infant education from the perspective of this ethos.

In this context the present teacher, by her relatively frequent use of the vocabulary, compared with her colleagues, has come to epitomize the radical child centredness in the ethos of the school. Her position as 'star'

(Breed, 1955) has high status, generated largely in the staffroom context of doctrinal reinforcement. Her classroom practice has an autonomy from the control of the head and reflects her 'stardom'. Given the highly problematic nature of the linkages between the child centred ideology and its operational philosophy, this teacher's practice is thought of as fitting most closely the ideal image. Thus, by playing the role most closely associated with the public image of the school as presented by the headmaster at a time when the school was felt to be under threat from reactionary outside forces of parent and vocal 'Black Paper Education-ists', Mrs Carpenter was able to generate a wide area of autonomy in her classroom practice and become a powerful member of the staff, particularly allied to the headmaster and his deputy. She is known in the school as a good teacher, able to handle the informal classroom organization and to be good with 'difficult' and deprived children. Her role as public conscience reinforces the purist aspects of the headmaster's public commitments and identity as the head of a progressive, child centred school.

This illustrates the paradoxical situation in which doctrine and commitment (Keddie, 1971) are empirically problematic *vis-à-vis* each other. The teacher's expression of the child centred doctrine has the significance of commitment to the official ideology and was, as such, rhetorical, having the function of reinforcing the present formal political structure rather than clearly explicating the child centred methodology. The paradox lies in that it is the power of the headmaster, as reality definer, to set the tone of the official ethos, and the public image of the school, which creates the opportunity for teacher autonomy in this way. The teacher perceives the head as ambivalent about the operational meaning of his child centred views, and to the present teacher he is 'really quite reactionary'. Thus the teacher's fluent use of the vocabulary becomes a presentational device (Goffman, 1959) which enhances her status and classroom autonomy. Thus autonomy cannot be explained simply as grounded in the intersubjective world of the staff's normative structure. In this convoluted political structure, where at one level power closely approximates the zero sum model (i.e. the headmaster has clear institutionalized power and authority over any of his staff), the generation of a legitimized vocabulary of motives, which is in structural terms a rhetorical expression of this power, gives at the level of classroom practice legitimized discretion to exploit the official will (that of the school ethos) against the 'real' will of the headmaster's own commitments. These latter are generated in the context of extra school pressures to deliver certain goods to parents and education administrators, such as higher than present levels of literacy and numeracy. There are structural features making for overall ambivalence in the headmaster's role in the structure of staff relations and perspective.[2] The situation is likely to be unstable, where the formal power-holder is torn between conflicting commitments. The headmaster represents the case of one undergoing a paradigmatic crisis where, having formal authority and established position, he adopts what he perceives as a revolutionary mode, and identifies himself, as a career bet, with a (in this case) radical child centred public image (Kuhn, 1962; Hagstrom, 1965). The outcome is difficult to predict. It will depend partly upon the movement of the extra school pressures upon him. So long as these external pressures pull him in the direction of formality in the approach to infant education while he retains the intra school stance of radicalism, ambivalence remains.

This section has illustrated an aspect of accounting in which the vocabulary of a social group concerning their work has objective status in two respects. It is, first, shared, and second, has implications for their practices. However, though the vocabulary is shared, meanings are not. The words are items of a vocabulary of obscure motives and have the main significance of identifying the user of the vocabulary in the political structure of common users. In this way the major implication of the use of the vocabulary is its constitution of commitment rather than doctrine. This then, adds a political aspect to Scott and Lyman's (1968) ideas on accounting, by including the rhetorical dimension. It illustrates a situation where the operational meanings of concepts central to the work of the members of an organization are highly problematic, but where these problematics are not aired, so that the words in the common vocabulary become badges or ritual symbols of commitment to the reigning political structure of that institution. The autonomy of Mrs Carpenter in this situation is grounded in the relative stardom consequent upon her fluent use of the vocabulary and thus role as conscience to the child centredness of the headmaster's perspective, which in turn constitutes the central ethos of the school.

Let us now move to a consideration of our second teacher, Mrs Lyons, whom we have already seen subjectively experiences a high degree of autonomy in the classroom but in terms of her practice deviates in some respects quite considerably from the radical child centred teacher projected in certain aspects of the school ethos. An initial explanation of the autonomy could be that it derives from her formal position in the school hierarchy, that of being deputy headmistress, but such an interpretation would, we feel, be oversimplified. By itself, the position of deputy head does not generate the degree of autonomy and areas of discretion which this teacher experiences. For example, the first deputy headmistress of the school, a teacher of considerable experience, left after only a short period of time after various disagreements with the head and the rest of the staff. As the headmaster explained:

'The woman who was deputy head before Mrs Lyons, she was chosen and I helped to choose her from a very limited field, and I thought she would have fitted in, but in point of fact she didn't but she had the good grace to say so, and after one year she departed amicably.'

Although the observers did not pursue in detail the reasons why she had left, it was apparent that certain doctrinal disputes which we have already referred to had arisen in which the deputy head came to be perceived as a formal traditional teacher who disagreed with the dominant child centred ethos supported by the head and most of the other staff. This then poses the question of whether the existing deputy head derives her autonomy from the fact that she agrees with the headmaster over the essentials of the school ethos especially regarding its prescriptions about how one should operate in the classroom. Our discussion of how she operates in the classroom could already lead us to suggest that such an interpretation is incorrect. Certainly when compared with Mrs Carpenter whom we have concluded has high autonomy, her classroom practice is different in a number of significant respects. She is far more concerned with order and discipline. She imposes work requirements on the children; she is more likely to engage in class teaching, and makes a clear distinction between work and play. In our discussion of Mrs Carpenter's autonomy, however, we suggested that there was an absence of unambiguous technical prescriptions and procedures which derive from the high level doctrine of child centredness, and that this situation potentially generates areas of discretion for the teacher to operate in the way she feels is appropriate. Moreover, it was the rhetorical use of the vocabulary in the context of staff relationships which marked the previous teacher's commitment to the political structure of the school and hence legitimized her autonomy, rather than the actual practices she used in the classroom.

If our interpretation is correct let us explore whether there are any similarities with Mrs Lyons. Like her colleague she is seen to be very fluent in the socially legitimated vocabulary and plays a leading role in defining reality for her other teaching colleagues in terms which are compatible with the view of the situation projected by the headmaster. The headmaster spoke very highly of her and obviously had full confidence in her both as a teacher and, from his point of view perhaps more importantly, as a source of support and loyalty, mediating between him and the staff and parents. Thus, he asked her to address the meeting of new parents where an account of the school and its practices was to be given, demonstrating both that she could do so in a way which he would find acceptable, and also that she could 'deal' with potentially critical parents efficiently and with diplomacy. Moreover, she seemed to be regarded by the other staff with respect and deference. Not only was she seen as an efficient organizer and administrator, but they seemed to look to her for reassurance and support in ambiguous or potentially difficult situations. Never was any staff member publicly heard to disagree with her on matters which were important to school policy.

Moreover, she seemed to have a great deal of power over day to day decision making controlling what sort of equipment should be bought, when the different teachers could use the hall for PT, what kind of show should be put on for Christmas, organizing the open day, etc.

Wherefrom came this power? On a commonsense level, she was more experienced than the other staff, and had been at the school since its inception, so had much 'knowledge' of the situation, the children, their parents, having been through the school's most difficult period when it had come under so much overt criticism from the parents. Moreover, she was regarded by the headmaster as highly competent to deal with the type of problems which Mapledene Lane presented and was consequently given more of her fair share of problem pupils; these she was seen to handle effectively, minimizing the disruption which might otherwise have been caused. She was also better qualified than they. She had an advanced diploma in psychology which gave formal recognition to the deference she was granted by other staff as well as providing her with the expertise and esoteric knowledge enabling her to handle 'these' children. But it was not merely her theoretical expertise which commanded respect but also her obvious competence in the eyes of other teachers.

In her classroom, she gave the impression of being fully in control. Order was accompanied by obvious productivity. The overt indicators the staff could use to assess each other's competence, like their pupils' productions or performances in the Wednesday assembly, school open days, the visible impression of activity which the decoration of the classroom presented, all these combined to reinforce her reputation of competence in the eyes of her colleagues.

Yet whilst these factors may go some way to explaining her power, and autonomy which the headmaster allowed her, it is ironic that autonomy should be granted to two teachers who differed so considerably in the way they interpreted the role. Whilst the former teacher, Mrs Carpenter, had high standing and was sponsored by this teacher and by the headmaster for a radical form of child centredness, which we have seen resulted from the ambivalence between the official will of the school and the headmaster's real will, Mrs Lyons seemed to have high standing precisely because whilst exploiting the real will of the head she managed to do so whilst presenting herself in terms of the official ethos of the school.

To expand this point further, it is necessary to reiterate that the headmaster experiences constraints impinging on him to achieve the same sort of standards in traditional areas like reading and writing that a more formally organized school might achieve and, perhaps additionally, he still thinks these traditional ways of measuring a school's competence are of importance. As noted in chapter 4, for example, while trying to defend the school's methods against what he feels to be outside criticism, he said

'But if we have achieved any success here, and I think we have . . . and the more I look around and the more I see, the more I think we have nothing to be ashamed of here—our standards in all the measurable things would compare favourably with schools that are run differently and the standard of behaviour is, in the main, quite good.'

This teacher also seems to attach a great importance to the acquisition of the skills of literacy and numeracy. For example, when enunciating the aims of the school to the parents she said 'The basic aims are still the same—children should learn to read and write but do it in a different way—by doing, they understand'. In addition, in her practice, she is far more directive regarding reading and writing than the other teachers—and makes it very clear to the children that they come to school to work not to play.

What is being suggested is that the teacher is acting in a way more formal than a radical interpretation of the school official ethos would permit. There is more direction, more compulsion, more group teaching than one would expect given her self-conception as an informal child centred teacher. That she is permitted such autonomy depends, it is suggested, on a number of factors, some of which have been mentioned already. In the first place the details of the teachers' activities in the classroom are invisible. It may well be the case that none of the teachers is aware of what goes on in each other's classrooms. Certainly it did not become apparent to the observers that either the head or the other staff knew of the extent of her deviation from a really radical child centred perspective where pupils would not be made to do anything except what their interests dictate. Second, in terms of the traditional skills like good reading and writing attainment, her pupils performed favourably thus satisfying one of the headmaster's and the parents' measuring rods. Moreover, she is a good disciplinarian. The headmaster respects her for her ability to maintain order and discipline; as he himself says to the children, 'you do not come here to do as you like, there are rules and laws' and a teacher who gives the appearance of managing these difficult children in an obviously experienced way demands respect. Parents also thought highly of her and defined her as more 'of the old school'.

But the main factor underlying the wide area of discretion permitted her is that she can in no way be regarded as a potential threat to the underlying structure of political relationships.

In spite of her rejection of a radical form of child centredness in her practice, she is a loyal and supportive deputy to the headmaster. Whilst appearing to join the staff in the kind of joking attitudes towards the headmaster behind his back, she mediates between him and them in a way which does not threaten him. She interprets his views to them—'he doesn't really mean that, you know'—and their views to him in a way which reinforces the sense of identification with a common purpose. And here her fluency in the child centred vocabulary assists her in that she, like her former colleague, is using the vocabulary not so much to provide some detailed operational definition of the situation and the practices, particularly the pedagogical methods expected therein, but as a rhetorical measure of commitment to the organization and its structure of power relationships of which she is a part.

We have thus an ironic situation that of our three teachers, and perhaps indeed, of all the staff in the school, the two who lie at the opposite ends of the informal/formal continuum in terms of classroom practices are at the same time those with highest autonomy in the sense of not being subject to any detailed overseeing or suspicion by the headmaster on the grounds of their ideological deviation or 'failures' as teachers and at the same time exhibit strong professional and personal linkages with each other. Indeed, Mrs Carpenter seemed to be brought closer and closer into the decision making process with the deputy head and was obviously being sponsored, out of several contenders with equal objective experience, for a post of special responsibility.

Nevertheless, in terms of the way Mrs Carpenter operated in the classroom, she far more closely resembled the third teacher whose position in the structure of staff relationships we are about to discuss. Where Mrs Carpenter differs from Mrs Buchanan, is in her lack of self-conscious ambivalence about her methodology, and its consistency with her educational aims and her public overt identification with the dominant ethos by fluent use of the vocabulary, public demonstrations of enthusiasm and support etc.

Now it may be the case that neither Mrs Carpenter or Mrs Lyons were aware of the extent to which their practices deviated from each other. Alternatively, it could be suggested that deviation from the official line is only permitted for those whose loyalty and allegiance is not suspected. As Gouldner (1959) argued, greater autonomy is permitted to those who ascribe to the basic norms of the system. In the same way that greater moral deviation was always permitted to the aristocracy because their moral deviancy could not be interpreted as in any way a threat to society, so the publicly acknowledged deviancy of a new low status entrant to the school, especially if it seems to be accompanied by a suggested critique of the legitimacy of the prevailing ethos, has to be effectively stamped on. In the meantime, the deputy head was allowed without criticism to organize her classroom in a way which Mrs Buchanan would have liked to do, but dared not, for fear of criticism.

Nevertheless, even if the headmaster were aware of the details of their classroom practice, it could be argued that such a variety of practices could all be legitimated and justified as falling within broad child centred rubrics. Such varied options derive from the basic ambivalence, and, in some cases, contradictions, within the philosophy itself. But it might be thought curious that the two people who were most obviously experiencing the ambivalence were those with the highest and lowest status and power in the community. Whilst the deputy head particularly, and to a lesser extent Mrs Carpenter, seemed very self-confident and secure in their ideology and relatively unreflexive in their practical activity, the headmaster particularly revealed a certain lack of certainty or unequivocal belief in what he was doing.

This ambivalence was noted by all the teachers who frequently commented on his style of teaching when he was forced to take a class in cases of staff absence. We have noted how he was observed by them to be directive, engaging in teaching the class as a whole, and indeed showing himself to be, in their terms, incapable of putting the methods into operation. It is interesting that the visibility of the head when he was engaged in teaching was high, compared with the other teachers. One wonders whether this was due to the other teachers' self-conscious feelings of insecurity in operating the methods when faced with the constraints of too many children and too little time, and a curiosity to see how the head as reality definer copes in the real situation. But his ambivalence compared with the other teachers was frequently publicly expressed. He was often to be heard saying such things as: 'I wonder whether we are doing the right thing' or 'I often have my doubts about whether these methods are suited for these children.'

Such ambivalence could be interpreted in several ways. It could be the case that his structural position as mediator between the expectations of outsiders, colleagues in the education field, administrators, social workers, parents and his own staff puts him in a position fraught with role conflict. On the other hand it could be that his self-doubt was a matter of hedging his bets in the presence of the researchers in case they discovered things which would be critical of the school's mode of operation. Or perhaps he was living out the role expectations of someone in a responsible position who would be expected to be constantly re-examining his philosophy and practices, amenable to argument and change, ready to act differently should circumstances prevail and so on.

Whichever interpretation seems more plausible, it should be stressed that the ambivalencies and self-doubt expressed publicly by the headmaster would not have been permitted by someone lower down in the school's hierarchy, our third teacher, Mrs Buchanan, for example. It is to her position in the context of the school ethos and the structure of political relationships that we now turn.

In our discussion of the previous teachers we have attempted to depict a relationship between, on the one hand, the ideology to which the teacher attaches, and on the other hand the managerial problems of the maintenance of formal order and control in the classroom which they, like any teachers, have to come to terms with. We have, for example, shown how the concept of busyness is not only central in terms of the teachers' attachment to a child centred pedagogy, but also legitimates the particular role which the teachers develop in the classroom towards their pupils in a way which is conducive to the solution of the management problems and has feedback qualities both *vis-à-vis* the ideology and *vis-à-vis* the reproduction of an ordered structure. We have also suggested that there is an elective affinity between certain kinds of managerial problems in an educational situation where the pupils may not necessarily be regarded as willing and captive clients, sharing a basic communality of meaning with their teachers, and the vocabulary which develops to deal with these managerial problems in ways which are non-threatening to the teachers and do not impugn their identity.

Our analysis might suggest the functionality of an ideology which looks at working class pupils in terms of a deprivation and pathology model, in that it legitimizes the use of concepts like 'odd', 'disturbed', 'peculiar', as explanations for pupils' failure which could be seen as militating against a sense of failure on the teachers' part. In so doing, there are produced feedback effects which reinforce the teachers' ideology and practices and sustain and legitimize their role behaviour *vis-à-vis* their pupils.

Moreover, not only have we tried to depict this circular relationship between management problems and typical elements of teacher role behaviour, we have also suggested that the performance of the managerial function is not unrelated to the career interests of the individual teacher in the school, and that these may well be bound up with the nature of the commitment to, and identification with, the dominant ideology within the school regarding pupils, parents, pedagogy, etc. We have tried to suggest how the ideology and the vocabulary has a rhetorical role insofar as it functions as a means whereby staff can publicly express and politically confirm their identification with the school ethos, their personal involvement in a common social enterprise and their unity of purpose with other community members; even though the ideology itself may be deficient at the technical level for enabling inferences to be made which can provide unequivocable guides for pedagogical practice.

The teacher we want to look at now, however, Mrs Buchanan, can in some senses be regarded as a deviant in so far as she both confesses some alienation from the school ethos and is regarded by others who know, and moreover, matter, to be not fully committed to the prevailing ideology. We could regard this teacher as simply a deviant case and attempt to explore the implications of her deviant perspective for her practice in the classroom, assuming a direct isomorphism between beliefs and actions, explaining any differences in social action in terms simply of the different meanings which she as a creative meaning-bestowing social actor brings to bear to the situation.

Such an approach, however, would undermine the theoretical perspective which we have so far been developing, that is to say, the need to see ideology or world views in relationship to the structure of the situation. For the situation itself contains irreducible structural features which in themselves will mediate and structure the patterns of social interaction developing therein.

These theoretical problems may be highlighted for us when looking at this teacher who, like her colleagues, is confronted with certain irreducible management problems of maintaining order and social control, and yet like them shares certain career interests in that she wants, in a minimal sense to stay in teaching, and in a more maximal sense to be regarded as proficient, competent, and capable of solving the difficulties which all teachers have to cope with. Mrs Buchanan is starting her career with certain deviant aspects in her ideology especially as regards her attitudes to the type of clientele and the kinds of pedagogical methods considered appropriate for this type of child. We have already seen how she starts off by rejecting the social and cultural deprivation model of the pupils' background, seeing them as different but culturally equal to other more middle class pupils, not deserving of moral denigration or sympathy. Moreover, we have observed how in some vague sense she would prefer a more formal approach to pedagogy for this type of child, who needs to be pushed and shoved, because of a lack of a natural interest in things educational due to his cultural background. Nevertheless, her precise objections to the official attitude towards pedagogy in the school are at a low level of specificity and, on closer examination, it is not easy to spell out very clearly precisely what her operational philosophy would be if given a free hand. This point has been illustrated by her own discussion of what she means by formal education.

The lack of clear cut operational definitions of certain key terms in the child centred ideology has already been commented upon before in our discussion of the previous two teachers. Moreover, we have noted that the teachers are rarely called upon in their everyday activity to give accounts of some key concepts in their perspectives on their work. Nevertheless, Mrs Buchanan's attitudes towards certain items like formality and freedom in the classroom are perceived by her as important in marking out, at least in political terms, the difference between her approach and that of the other community members, even though she confesses to not being aware of what goes on in other people's classrooms or, moreover, the precise form which her own deviation takes. Nevertheless, she experiences herself as being, on the one hand, out of step and, on the other hand, as powerless to create the kind of structure in the classroom which she feels is appropriate. This experience of a lack of autonomy is related not simply to the strength of the headmaster's personal influence on the school, but also, in this teacher's perspective, to her own lack of status as both a latecomer to the school and an initiate into the teaching profession. This is her probationary year and she feels that the probationer is not really accorded much autonomy.

She said when talking of what she would have done if given a free hand: 'I think if I had tried to institute anything like that I'd be criticized'.

Interviewer   By whom?

Mrs Buchanan   Well, for one . . . would criticize, well, I think the rest of the staff really generally . . .

Interviewer   Why do you think they would criticize?

Mrs Buchanan   I think some of them would say—'Oh, it's her probationary year and she's trying to re-organize the whole school'. I think that type of comment would come up. You see, if you have been teaching, say three or four years, and you think that you can, you know, work better if you do it in such and such a way, then you've got that much experience behind you to say, you know, 'Oh yes, she might know what she is talking about'. But with a probationer, I don't think it applies at all. So you've just got to do what the school does really.

But it is not simply that she feels her probationary status renders her powerless. She is also very conscious of the fact that in terms of her attitudes she is in a minority:

'But my opinions seem to be so contrary to everybody else's there, to a certain degree anyway, I never, or I, very rarely, entirely agree with anything that's said in the staffroom and yet I won't voice my opinion because I know they'll be about seven or eight voices banging away at me, you know — so I keep my mouth shut a lot.'

Thus both her probationary status and her minority opinions render problems for her to cope with. This feeling of a lack of power tends to be focused around the issue of what to do in the classroom. Even if she does not share in the school ethos and ideology—she must adhere to the form as far as classroom practice and behaviour is concerned, whatever her attitudes to the content. But to what extent is it sufficient to merely conform at the formal level to what the school ethos prescribes regarding appropriate teacher behaviour and practices? We have seen in the section on working in the classroom that this teacher seems to conform at the level of practice with the model of the good child centred teacher, but perhaps here behavioural conformity is not enough. Mrs Buchanan's private reservations about the ideology have certainly in the past been communicated to other community members. Moreover, her sense of personal integrity is such that she is not prepared to play at the role of being a good committed child centred teacher in terms of her public pronouncements, her use of the socially sanctioned vocabulary, and so on. But nor do her obvious career commitments permit her to come out into open conflict and hostility with the rest of the staff. In any case, she has already been witness to what happened to another probationary teacher who was openly, very early on, identified as somebody out of sympathy with the school ethos and too incompetent to deal with this type of child and eventually left the school.

We can see how Mrs Buchanan was faced with a series of role dilemmas which provoked considerable personal anxiety on her part and demanded some considerable skill in role playing and in resolving what might appear at first sight to be irresolvable dilemmas.

But, in spite of her self-confessed isolation from the other staff in terms of her attitudes to the children and pedagogy, etc., she is still faced with the managerial problem of, on the one hand, maintaining order and, on the other hand, of being productive. Like other teachers, this probationer has been socialized into the importance of keeping ahead of her pupils—not letting things go, not letting them get on top of her. She is well cognizant that her success or failure in this direction is crucial both for her own self-conception as a competent teacher and in terms of her identity *vis-à-vis* other community members.

She is aware that she is not producing in hard form, with conviction and vigour, the ideal child centred classroom where pupils are happily involved with enthusiasm, interest and self-confidence in productive activities. However, at the outset, she does not possess an appropriate ideology which would enhance her own identity by explaining the discrepancy between the ideal and the reality in terms of the individual and social pathology of the pupils. Hence, we would expect to see some considerable stress and anxiety on her part which could be coped with in a number of different ways. One possibility would be that the teacher would try to cope with these difficulties by withdrawing from her colleagues as a means of insulating herself from too much involvement in the affairs of her classroom by those whom she might reasonably expect to be critical. Certainly this was a response which Mrs Buchanan seemed to take initially. She admitted to the observer that things were not going well—and that she felt demoralized because of her own lack of experience and ability to achieve the ideal. She was well aware of a degree of disorderliness in the classroom but was initially inclined to blame herself and her own lack of organization for this unhappy situation. She expressed some anxiety that she was left by the other staff to sink or swim on her own and that little advice or practical assistance had been forthcoming from them about how to manage this type of classroom. She admitted to having been fairly aggressive at the outset:

'I was so aggressive at the beginning to everybody—and the organization. I wouldn't allow myself to talk to anybody. I hated it—I was obsessed with it—in case I should be thought an absolute fool. The only time I asked for help was when I was told it would come. I thought—well, I'll just carry on in my own sweet way and hope for the best.'

To withdraw, however, from involvement with the other staff, although self-protecting initially, might not have proved an adequate long term response and might have led to this teacher opting out of teaching altogether, or at least making some moves to transfer to another school in order to produce the kind of structure which she feels more appropriate to deal with this type of child.

However, as time went on, so two concurrent processes emerged which improved the situation for this teacher. First, as she got to know the other staff better so she began to discover that there was not quite as much homogeneity regarding the school ideology as she had previously discerned. Although she was aware that, in public, few would criticize any of the standard lines, she became more involved in an informal sub-group which seemed to provide its members with a realm of security where they felt they could talk more frankly about their problems and share their anxieties, articulate their difficulties without any feeling of threat.

As Mrs Buchanan put it 'We talk about it now with Sally, Vicky and Brenda, but more informally. I wouldn't ever say at a staff meeting—"Could somebody help me with the organization please?" but I can talk about it to them.' Again when asked whether others on the staff felt like she did, but didn't voice it, she replied:

'Mm—yes . . . I don't want to mention any names but I think Brenda would do a bit more formal work because she's only done formal teaching before she came here . . . Sally, I know, used to start off last year by getting all the children together to do their writing which I suppose compared with this situation, is formal . . . well, those two, you know—they won't say so in the staffroom but they don't entirely agree with everything.'

Here, we have a recognition that in the context of the school there are certain attitudes, etc., which can legitimately be expressed and others not. Nevertheless, within informal peer groups, a greater degree of variation in views is permitted, and these informal groupings provide a source of support for the teacher which at the official level she thought was lacking.

However, merely finding some degree of support from a somewhat deviant informal peer group would not by itself appear to be enough, especially since the managerial problem of maintaining some degree of order as well as trying to educate the pupils remains. However she tries to make out in the situation, she cannot let the managerial function slip completely, otherwise she is doomed. Given the inherent difficulty presented by a large class of working class pupils, who in her terms, do not appear to be interested in educational activities, we would expect that the teacher would undergo some degree of doctrinal conversion as a means of self-protection and identity preservation. It seems obvious that her adherence to a cultural difference rather than cultural deprivation and social pathology model was productive of demoralization and low self-esteem, and a strong tendency to blame herself for her failures. The observed tendency on this teacher's part to undergo some shifts in her perspective with respect to her role and her aims for these pupils, could be interpreted not simply because she holds a minority perspective and comes progressively under the influence of the majority who hold different perspectives, but because the majority perspective is a more appropriate ideology to mediate between the constraints of the situation and the identity and career interests of the teachers.

What actually happens is that over time Mrs Buchanan reveals a partial conversion towards a social pathology approach to her pupils and their backgrounds, and a reorientation at the level of goals, expressing far more concern with the emotional and social development of the pupils than with what was formerly her major goal—enhancing the level of academic attainment. Moreover, whereas initially she was constantly blaming her own lack of experience and organization for the pupils' failure—increasingly she began to resort to explanations in terms of the pupils' pathological backgrounds.

She said when talking at the end of the period of observation, about her early attitudes:

> 'When I first came, I wrote down my aims for seven year olds, six year olds, five year olds—I would have liked everybody to make a start on reading—I would have liked all my seven year olds to be able to write on their own, all the six year olds to be able to copy from one piece of paper to another—and so on. . . . My aims were mainly academic—but now I've seen changes in people like Lesley that have given me far more satisfaction than I would have thought. I just didn't think about it. At college you talk about emotional development but never have to think about that on teaching practice. The children are already moulded to what the teacher wants but, at least, in this free situation you get different types of satisfaction for each individual . . . so it's taught me not to expect too much . . . with expecting a bit less one gets more satisfaction.'

We see, here, and this was reaffirmed on several different occasions, that the teacher is beginning to relinquish her belief in the overriding importance of academic attainment. This fits in with her perception of the lack of stress given to academic attainment by other staff members:

> 'They don't even talk about academic goals. Of course, they would each of them like kids to do very well—but when the child is not getting on very well, then you've got to start thinking about other things, like his emotional background . . . something at home that stops him from getting on . . . No, they don't think a great deal about academic attainment.'

Similarly, whereas at the beginning of the period of observation, she rarely mentioned home background as an explanation for low achievement but rather tended to blame the inappropriateness of the methods, at the end of the period of observation, when talking with the observer about each child's performance in the classroom in detail, judgments of under-achievement were frequently related up to some known 'problem' which the child was experiencing at home, or the teacher, if not knowledgeable about the home situation, would argue that there must be something 'odd' going on at home otherwise the under-achievement would be inexplicable—as if, by definition, under-achievement is automatically associated with family pathology.

This gradual doctrinal conversion towards a social pathology approach to the situation could be looked at as an incipient perspective which develops over time, which negates the premises of the original perspective which she held, but which nevertheless accounts more satisfactorily, given the constraints of the situation, for the discrepancy between the teacher's goal and her perceived achievements.

It would be incorrect to try to account for this ideological development simply in terms of this teacher negotiating, at the ideological level, a perspective which integrates and adheres to the perspectives of the majority. Her ideological development should rather be seen as the result of the interplay between the forces of material and organizational constraints on the one hand and the problems of a middle class teacher confronting a working class clientele in a context of material scarcity on the other. Perhaps the case of this teacher reveals how social deprivation models can function as ideological mediators between a societal context, where at the macro level, there is structured inequality of material conditions and rewards which work against the working class, and a micro situation where a middle class teacher, socialized into the ideology of equality of opportunity, tries to educate and maintain social control when confronted by large numbers of working class pupils with cultural experiences which, from the educator's point of view, are viewed as alien and inappropriate.

Here was a teacher not initially socialized as a plausible member to the logic-in-use (Kaplan, 1964) but whose emergent perspective is related to the forces of constraint and control within the classroom and school situation itself, which cannot be reduced to mere constraint by ideas or ideologies. She has been socialized and initiated, not just into the prevailing concepts, or logic-in-use, but into the field of constraints. We are trying to look at her developing perspective not just as some hypostasized weltanschauung which phenomenological sociology might attempt to reconstruct and describe in all its intimate subtlety, but as an ideological perspective which is intimately related to the field of determinations. We are, perhaps, suggesting that a more fruitful approach to ideologies would be to attempt to locate them in the conditions in which they arise. In this way the frequently found relationship (HMSO, 1967 (Plowden); Clegg and Megson, 1968; Schools Council, 1970) between child centred approaches to pedagogy and a social pathology approach to certain categories of pupils would be interpreted not merely as some accidental or contingent association but as logically related to certain kinds of structural conditions the effect of which we have tried to sketch out in this chapter.

10

The parents

Parents have assumed some importance in our analysis so far in that within the teacher's perspectives the home is seen as having a crucial role in influencing if not determining the educability of the pupils with whom the school has to deal. Such a view receives official endorsement by social scientists who have explored the social roots of differential achievement. Amongst educational researchers it is widely accepted that factors to do with the home explain much of the differences in pupils' achievement and that, amongst home variables, parents' attitudes assume a crucial significance (Floud *et al.*, 1956; Douglas, 1964; Wiseman, 1964; HMSO, 1967 (Plowden); Goodacre, 1968). They function through their role in influencing the child's motivation and interest in school work, in facilitating the child's initiation into the school culture and in generally supplementing and giving support to the activities of teachers within the school. It follows from such a perspective that those committed to reforming education would be particularly interested in trying to bring about improved home-school co-operation. In so doing, hopefully, parents not presently contributing to their children's education can become more enlightened and thus better able to provide the kind of supportive environment their children need (Young and McGeeney, 1968).

We have already related how the headmaster accepts that Mapledene's relationship with its parents has not always been happy. Nevertheless, he, too, in line with prevailing views of 'good practice' (Craft *et al.*, 1967; HMSO, 1967 (Plowden) supports attempts to establish better relationship with the children's homes, without, of course, incurring any encroachments on his staff's professional autonomy.

Before proceeding with our own analysis of the role of parents it is perhaps germane to the discussion to mention some critical points about this view of parents which we have briefly characterized. From our observations and analysis we suggested that the child's educational identity and career is as much a function of the way in which he is differentially categorized and treated within the school itself as of any pre-school identity he originally possessed. Applying such an insight to the study of parents and their educational relevance it would appear that parents should not be studied atomistically but in relationship to other facets of the interactional nexus within the school itself. Second, it seems important to adopt a dynamic perspective to see how teachers' and parents' typifications of each other are generated over time as each attempts to negotiate a meaningful symbolic reality and further their ends in response to the situation they confront. Thus categories of good and bad parents, or good and bad teachers have to be seen in relationship to the past and present biography of the actors concerned in the ongoing process of their mutual encounters. Similarly there is a need, not merely to look at attitudes but also actions as teachers and parents develop strategies which both derive from and serve to stablize and reinforce the complex systems of meaning generated in specific situations. Finally on a methodological point, studies of parents or indeed of any social actors, must retain a sensitivity to the universe of meaning of the actors who are the object of study and not attempt to arbitrarily impose categories or indicators of such notions as 'parental interest' which may have no significance for the people they purport to describe but give more insight into the commonsense assumptions of the researcher.

We suggest that most studies of parents have been weak on precisely these points. Having argued this, however, it is important to point out that shortage of time, personnel and resources prevented us from carrying out the kind of study of our parents we would have considered appropriate. We were only able to interview each parent once, using an informal unstructured methodology designed to capture the universe of meaning of the parent and give some insight into the sorts of strategies employed to try to further their educational goals for their children. We were not able to trace the generation and development of these perspectives over time or witness many samples of parent-parent, parent-pupil or parent-teacher interaction which would have been necessary for a fuller picture to emerge. Nevertheless, our interviews we undertook with parents provided useful complements to the period of intensive observation within the school and some of the leads we have been following up there. It seems appropriate therefore to provide what we shall call an exploratory discussion based upon our limited data.

In our discussion of the teachers and their system of relevancies, we have already seen how the teachers develop differentiated typifications of the parents and interpret certain types of parental strategies in a much more favourable light than others. We were interested in whether these differential strategies reflected different universes of meaning among the parents and in what sense successful parent-teacher interaction involved some negotiation of a mutually agreed definition of the situation or intersubjectivity which might have beneficial consequences for certain types of pupils' career passages through the classroom. We were also interested to explore the kinds of strategies that parents and teachers use when faced with different and sometimes incompatible systems of relevancies to advance their interests, and the social significance of these strategies.

The analysis will be presented in terms of what we feel are key dimensions of the successful parent role. The more any of these elements are absent, the more likely it is that the parent will develop a relationship with the school which is potentially dysfunctional for his child's career.

What are these key dimensions? It is suggested that there are four which are of crucial importance. First, the good parent must be 'knowledgeable' about the way the school operates, the kinds of methods that are used and the pedagogical justification for them. The requisite degree or types of knowledge necessary is, of course, an empirical question. Previous studies have suggested that the problem with working class parents is that they are unfamiliar with the methods and underlying rationales of modern methods in primary education and therefore incapable of giving their children the right kind of support and preparation (Young and McGeeny, 1968; Musgrove and Taylor, 1965; Mays, 1962). We need to ask the extent to which 'understanding' the procedures and rationales of the teachers is a necessary precondition for developing a successful parent-teacher relationship. What criteria of 'knowledgeability' can we use and in what ways are these criteria of knowledgeability educationally relevant?

Second, the successful parent is one who is interested in his child's education and is motivated for his child to succeed. The difficulty with this area is that previous studies have tended to treat 'interest' in education non-problematically, as if it is something that can be measured objectively without specifying the normative standards built into the very way in which education is defined. In our discussion we have to explore and tease out what the school's clients, the parents, feel about education, how they define what it means to be educated and what they mean by success, as well as attempting to measure the extent to which their conception of the school deviates from what they think schools ideally ought to be doing for their children. It seems that a fairly obvious condition of a successful parent-school relationship is that the parent wants the child to get on, irrespective of how he defines getting on, and sees the school as in some way related to his child's subsequent success even though he may regard its role more as a barrier than a facilitator to his goals and aspirations for his child.

The third element in the successful relationship is that the parent is capable of cueing into the teacher's system of relevancies. By this we mean that the parent is aware, through whatever means, of what, in the teacher's view, constitutes the good parent. He knows what it is that the teacher thinks he should or should not do, how he should behave *vis-à-vis* his child and his teachers. Now this might be taken to suggest perhaps an over emphasis on the cognitive aspects of the successful parent-child relationship. We do not mean to suggest that there are not many exceedingly subtle criteria which are involved in the teachers' designation of parents as good or bad, over which, in many cases, the parent may have no control or of which he may be unaware. Nevertheless there must be some cognitive appraisal by the successful parent of how teachers think good parents should behave, at least with respect to those elements of parental role playing which are alterable.

The fourth element in the successful relationship is that the parent should be both able and willing to play the role of the good parent in a way which is concordant with the teachers' definitions. This does not necessarily mean that the parent should completely embrace the good parent role. What we are stressing here is that the parent should, if necessary through impression management, be able to 'convince' the teacher that he is a good parent. If this sounds too machiavellian we will suggest that the successful parent is one who is able and willing to engage in some degree of role segregation and differentiation and that completely to embrace the good parent role as teachers define it may result in consequences for the child which are actually dysfunctional for his educational career. We will present data to illustrate this point; it is sufficient, at this stage, however, to suggest that a degree of role segregation is possible precisely because the role regions in which parents operate, are separated in space, time and visibility from each other. Nevertheless, those who are party to the parents' role playing must in their different dramaturgical areas (Goffman, 1959) engage in some degree of audience tact. This particularly applies to the pupil if the relationship between parents and teachers is to be successful. The pupil may create difficulties for the parent if he 'lets on' in front of the teacher too many cues as to his parents' role playing in the home. In the same way the pupil may present problems for the teacher in the accounts that he renders to his parents of his activities at school.

Our approach offers a somewhat different interpretation of the good parent from that suggested in previous studies. It is not that the good parent *really is* knowledgeable about the school, *really is* interested in his child's education as the teacher defines it, and *really does* give the child and the teacher the support and encouragement which the child needs—but that he manages to *convince* the teacher through certain role playing devices that he is knowledgeable, interested and supportive and that it is his impression management which is most crucial. This impression management we have observed before but then by the teacher, presenting herself to parents as someone who is prepared to listen sympathetically to their views, giving them some credence, and thus projecting to the parents the image of a teacher having the 'real interests' of the child at heart, whatever views she may hold privately about the child's educability.

These four dimensions which are crucial in successful parent-teacher relationships will now be illustrated with reference to the empirical data. We discuss, first, the question of the parents' knowledgeability about the school and its *modus operandi*. This is a different area to deal with because the parents 'knowledge' of the school was gleaned from a variety of different sources and involved a complex mixture of quasi factual information and normative interpretations. Moreover, since the parents had no opportunity to spend any length of time observing the school functioning in its normal way, they were compelled to rely on various kinds of secondhand preinterpreted knowledge which the vast majority of parents recognized was likely to be partial and one-sided. Many of them had attended the school open meetings where the school ethos and methods had been explained officially. In addition, they cross examined their children about their activities, stared into those classrooms visibly accessible to the street, and exchanged information and interpretations at the school gate and in other types of informal social networks. In addition they made inferences from the kinds of 'products' their children brought home from school, their observation of public displays at the open days, and impressions gained from their short visits to the classroom. This information was supplemented by 'knowledge' gained from the mass media that modern methods in primary schools can be very different from those found in the sort of schools that most of the parents had themselves attended. As a result of these varied sources of information, nearly all parents seemed to be aware that the school was 'modern' in its approach but precisely what meaning could be given to the term 'modern' varied widely. The typifications of the school held by the parents were frequently vague and confused leading to the conclusion that the school had not managed to project a very clear unambiguous image of itself to its clients, except that it was 'different' and 'modern'. The following quotations reveal some of the impressions gained by parents about their children's school:

'They teach in small groups.'

'There's a lot of individual attention and they really care about each child.'

'It's play way, you know. They don't have them all sitting down at their desks doing what the teachers tell them - they do what they want.'

'They seem to play all the day at bricks and paint and things.'

'They teach the children to work things out on their own, they want them to have initiative.'

'They do sums in their head instead of writing them down in their books like we had to do.'

'The children learn through playing.'
Q. 'How do they do that?'
A. 'Well, now you've got me on that. Don't ask me - they just do - they learn when they're ready.'
Q. 'How do the teachers know when they are ready?'
A. 'Well, when they're ready, they learn them something, don't they?'

'They treat them as if they were at college'.

'They're very keen on art and things - but they don't bother about spelling or teach them tables.'

'They've got all these kids together of different ages and they just play with bricks all day. But the teacher says that's how they learn 'em to count these days.'

'There's a really happy atmosphere. It's playing you know, at least, they think they're playing but they don't really know they're really learning.'

A large number of the parents seemed very vague about the methods. If asked to explain the rationale behind the methods, few could make explicit links between their 'knowledge' of what their children did and the justification of these activities in terms of the stated intentions and rationales. Moreover, the vocabulary available to the parents to explain their conception of the school's methods did not assist in clarifying for them the specific pedagogical procedures and their underlying justifications. It also bore an extremely striking resemblance to the vocabulary used by the teachers when explaining publicly what the school's methods were all about, even to the extent that the same words and phrases were used. This came out particularly with those parents who claimed to be knowledgeable about the school and supportive of its general aims and procedures. There were hints of embarrassment among the parents when the researchers tried to probe more deeply into their knowledge of the methods and into their conceptions of how, in terms of procedure, the methods facilitated the attainment of the teachers' objectives.

Many parents admitted that they did not understand 'these modern methods': 'I don't really understand them myself but they know what they're doing'; 'I can see it's not what I've been used to but I can't make head nor tail of it myself . . . but it's their job and it's up to them to do what's best.'

These quotations have been used to illustrate the point that although nearly all the parents were knowledgeable to the extent that they could see the school was modern and different, there was some considerable degree of vagueness, confusion and ambiguity built into their conceptions as to how and why the school was different. Many explained their confusion by saying that they had not known or been told anything about the school and its methods before their child started school except what they had picked up through gossip with other parents of children already there and since they had no personal experience to go on, they had not known what to expect or how to interpret the cues regarding what their children were doing at school. In the absence of a relevant stock of knowledge at hand many of the parents, themselves, seemed to recognize that they were at a disadvantage and not necessarily in a good position to play the role of a good parent. However, we will suggest in our later analysis that a high degree of real 'knowledgeability' is not crucial, only an apparent knowledgeability may be sufficient, other things being equal, to further one's ends as a parent.

Let us turn now to our second dimension of successful parent-teacher relationship, that which pertains to the parent's interest in and commitment towards his child's success in education.

Here we are faced with the problem of what meaning the parents give to the notion of being educated and what counts for them as success. On this point there was far less confusion and ambivalence. Almost without exception they attached great importance to their children learning to read and write and developing numeracy and it was precisely with respect to this issue that the researchers discerned a degree of potential disagreement between the parents and the teachers. Nevertheless, although all parents regarded these skills as crucial, it was possible to differentiate several subuniverses of meaning among the parent group, for whilst some regarded the acquisition of the skills of literacy and numeracy, and the development of discipline, as the prime function of the school, others were prepared to accept a broader conception of the school's role; so long as it, at the same time, dealt with the transmission of instrumental skills.

'If she's all right at her reading, writing and arithmetic, then that is what I mean by getting on well.'

'For me, getting on means passing examinations, if they're going to get anywhere in their jobs.'

'I want him to develop all round but I shall get real worried if he don't pick up on his reading and writing.'

'I don't know whether they still have the 11+ but if they do then I shall want them to pass that. . . . Not that I did and it didn't do much harm though I might have got a better job, but well, if they don't pass the 11+ then I shall want to know what the school's been doing.'

'I don't like all this playing and drawing and freedom.'

'I think they should be getting on and doing real learning.'

Interviewer: 'What do they mean by that?'

'Well, I want the school to teach her reading, writing and sums and good manners, how to speak proper and respect for yer elders and all that.'

'They seem to do very little but paint and draw and do things with their hands. That's all right but it's not education. Schools should learn you how to read and write and do arithmetic and do as you are told—they don't do much of that there.'

'So long as they're reading, then the school should teach them good social relationships, to work things out for themselves—and to be adaptable . . . they should bring the kids out of themselves . . . but they've got to teach them to read and write as well.'

From the parents' point of view, the school's ability to transmit these skills was a vital measure of its effectiveness both with those who were favourably disposed towards the school and those who revealed more reservations or open hostility. Nevertheless, whilst those who were favourably inclined towards the school tended to articulate a broader conception of its role in terms of it developing initiative, flexibility, artistic endeavour, self-confidence and so on, the hostile rarely mentioned such things as compensating factors. Moreover, whilst a very high proportion were pleased that their children were 'happy' at school, only a very small minority regarded the happiness of the child as a measure of the school's effectiveness.

From our observations we seem to be suggesting a high degree of parental interest in their childrens' education which somewhat conflicts with the reified views of the parents which the teachers tended to hold. On what basis are we justified to make this assertion? What indicators did we use to identify parental interest? Here it seems important to stress the dangers of making *a priori* decisions regarding the indicators of parental interest in education. Parents' 'interest' will relate to their value conceptions about what they think education ought to be doing as well as to their definitions of what schools and educational systems actually are doing. People display their interest in different ways, having idiosyncratic or socially shaped reasons or justifications for the strategies and procedures to further their interests or cope with them. Suffice it to say that our interviews gave us the impression that parents were very ready to talk about their childrens' education, very articulate about their reasons for holding the views they had, and had readily available and, for them, adequate criteria for justifying them. Interest in their children's education seemed to figure centrally in their universe of meaning and they were generally prepared to take action when things were not going as they wanted them to. But this is not to suggest that their interest became translated into actions which the teachers themselves would identify as being indicative of parental interest and support. We will develop this point later when we come to deal with typical parental strategies. Nor is it to suggest a consensus among parents and teachers or within the parent group itself about what it means to be educated.

We now turn to the third dimension of good parent-teacher relationships, that which relates to the parent's awareness of the teacher's system of relevancies, how the teacher thinks the good parent should act and behave toward their offspring and towards the school. In this connection, since we have already mentioned the unfamiliarity with the school's ethos and practices which the parents articulated, together with the lack of specific advice the school had given them about how best to prepare their child and involve themselves, we suggest the parents here face a major stumbling block. Since there was a lack of socially available knowledge about how the good parent should act, it is, therefore, important how effectively teachers communicate their system of relevancies to the parents and through what cues and procedures their views are propagated. But the issue is not simply that of the ease of communication. The ability of parents to cue into the teacher's system of relevancies will not necessarily result in effective parental role playing, because the parents' actions and strategies will be related to their evaluation of the teacher's system of relevancies as well as to their desire to take the role of the good parent in order to further their ends, and this, of course, will be related to further issues such as the socially fashioned and socially prescribed ways of dealing with authority figures (Klein, 1965). Of this, more anon.

What perception did the parents have of the teacher's system of relevancies about how the good parent should behave? The following quotations illustrate a range of parents' awarenesses about different aspects of the 'good parent' role as defined by the teacher.

'I take her out, and talk to her and read to her. We've made her join the library and we take her to museums and things. That's what they suggested at the meeting.'

'I always help when I'm asked to—with the Christmas party, making clothes for the play, taking the kids to the zoo; and I go to all the meetings and appointments to see how she's getting on.'

'The teacher knows about what she's doing. I wouldn't try to contradict her, or tell her what she is doing wrong. That's her job, I try to help but not interfere.'

'Mrs X said I could help her with her reading now. I had been doing that already but I didn't say so.'

'We asked if we could buy him books to help him read but the teacher said no, we prefer to do it ourselves, so we said, fair enough.'

'We don't think we can help them very much because the teacher said that they have their own methods and it really wouldn't help them very much—only muddle them if we took a hand—but we try to take them out to museums and exhibitions and things.'

'They suggested I should play with her. I suppose they thought I should get down on the floor and play about with her.'

'They get their clothes filthy and their jumpers ruined. Their paint won't come off; the teacher said just soak it, but it doesn't come off. If she had children of her own she'd realize just how expensive kids' clothes can be. They expect you to say nothing when they come home from school filthy.'

It will be noted here that little has been said about how the parent, himself, thinks the good parent should act. All sorts of actions could be cited which relate to the way in which parents thought they could help their children—'making him do as he is told'. 'We teach him his tables and make him sit down and do adding up and taking away.' 'We've taught her the alphabet and we give her spelling tests every night', etc. What we are suggesting is the irrelevance on its own of what the parent feels should and should not be done. It is crucially important for the parent to cue into what the teacher feels should and should not be done, to understand how the teacher defines the situation. Without this information the parent can not only do all the wrong things, but if he persists with all the wrong things and yet still wants to appear a good parent—fail to develop strategies to cover up what he is doing, withhold information or selectively filter the information he makes available to the school.

This brings us to the final dimension of the successful parent-teacher relationship, the ability and willingness to play the role of the parent in a manner which fits with the teacher's normative conceptions of how the good parent should act. The ability may depend upon the other factors mentioned previously. But it is not simply the role taking ability that matters. The bad parent may be aware of how the school would like him to behave, perfectly competent to do so but be unprepared to engage in the kind of role playing expected. What seem to be the essentials of good parent behaviour? The good parent is one who appears to defer to the teacher's superior knowledge, expertise and competence. He will give the appearance of trusting the teacher's judgment and definition of the situation whilst at the same time giving the impression of being in a supportive role to the teachers. Such a parent may well be one who develops fluency in the vocabulary of the school ideology regarding its methods and aims, using key words like readiness, needs, stages of development, etc. We have, however, already hinted at the vagueness and ambiguity surrounding the vocabulary of methods. The use of the teachers' vocabulary by the parents may do no more than demonstrate a communality of interest and commitment to the school in general and the child's progress in particular and enables the parent to present himself as one who is on the teacher's side, but yet has expectations and trusts the teacher to do the right thing and do what is best.

Here again we are hinting at the rhetorical nature of the vocabulary not for arriving at genuine intersubjectivity and consensual meanings, but as a means of demonstrating commitment, setting the scene for an appropriate working role relationship which is both unthreatening for the teacher and enables the parent to further its ends. At the same time, the use of the teacher's own vocabulary by the parent appears to suggest the parent's deference to the teacher's worldviews but makes it more difficult for the teacher to fend off criticism from the worried parent by quasi scientific terms as a means of social control. Fluency in the vocabulary can pre-empt issues both by the parent as well as by the teacher.

We have stressed the parent's role taking ability and in doing so there arises the question of the degree of role embracement required in order to be a good parent. We are suggesting here when we emphasize the question of the parent appearing to do something or be something, that fully to embrace the role of the good parent as the teachers define it may, in fact, be dysfunctional. The irony is that if the parent really trusts the teacher and does what she suggests, then the parent is exposing the child to the elements of chance and accident and the results of scarcity of time and resources which we have seen are so crucial in the classroom. The good and effective parent is one who can engage in some degree of role segmentalization and play the role of directing and dominating working class parent at home but not appearing to be so at school. What came out very clearly in the analysis is that those children whom the teachers defined as good or bright pupils at school had parents who had, in fact, taken upon themselves the role of the teacher at home, in defiance of what they knew to be the teachers' frowning on parental interference with respect to activities like learning to read and be numerate. Nevertheless, at the same time as they were, in fact, interfering, they had to manage the nature and extent of their involvement in order for it not to appear that trust had been taken away from the teacher. Such parents could be seen as engaging in some kind of compensatory education for what in their actions they saw as the failure of the school to do what the parents regarded as important, i.e. teach. If the parents went about this task subtly enough and trained their children to exercise sufficient tact, their children would then display the right amount and kinds of readiness which would then pay off in terms of continued teacher interest in and support and sponsorship of their child. The irony here is that whilst the teachers think that they are engaged in compensatory education providing a wide variety of experiences for deprived children to work through their needs and become ready to learn, the differential readiness to learn is related to the extent to which parents have engaged in compensatory education to compensate for the deprivation in learning experiences that they feel their children have suffered at school. Additional irony—those parents who are most in favour at the school are usually those who, amongst other things, appear by their actions in consistently teaching children to read, etc., most critical of it.

The good parent, however, must train his child to act discreetly at school. He mustn't let on that his parents are teaching him or that they are telling him what to do at school. The classic gaffe which a child can make in school would be to say 'My mum said I've got to do reading and writing every day' or 'My mum says I've got to do some sums'. Were he to do this, the teacher may sense the incursion into her autonomy and the implied denigration of her competence and deliberately deny the child the opportunities to read and write. Such a child would be defined as being unduly pressurized beyond his particular stage of 'readiness'. Since his interest in these activities merely reflects, for the teacher, parental pressurizing, rather than any spontaneous choice of his own, we might at this juncture ask why little attention is given to the child who spontaneously chooses to please his parents by choosing to do what the parents are pleased with?

The child, thus, is crucial as a mediator in the successful parent-teacher relationship. Since he is the only role player who directly experiences both the world in the classroom and the world at home, a great premium is placed on the child's role taking ability, the degree to which he can engage in role segmentalization and role differentiation without breaking audience tact and revealing inconsistencies and incompatibilities between the parents' system of relevancies and the teachers'.

By contrast, the unsuccessful parent may be one who fully embraces the role of the good parent, i.e. the one who accepts that it is the teacher's responsibility and duty to teach the child without interference from the parent, the one who does not try at home to shape what the child does at school on the grounds that the teacher knows best and will see that the child does what he ought to. His child is one who, as we have seen in our discussion of the classrooms, becomes exposed to the hurly burly of activity in the classroom, who because he may not immediately appear to be good at or interested in reading, etc., is perhaps more likely to be unsuccessful, becoming defined as backward, abnormal, or disturbed in some way. This kind of unsuccessful parent may find these categorizations acceptable, if worrying, explanations for the child's low achievement.

The other main type of unsuccessful parent is one who is not prepared to take the role of good deferent parent but rather communicates to the teacher his dissatisfaction with her competence and her failure to produce results. His interactions with the teacher will be denigratory, undermining her authority and identity as a competent teacher. This type of parent is likely to find himself categorized as disturbed or unstable, given to projecting his anxieties and inadequacies on to the school. His child will be seen to reflect these family pathologies which explain his failure to achieve. However much he tries to intervene to assist his child, because he will not accept the teacher's terms, his interventions accentuate a spiral of mutually disconfirming cues, worsening a relationship from which it is very difficult either for the teacher or the parent to extricate himself.

At this point, it is perhaps worth asking why it is that certain types of parent successfully manage to play at being model parents whilst others do not. We would hypothesize on the basis of our observations, that, had it been possible to explore much more fully the worldviews of the parents, we may well have been able to further substantiate a suggested relationship between the different kinds of parental role playing and the parents' views of authority and the social structure. There were some indications that our really 'bad' parents resembled Mogey's status dissenters (Mogey, 1956). They were the ones who caused trouble, who privately and publicly denigrated the school and questioned the teachers' competence, who refused to accept the school's right to lay down policy on such issues as school clothes, discipline, leisure activities and so on, saw the social structure as illegitimately overbearing and teachers, along with other authority figures, as representatives of this overpowering structure of oppression. Such parents may well have privatized ends for their children in the sense that they would like them to get on, but they define teachers as people who are out to deny them their wishes, who impugn their essential selves and deny them legitimacy. Unlike our instrumental parent who plays at being a model parent, he is unwilling to become instrumentally engaged with the teacher to translate his aspirations for his child into objective results. Instead he castigates the school and the teachers for their failure, in his terms, to educate the child and thereby sets himself into an ever increasing spiral of further alienation. In one sense, however, he is like our first type of unsuccessful parent—he embraces one aspect of the good parent role—he leaves it to the teacher to produce results, but when the teacher fails to do so, he directs his antagonism not on the child as being too stupid or insecure, disturbed or unready but on the teacher who in his terms has failed to teach.

Our instrumental parent, on the other hand, is a status assenter (Mogey, op. cit.). Although he also may hold critical and ambivalent views about the teachers, he uses very different kinds of strategies. He may have a more pluralistic conception of the social structure, seeing it, not in terms of a them/us situation, but as a mobile world in which 'you've got to play their game whatever your private feelings if you want to get on in their world'. The consequence, for the parent, of this type of role strategy is the acquisition of a favourable identity as a parent in the teacher's eyes. Now this, together with the way in which the child behaves at school, may have a favourable feedback effect on the child's career in the classroom. Such instrumental role playing, therefore, whatever the initial private feelings and attitudes towards the school, may lead to a genuine supportive and non-antagonistic attitude towards the school.

So far, we have been attempting to explore the realms of meaning and system of relevancies of the parents by trying to draw out the accounting procedures and interactional strategies that characterize the successful parent-teacher relationship. From a social phenomenological point of view it might be suggested that the diverse relationships between home and school can be explained and conceptualized in terms of the co-existence of various subuniverses of meaning which coalesce or fail to cohere at the level of the school. Our approach, however, casts doubts as to the extent and nature of the negotiation of meanings which goes on in the successful parent-teacher relationship; as ordered and stable interaction may as much depend upon mutual deception and misunderstanding as on genuine communality of meaning. We want to proceed, however, with a return to one of our original theoretical questions; the extent to which a phenomenological account can be a completely adequate theoretical framework to understand the structure of the relationships that exist between parents and teachers. From a phenomenological position we might conclude that a major element in some working class children's lack of success in the educational system is misunderstanding. On the one hand, teachers fail to give credence and legitimacy to the world of the parents, they fail to interpret or they misinterpret educationally relevant cues; and on the other hand, parents have a different stock of knowledge at hand with a different system of relevancies which clash with those of the teacher. Moreover, the interactional strategies that each uses to further its ends is likely to be misinterpreted by or miscued into the system of relevancies of the other. Since it is mutual misunderstanding which is at the heart of the problem, policy implications which would follow might involve the de-reification of each party's views of the other. Given such changes in attitudes, each could be taught to be a more effective role player to further his ends.

It will be suggested here, however, that such a phenomenological account only captures the surface character of the interaction, and seems to avoid any attempt to come to grips with the underlying nature of the social totality in which parents and teachers are embedded. Merely to expose the others' meanings and encourage parents and teachers to be sensitive about each other, think differently and use different strategies, may be feasible or satisfactory for the individual parent or teacher, or indeed a particular school, but by itself is not going to alter the underlying structure of the social totality in which parents and teachers (as members of groups who have definite structured relationships with each other) are embedded. An individual child may become socially mobile but this by itself has no implication for the overall way in which power and resources are generated and distributed. The surface structure of the interaction between parents and teachers may be dependent upon a latent structure which a phenomenological account will not necessarily reveal. The teacher, for example, is enmeshed in a status and interest structure to which his ideology attaches which sustains and reinforces his reified view of the working class parent; the same can be said of the parent. The teacher's worldview about working class parents can only be understood if one renders problematic their position in the social structure, their quasiprofessional but marginal status position in the competitive struggle for power, prestige and economic rewards which characterize a stratified society. Their ideology about working class parents and their pathological attributes are only one part of a whole ideological superstructure which is self-maintaining and self-fulfilling in a context where resources and power are unequally distributed. Without some conception or theory of the social totality, such differentiated systems of relevancies and realms of meaning become merely accidental or contingent, something which can merely be described but not explained. As we have suggested in chapter 2, phenomenology cannot provide us with the analytical tools whereby we could cope with the social structuring of worldviews and their interrelationships; and it cannot do this because it lacks a theory of the social structure. It is engaged in what we referred to above as methodological localism, i.e. the social structure is generated by the face to face interactions and encounters at the local level. We have, however, throughout the book been raising the extent to which interaction is structured by elements over which the parties to the interaction have no control and may not even be aware of.

It is this lack of an adequate theory of the social totality that a phenomenological account of the 'problem' of parent-teacher relationships shares with what we could call the dominant structural/functionalism of many educational researchers' views of the role of parents in the aetiology of pupil achievement, and with the worldview of the teachers. To see the social structure as a construction of myriads of individuals is in one sense a truism but in another sense highly misleading in that social action is constructed within a context of constraints which pre-exist the social actor. Unless we can generate a theory which can render those phenomenological accounts themselves problematic, we will never be able to discern the latent structuring of opportunity behind the surface character of interaction.

We have indicated that a major social structural feature which an adequate theory must come to terms with is the question of the differential distribution of power as one of the contexts of constraint within which teacher-parent interaction took place. Now although not all parents expressed a lack of power, among parents who were hostile to the school and the teachers, a sense of powerlessness was openly admitted. This powerlessness revealed itself in a number of ways; a recognition that their geographical and economic position gave the parents no choice of school; a realization that the parent had no sanctions he could bring to bear whereas the teachers had, which might result in the child being 'done down'; a lack of institutionalized authority behind the parents to give legitimacy to their complaints; a feeling of being deprived of access to information which might assist them in their case against the school; a realization that if the parents and teachers are going to get on well, then it must be on the teachers' terms.

'I've got to do it like they say—I've got to put up with it their way.'

'If I was prepared to do that, then I'd get on all right. But I keep saying to myself why should I? They're my kids. Why should they have the right to push me around?'

'The catholic schools are a long way off. There is one on the other side of Mapledene but it would be impossible to get the girl in there. That's the posh end of Mapledene, and they don't want people going there from the estate.'

'They couldn't have gone to any other school. You see, Mapledene Lane is our school. The other schools would all be too full up. They wouldn't take children from the estate. He is always saying if you've got any complaints and worries about the school to go down and discuss them—but if you do, you just get shouted at. We've got no choice, you see. We just have to put up with it.'

'Our friend wrote to the chief education office about Mr McIntosh not letting the boys wear long trousers. The reply came back that Mr McIntosh has a complete right to decide how his school should be run. Somebody took their child away and sent them privately—but we can't afford that.'

'All schools ought to be the same. They ought to abolish public schools and grammar schools. They say that would mean ending freedom of choice but we haven't got freedom. Only people who are well off have got freedom. I haven't got any freedom to choose my school for my kids. It's a good job I am happy with that school because it wouldn't make any difference if I wasn't.'

'I asked him (the psychologist) what could I do—he said he didn't know. I was upset about that 'cos it's his job to give advice. There's nothing we can do—that's why we're so worried.'

One could argue, from the phenomenological position, that this sense of powerlessness is interesting as data but does not necessarily reflect reality. Then we could cite examples of parents who appear to establish a very successful relationship with the teacher where some degree of negotiation is possible and where the parents seem better able to manoeuvre themselves into a favourable position with the teachers. Nevertheless, from an objective point of view, whether the parent feels powerless, or not, we are facing a dynamic situation where there is an effective asymmetry in the situation. Parents tend to be fairly privatized and isolated except for a few neighbours. The conditions for successful organization for them as a group are not present. Parents are invited to the school to talk about their child, to be told about the school's methods, to be given entertainment in the form of a play or a concert, etc., but there is an absence of channels whereby parents' views and opinions are invited in the sense that a discussion of the underlying basis of the school's approach is permitted. In addition, parents do not have access to research or objective information that they could use to start to challenge the school. Moreover many can be put down by vocabulary. They can complain, but if they do so and are not satisfied they can move, grumble or send their children privately if they can afford it. Apart from these, there is little they can do.

Even if we think of those parents who were happy with the school, they had not set the terms of the interaction but had accepted them by others and used them to their own advantage.

What we are faced with, then, is different realms of meaning co-existing but the holders of one having more powerful purchase on the situation than the others. There may be a structured similarity in the worldview of parents and teachers which despite variations in detail remains relatively constant from school to school. Why is this and with what significance?

In conclusion, we want to turn back to the questions raised at the beginning of the study. Better participation and co-operation with parents need to be considered in relationship to the structural precondition that might make this possible. In the same way that we have suggested a structural discontinuity between the elements of the teachers' ideology and the structural components of the situation, so we believe that parent/teacher interaction should be assessed not simply in terms of the varying worldviews and typifications that they hold but in terms of the latent structuring of their relationships as members of groups in the wider social structure. It is to some of these wider structural parameters that we now turn in our conclusion.

11
Summary and conclusion

It is important to reassert that this study is essentially exploratory. No claims are being made that any of our propositions have been positively verified. The empirical materials have been illustrative and the theoretical categories are no more than minimally saturated (Glaser and Strauss, 1968). The main aim has been to illustrate a substantive area of infant education within the context of a critical perspective towards certain current theoretical developments in sociology.

With regard to the substantive aspects of the study, in our analysis of the theory and practice of the teachers in their classroom activity, we observed them subject to conflicting expectations and ambivalencies stemming from several sources. The practical implications of the child centred methodology were not clearly articulated amongst the staff community. In operation they tended to mean the 'free day' or the 'integrated curriculum', both these and other notions being loosely formulated. These became, in practice, organizational precepts whereby children tended to be given wide discretion to choose between many activities, and in so far as they appeared to choose to do things, i.e. satisfied the conditions for 'busyness', the child centred approach was assumed to be in operation. The teachers seemed to be left unclear as to their precise role in interacting with their pupils to further their development in various approved areas of knowledge. The vocabulary appealed to such concepts as 'needs', 'interests' and children's 'readiness' without specifying their operational indicators. The teachers' rationales fall back upon the idea that 'what children do they need to do', 'it is important for children to be happy at school' or 'play is work'. These are operationalized or informed in practice by the teachers' common sense concerning how normal children behave, derived from their immediate colleagues, from the wider context of their professional relationships and from their continuing biography as lower middle class members of society. Their rationales have strong undertones of deprivation and social pathology perspectives towards their clients which legitimizes their therapeutic ideology. Thus the high level theory with its ambivalent concepts has superficial connections with the teachers' operational philosophies when interacting face-to-face with their pupils. The teachers are able to organize the environment of their classrooms to allow a wide range of choice but have to generate their own theory of instruction for the children.

The headmaster publicly endorses the view that the school is committed to the teaching of both traditional and new types of knowledge. As a progressive school the children should be allowed to integrate their own knowledge, develop at their own pace, according to their own present needs and interests. But the school has also to account for itself in the established way by teaching literacy and numeracy. The teaching of reading, writing, mathematical concepts and computing skills are thus recognized as important in the teacher's work. The teachers are, however, in a difficult position because it is not immediately clear how these can be 'developed from within' the child rather than through the routine intervention and structuring by the teachers of their pupils' activities. They are confronted with the complex problem of cognizing, monitoring and further facilitating the children's development without adopting a too directive or formal approach. This is compounded by the age range of the children and their clearly differentiated levels of achievement.

The solution adopted by the different teachers we have observed consists of operationalizing in varying ways the 'integrated day' with a tendency to adopt the therapeutic ethos or image of the school as presented by the headmaster. Publicly, the school operates as a progressive educational establishment while in the practice of these teachers and in the private views of the headmaster, it is also a socializing institution, civilizing a deprived portion of the population. We have illustrated aspects of the social structuring of the classroom practice of the teachers at the intra classroom level and tried to show how this is situated within the context of staff relations.

Perhaps the central paradox[1] of the substantive level of our study relates to the operationalization of the child centred methodology and the relationship between intentions and outcomes. In the abstract, child centred ideology, the teacher operates by 'knowing the child'. Intersubjectivity is assumed to be unproblematic. The individual child in this situation, unlike in more formal and traditional approaches to education, really matters. At the level of the teachers' classroom practice and in the ethos of the school, the aim is towards a fluid harmony of co-operative actors allowing full and free expression on the part of the children. However, the structures generated reflect the teacher's attempts to combat anomie (Horton, 1964). We have tried to show how the constraints beyond and within the classroom situation prevent the teacher from achieving the high degree of consociality which the abstract ideology requires. Certain pupils are being denied 'their reality' and the opportunity to orient themselves towards the hidden curriculum. This curriculum is an aspect of the teacher's real power and reality defining functions. Such a process occurs in the absence of any adequate theory of instruction, in a context, moreover, where there is a liberal and relativistic denial that any such theory is necessary. (See Bruner, 1966). Here the open classroom is epiphenomenal to a latent structure of control and the consequences we have described are generated in order to make the teacher's task manageable.

Rather than an unalienated, non-reified harmony of true selves we find a tendency towards the hardening of certain pupil identities of an alienated nature based upon problematic ignorance at one level of the teacher's practice, where pupil-teacher intersubjectivity is low. At the opposite extreme was the unalienated consocial intersubjectivity constituting the central mode of sponsorship in this social structure (Turner, 1961). Between these, at points on the formal continuum thus constructed, are the various identities and positions of normal pupils. These constitute a 'bedrock of busyness' crucial in structuring the teacher's ability to sustain the classroom as a manageable entity. This structure generates positive advantages for the 'ideal' client while the reification of deviant identities and social positions is a strong possibility. Thus, whilst the teachers display a moral concern that every child matters, in practice there is a subtle process of sponsorship developing where opportunity is being offered to some and closed off to others. Social stratification is emerging.

We have tried to show how these practices are a function of the constraints both ideological and material which influence the practice of the individual teacher. Far from the stratification system being a mere product of interaction patterns at the micro level, we have suggested that such interactions are socially structured by the wide context of which they are a part and whose major features they reflect and in turn reproduce. Our analysis stresses the phenomenon of control and the social construction of the opportunity for some social actors because of their situation to directly influence the social careers of others. The outcome may be constituted as the unintended consequences of co-operative activity which masks a hierarchical structure of differential power and control. It is interesting in this context to suggest that disequilibrium in the structure of classroom relations was more likely to occur with the 'bright', 'ideal client' than with the 'dim' or 'really peculiar' child who presented few behaviour problems. The former were more capable of exposing the reality of power and control underlying the child centred harmony of the classroom (Dreitzel, 1970).

Similarly in terms of relationships among the teachers themselves and between teachers and their clients, the parents, good relationships depended upon a refusal to call into question established power positions and their legitimacy. Apparent recognition of the underlying structure and acceptance of power and control which did not prejudice the positions of each party to the interaction led to a greater opportunity for flexibility and manoeuvre, within certain limits.

We have tended to confine our substantive analysis to the level of the school in which the research was undertaken but clearly this context is situated and transcended by other factors which focus upon the classroom and the teachers' activities within the school. To extend the argument further one would need to relate the analysis of these social processes to other institutional processes. Whilst we have emphasized the central problematic of control in the context we have been observing, we have continually suggested that the analysis of the problem of harmony and order in micro institutions like schools interrelate crucially with more macro institutional features which differentially structure opportunity, resources and power.

To stress the need to integrate the analysis within a more macro perspective does not by itself entail the distinctiveness of the approach adopted here. Indeed we have argued in an earlier section that much of the sociology of education is premised upon a structural functionalist perspective towards macro societal processes and the specific role of education. Our approach is, however, critical of the analysis of social order which structural functionalism embodies. We reject the view that systems of values and normative rules are the basis of social order in society. Moreover we are critical of social phenomenology which some have described as a sophisticated modern variant of social order theory.

With its assumption that social order is ultimately dependent upon an underlying, taken-for-granted structure of rules which regulate and define social interaction, there is a tendency to overemphasize the rule governed nature of social discourse and to underestimate other sources of order such as the operation of power and constraint.

Although it would be almost impossible to develop from phenomenological assumptions any general theory of the role of educational systems in complex social structures, in structural functionalism educational systems are accorded great significance in the maintenance of social equilibrium (Durkheim, 1965; Parsons, 1959). In a complex and differentiated society education is a crucial mechanism for socialization and social control initiating people into those skills, attitudes, and values which are essential for effective role performance. It is thus involved in social selection and role allocation. In so far as there may be a discrepancy between ability and performance this tends to be explained in terms of individual or social pathology models of the pupils (Riessman, 1962) rather than in terms of any necessary structural incongruities within the educational system or society itself. A completely self-equilibriating society would be one in which all adhere to sets of common values, and individuals' positions in the social hierarchy would be commensurate with their 'talents'. The existence of the hierarchy is a function of the need to mobilize power in order effectively to pursue common goals, a structural device which responds to the functional requirements of the system (Davis and Moore, 1945).

This approach to social order follows from the failure to recognize that societies are structured not merely by normative systems but also through the mode of organizing material reality and the related social and political relationships. The maintenance of social order may be as much a function of these aspects of social structure as of the initiation of the population into sets of common values. Our approach to macro sociological issues reflects this. At the micro level we have observed in our analysis how there is a social distribution of opportunity to control resources, mobilize power and influence and alter the life chance of self and others and that this differential opportunity is related to the individual's social location in the macro structure of society. What would, however, comprise an adequate theory of the macro structure is, of course, highly problematic. Our own perspective has been influenced by Marxism whilst recognizing that the specific articulation of Marxian concepts for the analysis of latter day capitalist societies has not yet been adequately accomplished. A satisfactory theory would have to resolve the problems of how the social structure generates the differential resources, facilities and power which constitute part of the context of action in the kinds of situation under analysis in our work. Unfortunately modern sociology has moved away from asking such grandiose questions and, in its search for security has become preoccupied with lower level problems which has resulted in the fragmentation of the discipline into ever increasing sub-areas of specialization. Such a trend is particularly consequential for those interested in the analysis of education. As Lukács and Mészáros have argued in other contexts, (Lukács, 1971; Mészáros, 1972) to isolate specific instances of social life from the complex totality of which they are a part can only obscure the horizons of the problem. There is a need for a general theory which can serve as a framework within which to conduct lower level analyses.

But whence comes a theory of the social totality, and how, given the absence of such a theory, is it possible to conduct inquiries into social interaction in a specific set of social institutions as, in the case of this study, classrooms? Must one, indeed, wait until such a theory is forthcoming before one attempts to explore the kinds of contexts in our own work?

Such a view, we believe is mistaken. The study of education is particularly crucial for the understanding of a society. To ask for a theory of the social totality is to ask how the society reproduces itself, how it perpetuates its conditions of existence through the selection and transmission of knowledge upon which a complex industrial society depends, and how it maintains the cohesion of a social formation through its reproduction of class relationships and its propagation of ideologies which sanction the *status quo*.

What is the relevance of our own study to such issues? The processes we have observed in the classroom and referred to as the social structuring of pupils' identities can be seen as the initial stages of the institutionalization of social selection for the stratification system. As studies of differential achievement have shown, early success and failure in the classroom is of crucial importance for entry into the occupational structure, and hence the class structure at different levels. Moreover we have suggested not merely that there is a developing hierarchy of pupils but also the content of education is being selectively organized and socially transmitted. The social stratification of knowledge and ignorance which characterizes the wider society thus impinges on the child in his earliest encounters with formal institutional mechanisms. In addition within the school, social control is being maintained through the initiation of pupils, teachers and parents into appropriate attitudes and modes of action and, when these break down, through the operation of constraint against those who challenge established interests. Such processes are typical of the way in which ideological legitimation of the stratification system is articulated.

It is of course problematic to employ evidence from a single case study to support propositions about the workings of educational systems in societies like our own. Nevertheless, if the processes we have explored in our own study are typical then we would be justified in arguing that educational institutions are not merely involved but have a crucial role to play in the reproduction of socio-economic systems that depend at one level on the production of human capital through the inculcation of knowledge and skill and at another level on the social transmission of varying levels of ignorance (Moore and Tumin, 1949). Sociologists of varying theoretical persuasions seem to be agreed that the development of education in industrial societies is causally related to the transformations of the socio-economic structure. Nevertheless whilst education has expanded and taken on such significance for the reproduction of the socio-economic structure, its development has not been without problems. Industrial societies are faced with the problem both of satisfying a demand for skilled and trained personnel and for providing some institutional means for soaking up or consuming surplus labour which results from advancing technology. This has led to a great expansion of educational provision at all levels. This expansion of educational provision has in its turn been associated with a developing mass demand for education which overtakes not simply the educational opportunities available but the structure of occupational opportunity. In both advanced and developing societies there is a growing problem of absorbing the overproduction of educated personnel at one end of the occupational spectrum (Lewis, 1967; Myrdal, 1969; Foster, 1965; Malenbaum, 1957; Callaway, 1961; Clark, 1960); and, at the other, of absorbing that surplus labour which has been shaken out through the changing structure of the economic base (Tannenbaum, 1966). Many societies seem, thus, to be faced with irreconcilable dilemmas since they both raise people's aspirations and yet fail to give access to the sort of social roles in society which the educated believe they have a right to occupy (Hopper, 1970). Where mass demand for education and expanded educational provision are not associated with great changes in the occupational structure and a proliferation of middle and higher range roles, there will tend to be a continual downgrading of educational qualifications and a potentially disruptive situation for the society which is faced with alienated disaffected groups who form a major focus of threat to the established interests in the social framework (Coleman, 1965; Eisenstadt, 1966).

Many underdeveloped societies which have experienced these phenomena developing over a comparatively short period of time are unstable in their political and social frameworks and have been unable to contain the widespread tensions which have resulted from the rapid breakdown of traditional culture and social relationships with the onset of modernization. In well developed industrial societies, however, where the process has been more gradual, there has been a progressive modification and adaptation of traditional institutional and ideological forms of control such that instability and dissent are less apparent. Nevertheless, the analogy with underdeveloped societies is not inappropriate. Although industrialization leads to increase in the possibility for mobility for lower social categories due to the growth of bureaucratization and service industries which results in a greater proliferation of medium range roles (Lipset and Bendix, 1960; Smelser and Lipset, 1966), there is no evidence in Britain, for example, that those groups who have traditionally hegemonized the upper levels of the social hierarchy are declining in significance (Copeman, 1955; Clements, 1958; Kelsall, 1955; Guttsman, 1965; Westergaard, 1965). Whilst there has always been some upward mobility into these levels, high rates of self-recruitment continue. Although students of social mobility argue that the rate of upward mobility in advanced industrial societies is high, most mobility which occurs is small scale, from unskilled to semi-skilled, from skilled to white collar work—and the rags to riches transformation is an unusual occurrence. The increasing significance of education as a means of mobility does not necessarily reveal in real terms the institutionalization of equality of opportunity but only the decline in the significance of other routes of mobility, like the acquisition of wealth, mobility via marriage or sponsorship within bureaucracies, etc. Whilst educational institutions increasingly are the determinant of the level at which one enters the occupational structure and set limits on the amount of mobility possible thereafter, social origin is still the major determinant of occupational destiny. The great expansion of educational provision has not resulted in significant changes in the differential class chances for achievement (HMSO, 1963 (Robbins); Coleman, 1966).

The increasing involvement of education in advanced industrial societies in social selection through the role allocation of its inmates to different locations in the stratification hierarchy has rendered educational institutions increasingly exposed and vulnerable to incipient conflict. Durkheim, in stressing the integrative role of education, failed to appreciate the implications of education's involvement in role allocation in the division of labour. Had he developed his analysis of the various categories of 'abnormal' forms of the division of labour he might have modified his faith in the ability of educational systems to build consensus and maintain equilibrium. Whilst they may believe in equality, educators are operating within a stratified society where there are structural incongruities at the level of material interests which play havoc with the ideal of equality of opportunity, a mere surface phenomenon. As noted in our own substantive work the character of interaction and the perspectives of the actors involved may camouflage the real structure of relationships in which groups and individuals are embedded. Whilst educators and parents may view the educational system as the locale where talent is developed and individual needs responded to, its 'real' function may be very different and related more to the social demands of established interests in the macro structure than to the requirements of individual pupils. As we have observed in the classroom, the social advancement of the few depends upon a denial of the same for the many, as pupils' careers are socially structured through the activities of educators who are themselves enclosed within a wider structure of constraints over which they have little control.

It is here that the real irony and paradox of child centred progressivism as an educational ideology is revealed. Developing as a reaction to what was held to be the rigidity of traditional educational structures which denied opportunity to the many, the progressive child centred movement was impelled by a moral rhetoric which sought to re-establish the rights of the individual for freedom, self-development and individual expression, over and above the demands of the society (Entwistle, 1970).

Yet, it is possible to suggest an intimate connection between the development of progressivism in education and the 'demands' of society. The rigid hierarchical notion of fixed abilities is incompatible with the requirement for the maximization of skilled and trained personnel, whilst at the same time there is a need to socially structure over-optimistic aspirations as a result of the disjuncture between the mass demand for education and educational provision and occupational opportunities available. We suggest that the rise of progressivism and the institutional supports it receives are a function of its greater effectiveness for social control and structuring aspirations compared with more traditional educational ideologies whose legitimacy was already being questioned.

Within child centred progressivism, far wider ranges of the child's attributes become legitimate objects of evaluative scrutiny and explanatory variables in the construction of success and failure. Not merely intellectual but social, emotional, aesthetic and even physical criteria are often employed in the processing of pupils in educational institutions, the social control possibilities thus being enhanced. Moreover the development of a quasi therapeutic orientation to the educational task which we have suggested characterizes much of 'progressive child centred' thought (Clegg and Megson, 1968), impugns those who fail in ways which are non-threatening to established interests, thus 'cooling people out' and moving more and more people into soft control areas. The incorporation of social and individual pathology views of certain categories of pupils has its counter-part in other substantive areas of social policy, in attitudes towards criminality, mental illness, and so on (Miller and Riessman, 1968; Valentine, 1968) where increasingly social problems have come to be conceptualized in the same way. Such developments pose interesting questions for the sociology of knowledge regarding the institutional basis and supports for these ideas and the established interests which they serve. It is not possible in the present state of theory about such issues to do anything more than pose tentative questions.

Within educational contexts and elsewhere the ideal of equality of opportunity has replaced the institutional justifications for ascribed status. Nevertheless subtle modes of ascription continue to operate (Cicourel and Kitsuse, 1963) which have resulted in little change in the underlying structure of opportunity. Our work has illustrated how the ideologies which provide a legitimation for the discrepancy between intentions and outcomes often serve to reproduce those very structures in which this comes about. However the disjuncture between the moral aims of the educator and the outcomes of his educational practice is not confined to the progressive child centred educationalist alone but has characterized most educational theory. Whilst educational theory is intimately involved with value questions concerning the nature of the good society, knowledge, the proper role of man, etc., it has, additionally, to deal with empirical questions if it purports to explain how these desirable end states can be achieved. Without wishing to suggest that the empirical aspects of educational theory can be completely separated from the moral, any sound educational theory must be based upon an adequate appreciation of the social and psychological parameters of the educational process. Whilst progressivism, as we have seen in our analysis of the perspectives of the educators depicted in this study, claims to be based upon some sound 'reputable' psychological principles concerning the nature of child development, the sociological dimension of the progressive educationalist ideology is far less well developed. If the educators we have observed are typical, the sociological assumptions they are using are little more than a version of the prevailing common sense, which, if elaborated in sociological language, bears strong resemblance to the conservative social order perspective which has characterized much sociological thought about education. We have suggested that the educational ideology of child centred progressivism fails to comprehend the realities of a given situation of a stratified society where facilities, prestige and rewards are unequally distributed. It cannot explain these phenomena but takes them as given.

Without some clearer conception of the character of industrial societies and the limits on effective intervention that are imposed one can only depict progressive educators as utopian. The failure to consider the social preconditions for the effective institutionalization of their moral ideals which would involve a trenchant analysis of the social parameters of the educational system, reduces the progressive educator to little more than an unwilling apologist of the system and his utopian solutions ineffective. He is in the same dilemma as Matthew Arnold in the first stage of the drive to mass education. Arnold sought the solutions to the social crisis, brought about by industrialization, through the transformation of the individual through culture, an idealist solution which failed to provide an adequate account of the causes of the crisis which Arnold observed, and which was ultimately tautological (Arnold, 1963 edn; Williams, 1958). If the lack of culture is the cause of our social crisis, then merely to advocate culture to cure the crisis ignores the reasons why culture was absent or had become so degraded in the first place. Similar difficulties can be noted in the ideology of the progressive educator. Ironically he often sees himself as totally opposed to Arnold's élitism. If advanced industrialization has led to a devaluation of the individual, it is not enough merely to assert that the individual matters but to attempt to transform the character of the institutional framework which differentially stifles talent, dispels initiative and individuality and renders the vast majority of the population 'reduced' and 'alienated'.

Both Arnold and progressive child centred theorists typify the 'faith' in education as the resolution to all social ills. Comparative and historical studies suggest that attempts to bring about radical solutions to a variety of social problems through education are likely to fail—unless systematic attempts are made to alter the structure of incentives and manipulate and control other aspects of the social structure through direct political intervention. We are suggesting that modern child centred education is an aspect of romantic radical conservatism which involves an emotional turning away from society and an attempt within the confines of education to bring about that transformation of individual consciousness which is seen to be the key to social regeneration. This romantic conservatism characterizes both the institutional forms of educational progressivism in the state primary sector, and, as Gintis (1972) has argued, in the radicalism of the de-schooling movement.

Unless or until educators are able to comprehend their own structural location and develop theories of the limits of feasible political action to transform that location, they will continue to be unwilling victims of a structure that undermines the moral concerns they profess and which, we have observed, so informs their own perspective on their activity. Such a theory is as yet only in the most primitive stage of formulation but it is suggested that the attempts to integrate the study of education into the much larger concern to comprehend the structure of social processes in advanced industrial societies will perhaps ultimately provide the answer. What is needed is to go beyond the perspectives of individual actors and to explore the tensions which occur in social structures between meanings and actions, intentions and outcomes, consciousness and rationality. Unfortunately the magnitude of the sociological endeavour is only just being appreciated but the importance of the task is surely enormous not merely for those with a desire to know, but for those with a moral commitment to a society in which man as a rational being can realize his true potential.

Appendix:
a note on methodology

In this extended note we will discuss some of the major features and problems of methodology associated with this account. It appears to be useful to draw an analytic distinction between the 'practical' and the theoretical-conceptual aspects of methodology. That is to say, between the collection of 'data' and the problems encountered during the processing and evaluation of the data leading to the account thus offered. Clearly, at certain points this distinction breaks down and the activities associated with each are fused. We do not intend to present a full picture or a complete natural history of our methodological decisions, techniques, and difficulties, but rather to illustrate some of them in order to give an idea of our procedures and the way we arrived at our final account. However, before embarking upon this, it is important to emphasize the essentially exploratory nature of this work. As was stated elsewhere our substantive and 'empirical' work has proceeded against the background of concern with theoretical and epistemological issues current in sociology generally and in particular, recent developments in the sociology of education. We recognize the danger that the term 'exploratory' is often used as a convenient 'catch-all' which might entail it acting as a rationalization for shallow or essentially incoherent work. However, we can do little more at this stage than offer this account as a finished but essentially open-ended product to be judged by the interest it generates and insights it may offer.

The method by which the account came to be written cannot be stated according to some readily recognizable formula. It was not a one-off event but arose during a process of sustained negotiation at all levels, from decisions and wrangles over metatheoretical standpoints to the day to day activity of deciding what to observe and how our work was developing in terms of our changing conceptual apparatus. To give an account reflecting the intricacies of this complex and reflexive process is, we suspect, virtually impossible. There is much we are unable to articulate ourselves and, of course, to do so would require another very long account.

First, we will discuss some of the technical decisions faced during the course of the research as part of the practical aspect of the methodology. It had been decided in the late spring of 1970 to undertake an exploratory study from a sociological point of view of schools in the primary sector. Our intention was to attempt to find two primary schools as a basis for useful comparison; in particular, two schools with a broadly similar composition in terms of the social class background of the pupils but which varied according to pedagogic regime. There are major difficulties for this kind of work, not only because of technical problems of setting up such a basis for comparison for instance, which would require fairly extensive knowledge of various schools in order to be able to set up the comparative situation but also of being granted entry in the first place. Permissions had to be obtained from LEAs, who then listed the headteachers who they thought might be willing to allow their schools to be studied. It was then up to the headteacher to decide. Understandably we were treated with suspicion by many of the groups of staff whom we visited, partly, we believe, because we were unwilling to present ourselves according to the then dominant image of educational researchers. We wanted their permission to do relatively unstructured observation, rather than use the more formal psychometric and sociometric techniques with which they were familiar. We made it clear that our aim was to observe children in their work groups and their spontaneous social organization, where it occurred. In doing this, we underplayed our interest in the activities of the teacher in the social organization of the classroom. It was emphasized that we were not qualified teachers and were not interested in making assessments of their personal teaching competences. It was also made clear that we were completely independent of the LEAs which had provided the names of their schools or which paid our own salaries.

By a process of self-selection on the part of the schools we were left with only three. Nevertheless, two of them looked as though they would provide useful comparative material. It must be constantly kept in mind that we did not regard this lack of choice on our part as a serious problem because of our exploratory orientation. We recognized that there was very little sociological work done in this country on teacher-pupil relations and classroom social structures which was linked to a consideration of educational ideologies. Though, in a sense, we had adopted elements of a quasi experimental and neo-positivistic research 'design' in attempting to arrange a comparative situation, this was less crucial than having the opportunity, as sociologists, to spend time with teachers and children in their schools. As the research progressed, the comparative aspect of the project collapsed. We began to find ourselves increasingly interested in the first school we had entered and thus anxious to devote more time to developing an understanding of what we were observing there. The perspective we came to adopt was that this school might usefully be regarded as a critical case.[1] It is upon this school, the basis of our substantive report, that we will concentrate.

Our reception into this school was such that we were given the impression of an atmosphere of openness and a willingness to allow us in as observers. As noted above, we underplayed the attention which was to be paid to teacher-pupil interaction, the teacher's behaviour in structuring the classroom situation, teacher's consciousnesses and their social construction of meaning in these observations, because it was felt that to alert their attention to these aspects of the school would radically influence their action in ways we would find difficult to assess. In our initial discussion with the staff of the school, we attempted to be as open ended as possible when answering questions about our work. Thus, while emphasizing its exploratory nature and that we were unclear as to what we would find, we negotiated as wide an area of discretion as possible, while leaving the staff with the required initial security to allow us in. They appeared to accept the broad rationale that we were interested in children's behaviour in the classroom, as this constituted pupil-pupil interaction, group formation, and activity because this would help in the understanding of differences in children's achievements. This is not to suggest that the teachers were unable to perceive that they would be under observation to a certain extent, indeed this was specifically mentioned by them in our initial discussions though it did not appear to raise any serious anxieties.

It appeared from our initial experiences in the school that our entry may well have been facilitated by the headmaster's interest, in that his keenness for our work, which was itself to present problems, may well have been crucial in persuading this young staff that the work could be useful. However, there was certainly no suggestion at any later stage that we had been imposed upon them against their will. The point is that the headmaster understandably had an interest in the work. Having established a working regime upon novel lines he was keen to receive an assessment of it. The difficulty for us was that we had constantly to avoid leading questions on this point and so being unconsciously influenced, or revealing our developing perspective which may have radically altered the field.

The methodological problem thus became one of constantly negotiating our autonomy *vis-à-vis* the headmaster, of retaining a reflective interest in his problems without adopting his problems and so 'going native'. In the case of the other teachers there appeared to be a much greater willingness for us to proceed without question on their part. Clearly, as with all aspects of methodology in this kind of research, these problems constitute both part of the practical difficulty or facility we faced in gaining access to different settings in the school and important elements of our data and growing knowledge about the school and its social structure. Having gained entry to the field, it was decided to spend about six days observing generally to familiarize ourselves with its significant routines, identifying specific settings for subsequent more intensive observation, and arranging a working division of labour. It will be useful to mention the composition of the research team at this point. The team consisted of Rachel Sharp, Anthony Green and Jacqueline Lewis. Sharp formally led the research, taking formal responsibility for its development *vis-à-vis* Enfield College, who were financing the project, and the school in which the research was carried out. The college employed herself and Green, while Lewis was 'on placement' with the project for the year 1970-71 (as part of a course for a degree in Social Science under the auspices of the CNAA). Our intention was for each of us to select a classroom on which to concentrate our attention, so that much of our early period of observation was directed towards familiarizing ourselves with each classroom in order to make the crucial early choices about where we would subsequently focus our resources. Each of us spent time in every classroom noting the organization, style of the teacher, types of activities the children were engaged on and thus trying to make some rudimentary assessments of the social organization of each and the personality of the teacher. We were encouraged to view all except one classroom, where the headmaster felt the teacher, a probationer, was rather insecure. During this early period we also devoted time to acquiring a picture of the general rhythms and atmosphere of the school by attending the morning assembly, lunching with those children who took their midday meals at school, and by joining in staffroom conversation.

In these, our 'first days in the field' we reached a decision to concentrate upon the Infant department of the school and for each to adopt a class and its teacher for intensive observation. There were several reasons for doing this which reflect a change in the orientation within the team. Initially it was felt, particularly by Sharp, that we would look at the older children to see how the teacher-pupil interaction at that level was accommodated to the child centred ideology. This would have been useful to the extent that it was a logical step in the development of work on labelling which had become salient in the sociology of education which, at that time, concentrated mainly on secondary education. Thus the process of transition from the primary to the secondary stages of education could have been monitored to throw light on the way in which their identities as actors in, or objects of, these educational institutions were crystallized, amplified, or changed. However, by a process of elimination it became apparent that we would have been unable to do much comparative observational work in the Junior department. One class was felt to be unsuitable by the headmaster, as we have previously mentioned. There were few parallel aspects to the other three classes in terms of age composition. Two contained rising 8s to rising 10 year olds, while the other contained 10s and rising 11s. In addition there was a student doing teacher practice in one of the classes at the time. These, however, were not the major reasons for our eliminating the Junior department during our period of initial observation. Our reasons were concerned more with the attitude of the school staff to the children, namely that they were not 'our children'. It should be recalled that the school had only recently opened and in order to recruit to the Junior department they had to take children from other schools, and these children were generally unfamiliar with the sort of regime they found at Mapledene. The staff took the view that the juniors did not represent what was characteristic about the school and in this sense did not reflect the methodology employed there. In contrast, the infants were wholly their responsibility and the child centred methodology was being most clearly applied with them. This kind of decision raises one of the most frustrating aspects of attempting to do a study of an institution in its structural setting, that is as an individual or in a team: only so much can be accomplished. There is the problem that while, on the one hand, we have tried to present the school as a whole, and feel that, in terms of presenting major aspects of the ideological dynamics in the school we have been fairly successful, in other areas there is a lack of focus. In particular, the teachers in the Infant department are clear, as are the social structures of their classrooms, and the main feature of the politics within this part of the school. However, the other teachers are less clear, and appear mainly as vehicles of the school ethos. We feel that this is virtually unavoidable given the resources at our disposal.

During this early stage we thus decided to concentrate in the Infant department, with its four parallel, virtually grouped classes. Our overall approach of looking for the techniques of social control, labelling and classroom management could apply equally well here, and in fact what became salient for us during this period was the crucial importance of defining children as they entered formal education. This formed a rationale for our working specifically with three infant classes. It was decided that we should each adopt a class and teacher to observe, and the process of selection was again one of contingency and positive self-direction on our part. We felt that at this point the most crucial aspect of doing unstructured observation in this natural setting was that both observer and observed should be as comfortable or relaxed as possible. The teacher and children should, so far as is possible, be able to proceed with their normal routine and non-routine activities without the observer being a factor to consider. With this in mind we took care to observe our own effects upon the teachers and children, looking, for instance, for signs of nervousness or apprehension in our presence. With this in mind we decided that one of the classes was unsuitable particularly because we felt that we would have been unable to develop the rapport with the teacher necessary for the subsequent observation and more structured interviews we intended to carry out at a later stage. Thus the three remaining classes were selected and each observer attached to one of them, remaining with this classroom for the whole of the rest of the school year.

Although the styles of observation and staff interviews adopted by each of the fieldworkers varied quite considerably—from virtual observer (Green) to virtual participant (Lewis), with Sharp more clearly negotiating positions between these ends of the continuum (Gold, 1958)—we were fairly confident that comparability was developed by the process of regular fieldwork conferences in which time was spent discussing and structuring our findings. However, as others attempting this kind of work have noticed, it was only when we had left the field that many of the crucial insights emerged and with them the crystallization of the overall approach to our accounting. Thus we cannot claim to have done a piece of 'grounded theorizing' of the radically empirical variety Glazer and Strauss describe and claim to have adopted. Our categories are often minimally 'saturated', and our theoretical propositions go beyond and are not induced from our empirical evidence but rather are deduced from the wider context of negotiation after the fieldwork stage over our broad theoretical perspective. For instance, our evidence suggests that in many respects the social structure of each classroom is different, the teaching styles are somewhat different, as well as pupil organization; however, we came to the conclusion that these variations did not outweigh the overriding structural similarities. This, in turn, relates to changes in our overall theoretical stance during the course of the research, from an initial central adoption of key features of an interactionist perspective, focusing almost exclusively upon the symbolic and labelling processes to a disenchantment with this as a viable approach as such. It became increasingly clear to us that what is significant about such processes is to construct an accounting for the opportunity structure within which they occur. Thus the account we have produced does not resemble the way in which 'scientific research' is usually conventionally presented: a problem is identified, a method adopted to investigate it, the data collected after the design has been formulated, and the evidence then brought to bear upon the problem. We found it difficult to adopt a clear-cut view of how the problem should be formulated once we had, in a sense, started collecting the 'data'. How to save this smacking of methodological heresy and/or downright confusion on the part of the researcher? Such a judgment, in our view, reflects a certain misplaced confidence in the perspectives and methods currently available in sociology. There is a need to attempt to operate simultaneously at the epistemological, theoretical, and empirical levels with self-awareness given that there is no ready made formula for producing knowledge, let alone truth. However, we would be the first to recognize that what is thus produced may not be a tightly articulated whole. Our point in publishing it is that it may well raise more questions than solutions. That would be its central value. Again it is for the reader to judge.

Notes

1 Sociology and the classroom

1 It is crucial to recognize the implications of the word 'Ideally' opening this sentence. The effect is to make the approach formal and idealist in the sense that it both treats this ideal as a starting point for analysis but it is also the conclusion. That is to say, the ideal of perfect integration is projected on to empirical reality. Where there is a lack of fit, between this ideal and reality as observed, this does not provide the starting point for an historically situated scientific analysis, as in the case of Weber's conceptualization of the role of ideal types but the concluding point where a direct moral judgement is made. For instance malintegration, malsocialization or anomie are thus identified but not explained.

2 Clearly, there was a strong commitment generated during Lewin's biography away from authoritarian government and social control.

3 For developments of this work, plus critical appraisal, see Brophy and Good (1970) and Clairborn (1969).

2 Theoretical considerations

1 To use the term sociological phenomenology does not necessarily imply that the authors accept that sociological phenomenology necessarily derives from or is consistent with the phenomenological tradition in German philosophy. Indeed, a case could be made out that, in spite of the use of many phenomenological concepts and categories in sociological phenomenology, there is a fundamental inconsistency with some basic tenets of the philosophical movement on which phenomenological sociologists claim to have based their approach. See Hindess (1972) and Best (1973).

2 In recent years many sociology departments in universities and colleges in Britain have experienced the 'wind of change' associated

with 'sociological phenomenology'. It is interesting to speculate why the approach should have aroused so much interest. The answer must obviously be sought partially in the intellectual poverty of British sociology, its tendency towards scientistic empiricism and the fact that it has produced no major sociological thinkers to compare with current American writers, such as R. Merton, A. Cicourel, T. Parsons, A. Gouldner, etc. However, a more searching attempt to explain the 'success' of sociological phenomenology would require a simultaneous examination of the interrelationship between, on the one hand, the dominant structural features of an industrial society and, on the other, the 'forms of social consciousness' which develop in such a society providing a philosophical vision in which both man and society are understood.

3 To argue for the linkages between the various levels of analysis to be clearly articulated is in no way inconsistent with an argument against reductivism. One can both accept the validity of the notion of 'emergence' in social reality whilst still recognizing that psychology has a valid area of study. Difficulties arise when the theorist, for example the psychologist, fails to take account of the social context of the psychological processes in the theories which he is developing to account for those psychological processes. See, for example, studies of authoritarian and democratic leadership.

4 There are some commentators who would accuse Durkheim of this. See J. Monnerot, 'Les faits sociaux ne sont pas des choses' (1946), quoted in Berger and Luckmann (1967).

5 There are, however, historians who would reduce history to merely the history of individuals' thoughts and projects. We would accept Gellner's argument (1956) that historians are not 'biographers en grande série'.

6 See for example the following: Manis and Meltzer (1972), Douglas (1971), Blumer (1962), Schutz (1962), Mead (1934), Berger and Luckmann (1967), Cicourel (1973).

7 See Korsch's (1970) criticism of the vulgar materialism into which Marxism degenerated in the 1920s and 30s.

8 See Poulantza's critique of R. Millband's *The State in Capitalist Society*, and Miliband's reply on the relationship between theory and empirical reality in Blackburn 1972.

9 The phenomenologist does provide an explanation for the emergence of social meanings by assuming that they are embedded in an epistemic community. But this explanation is unsatisfactory and ultimately tautological in that an epistemic community is defined by consensual meanings. See Holzner (1968).

10 Although we are using Marxian concepts here, we do not want to suggest that in Marx's formulation there is no ambiguity attached to the concepts 'modes of production', 'forces of production' and 'relations of production'. Rather we would suggest that Marx's work can be used heuristically to direct attention to the fact that the particular organization of the conditions or production will be related

'in some way' to the relations of domination and subjection in society as it grows out of and in turn influences production. See Karl Marx, *Capital*, vol. III, p. 841. What is still problematic is the explicating of the term 'in some way'. The failure of Marxists to provide a satisfactory analysis of the development of capitalist society since Marx needs to be explained perhaps not in terms of the falsity of Marx's insights but in terms of the failure to move beyond him to develop new categories able to grasp the great complexity of capitalist social formations.

11 It is ironic that although great stress is put on the antipositivism of the new perspective, its approach to analysis seems fundamentally empiricist. However their view of 'empirical reality' is not synonymous with material objects but 'cultural' objects.

12 This is not to suggest that history consists in some supra-individual or supra-societal forces which operate with an immanent logic irrespective of the action of individuals. Rather, that there are some categories of historical (and sociological) problems which involve relationships between institutions or classes or other societal features which are not explicable in terms of what individuals think and feel or do.

13 The phenomenologist might also be interested in this, but since he has no theory of history which transcends the history of individual consciousnesses and since his framework only enables him to focus on 'mind' and its relationship with other minds, the kinds of problems we want to pose about 'history' would be excluded.

14 Berger and Luckmann's treatment of reification as further along the continuum of objectification makes reification simply a product of the objectifying consciousness. Reification implies that man is forgetting his own authorship of the human world and further that the dialectic between man, the producer and his products is lost to consciousness (1967, p. 106).

There is a need to distinguish between objectification and alienation. The former refers to a state of 'mind' the latter to a social condition which may have consequences for 'states of minds'—among other things.

15 See also Marx's critique of the Young Hegelians in *The German Ideology* (1964).

16 Whilst Durkheim's notion of social facts being external and constraining refers primarily to the normative structuring of social activity, Marx's notion of constraint is very different. Men are 'constrained' by factors other than mere ideas or normative systems in their alienated existence. Similarly we are critical of Berger and Luckmann's notion of constraint. Although in their analysis of 'order' they do not take the verified character of the world as it is (in Durkheimian fashion) they describe in formal and abstract terms how it inevitably became verified as a necessary result of constructing an orderly account of the world (Horton, 1971). Nevertheless it is clear that their discussion of institutionalization constitutes a version of

that approach to social order in terms of shared meanings if not shared evaluations.

17 See Strauss (1964) and Cicourel (1973) for their use of the term 'negotiation'.

18 In an oral comment at the Ethnomethodology Conference, Edinburgh, 1972.

19 See the following for approaches to role and role conflict with reference to teachers—Gross (1958), Westwood (1967), Getzels and Guba (1955), Kelsall and Kelsall (1969), Musgrove and Taylor (1969), Grace (1972).

3   Mapledene Lane: the school and its environment

1 Some of the trained schoolteachers whom the authors have encountered have commented on the irony in the situation where an educational ideology, which stresses the importance of child centredness and the child finding out on its own, should be imposed often in a very authoritarian way upon trainee teachers in colleges of education. As will be further explored in later chapters, Mrs Buchanan's position in the school is essentially paradoxical for similar reasons.

2 Central but not necessarily exclusive to progressive ideology. It is the combination and emphasis accorded them which is significant.

3 There are structural resemblances to the monitorial system here.

5   The teacher's perpesctives

1 The initiation of seasonal themes into the curriculum poses interesting questions for the sociologist. Whilst for the individual teacher Christmas and Easter may provide easy pragmatic solutions to the problem of how to involve the pupils in 'interesting' pursuits which have obvious meaning to the child, the social implications of such seasonal themes may be far-reaching over time, reinforcing in the child a sense of time and tradition through ritual celebration. Whilst the conservative implications of religious festivals (and royal visits or weddings) are clear, it is interesting to speculate on how societies dedicated to radical social reconstruction socially structure a different sense of time and change in the young. Are there similar conservative implications in the recurrent celebrations of 'heroes' of the revolution?

6   Social stratification in the classroom: an ideal type

1 To make a distinction between social or symbolic constraints, on the one hand, and physical constraints on the other, may suggest a dualism which we have argued in chapter 2 needs to be transcended. It

is recognized that many physical features in the social context of the teacher's practice are artifacts and as such embody norms, values and cognitions. Nevertheless the social definitions embodied in the physical environment themselves have a history reflecting the political-economic aspects of the totality of historical conditions in which the school is embedded. This, we have argued, is crucially related to material/physical reality and its control.

2   It might be thought that we are suggesting unproblematically that the teachers 'choose' between a restricted range of *a priori* alternatives which allow them to cope. A sociologist must be concerned with the philosophical basis of the notion of freedom and rationality. Whilst the teachers may cognize alternative operating procedures, both these cognitions and their subsequent choices may be due to the unique biographical experience of the individual which itself is socially structured. Whilst the philosophical arguments against determinism seem irrefutable, a satisfactory alternative which enables one to relate rational decision making to individual biographies and social structure seems to be lacking, and we still need to ask what constitutes 'freedom to choose'.

3   In this case study the social worker who 'dealt' with the school pupils and their families certainly tended to reinforce the teachers' reified conceptions of the 'problem pupils' although the manifest function of close co-operation between the teachers and social workers was to increase teacher/pupil rapport or, in Schutz's terms, benevolent consociation. However, it would be interesting to speculate on the implications for teacher-social worker co-operation of the recent development of radical welfare ideologies among some social workers. A teacher, who receives no 'props' to her solution, may proceed to denigrate the welfare worker, followed perhaps by an intensified covert reification of the child in question, or, possibly more likely, if there is an increase in the social status of the welfare worker, experience anxiety and identity crisis.

4   It could be argued that not enough consideration has been given in this chapter to the effect of peer group influences on the pupils' career, nor has enough attention been paid to the pupils' phenomenal world. In mitigation, it is worth noting that most studies of peer group influences and pupils' world views have been carried out on older children. The authors found it difficult to interview such very young children in any systematic way and had to make inferences from, usually, 'external' indicators like seating arrangements. Nevertheless, they recognize that a further composite picture would have emerged if time and resources had permitted a more intensive examination of such issues. However, such data as was obtained leads us to the conclusion that the analysis presented here would not be substantially undermined, but rather, refined.

9   The child centred ethos as an accounting system

1 Whilst neo-psychiatry assists teachers to maintain discretion from parents, this may be seen as merely the latest support to teachers' endeavours to keep social distance over a long period of time. As Baron and Tropp (1961) point out the evident educational knowledge gap between teachers and parents in England has long been a factor in their discretion. It is interesting that the development of 'progressive' educational ideas amongst infant teachers may be associated with attempts on their part to generate a professional ideology and occupational structure in order to increase their autonomy and status.

2 It could be suggested that the headmaster's ambivalence would occur whatever his career motives. As Gross points out, he is likely to be subject to conflicting and different pressures due to a heterogeneous role set exerted by others with power and by those whose values he subscribes to. To cope with these he has to speak out in ambivalent ways. The headmaster's personal charismatic qualities were in his actually coping; his ambivalence, a part of the enigmatic qualities of the person who successfully manages to do what appears in principle impossible. Nevertheless, it is not merely his charisma which enables him to exercise power. His power is vested in the office of head, and its strategic locale for mediating extra school and intra school interests. The office of the headmaster is embedded in a network of social institutions which buttress the headmaster's position to the extent that men without any of Mr McIntosh's personal charisma, professional skill and diplomatic tact would not remain long in that role without any real threats to their position.

11   Summary and conclusion

1 When using the term 'paradox' it should be noted that we mean more than the contradictions within ideological perspectives, which tends to be focused upon by such writers as Keddie (1971) and Esland (1971). The paradox lies in the structural underpinning and determination of the teacher's practice whereby, although they appear generally to be satisfying their own ideological commitments, they are unconsciously accommodating to a situation which renders it impossible to realize their commitments.

Appendix: a note on methodology

1 For a discussion of some of the methodological issues involved in the idea of a 'critical case', see Westergaard (1970).

Bibliography

ADAMS, R. S. and BIDDLE, B. J. (1970) *Realities of Teaching: Explorations with video tape,* Holt, Rinehart & Winston.
ALTHUSSER, L. (1970) *Reading Capital,* New Left Books.
ANDERSON, R. C. (1959) 'Learning in Discussions. A Resumé of the Authoritarian-Democratic Studies', *Harvard Educational Review,* vol. 29, no. 3.
ARNOLD, M. (1963 edn) *Culture and Anarchy,* Cambridge U.P.
BACHRACH, P. and BARATZ, M.S. (1963) 'Decision and Nondecision: An Analytic Framework' *American Political Science Review,* vol. 57.
BACHRACH, P. and BARATZ, M.S. (1962) 'Two Faces of Power', *American and Political Science Review,* vol. 56.
BARON, G. and TROPP, A. (1961) 'Teachers in England and America' in A. H. HALSEY *et al., Education, Economy and Society,* Collier-Macmillan.
BECKER, H. *et al.* (1961) *Boys in White,* University of Chicago Press.
BECKER, H. (1963) *Outsiders: Studies in the Sociology of Deviance,* Free Press.
BEEZ, W. V. (1970) 'Influence of Biased Psychological Reports on Teacher Behaviour and Pupil Performance', in M. B. MILES and W. W. CHARTERS (eds), *Learning in Social Settings,* Allyn & Bacon, 1970.
BENNETT, D. J. and BENNETT. J. D. (1970) 'Making the Scene', in G. STONE and H. FARBERMAN (eds), *Social Psychology through Symbolic Interaction,* Ginn-Blaisdell.
BERGER, P. (1967) *Invitation to Sociology,* Penguin.
BERGER, P. and LUCKMANN, T. (1967) *The Social Construction of Reality,* Penguin.
BERNSTEIN, B. and DAVIES, B. (1969), 'Some Sociological Comments on Plowden', in R. S. PETERS (ed.), *Perspectives on Plowden,* Routledge & Kegan Paul.
BEST, R. (1973) 'Misdirections in Sociological Theory: A Critical Evaluation of the Paradigm of Phenomenological Sociology',

241

unpublished dissertation for B.A. in 'Sociology of Education', Middlesex Polytechnic.

BLACK, M. (ed.) (1961a) 'Some Questions about Parsons' Theories', in M. BLACK (ed.), *The Social Theories of Talcott Parsons.*

BLACK, M. (ed.) (1961b) *The Social Theories of Talcott Parsons: Critical Examination*, Prentice-Hall.

BLACKBURN, R. (ed.) (1972) *Ideology in Social Science. Readings in critical social theory*, Fontana.

BLUMER, H. (1962) 'Society as Symbolic Interaction', in A. ROSE (ed.), *Human Behaviour and Social Processes.*

BLYTH, W. A. C. (1965) *English Primary Education, a sociological description*, vols I and II, Routledge & Kegan Paul.

BOLTON, C. D. (1963) 'Is Sociology a Behavioural Science?' in J. G. MANIS and B. N. MELTZER (eds), (1967) *Symbolic Interaction. A reader in sociology* (extract only), Allyn & Bacon. Complete in *Pacific Sociological Review*, VI (Spring 1963).

BOOCOCK, S. S. (1966) 'Toward a Sociology of Learning: A Selective Review of Existing Literature', *Sociology of Education*, vol. 39, no 1.

BOOCOCK, S. S. (1972) *An Introduction to the Sociology of Learning*, Houghton Mifflin.

BOYCE, E. R. (1945) *Infant School Activities*, Nisbet.

BRAYBROOK, D. (ed.) (1965) *Philosophical Problems of the Social Sciences*, Macmillan.

BREED, W. (1955) 'Social Control in the Newsroom', *Social Forces*, vol. 33, May.

BREWSTER, B. (1966) A critical note on P. Berger and S. Pullberg, 'Reification and the Sociological Critique of Consciousness', *New Left Review*, no. 35.

BRODBECK, M. (1958) 'Methodological Individualism, Definitions and Reductions', *Philosophy of Science*, vol. 25.

BROPHY, J. E. and GOOD, T. L. (1970) 'Teachers' Communications of Differential Expectations for Children's Classroom Performance', *Journal of Educational Psychology*, vol. 61.

BRUNER, J. S. (1966) *Towards a Theory of Instruction*, Norton & Co.

CALLAWAY, A. C. (1961) 'School Leavers in Nigeria, 1', *West Africa*, no. 2286, 25 March.

CICOUREL, A. (1970) 'Basic and Normative Rules in the Negotiation of Status and Role', in H. P. DREITZEL (ed.), *Recent Sociology*, no. 2, Macmillan.

CICOUREL, A. (1973) *Cognitive Sociology*, Penguin.

CICOUREL, A. and KITSUSE, J. (1963) *The Educational Decision Makers*, Bobbs Merrill.

CLAIRBORN, W. L. (1969) 'Expectancy Effects in the Classroom: a failure to replicate', *Journal of Education Psychology*, vol. 60, no. 5.

CLARK, B. (1960) 'The Cooling-out Function in Higher Education', *American Journal of Sociology*, lxv, May.

CLEGG, A. and MEGSON, B. (1968) *Children in Distress*, Penguin.

CLEMENTS, R. K. (1958) *Managers*, Allen & Unwin.
COLEMAN, J. S. (ed.) (1965) *Education and Political Development*, Princeton University Press, 1965.
COLEMAN, J. S. *et al.* (1966) *Equality of Educational Opportunity*, Office of Education, Washington, D.C.
COLLINGWOOD, R. G. (1954) *The Idea of History*, Oxford U.P.
COPEMAN, C. H. (1955) *Leaders of British Industry*, Gee.
COX, C. B. and DYSON, A. E. (1971) *The Black Papers on Education*, Davis-Poynter, rev. edn. of *Black Paper*, 1–3, first published by Critical Quarterly Society, 1968-70.
CRAFT, M., RAYNOR, J. and COHEN, L. (eds) (1967) *Linking Home and School*, Longman.
DAHRENDORF, R. (1958) 'Out of Utopia: Towards a Reorientation of Sociological Analysis', *American Journal of Sociology*, vol. 64.
DAVIS, K. and MOORE, W. E. (1945) 'Some Principles of Stratification,' *American Sociological Review*, vol. 10, no. 2.
DOUGLAS, J. B. (1964) *The Home and the School*, MacGibbon & Kee.
DOUGLAS, J. D. (ed.) (1971) *Understanding Everyday Life*, Routledge & Kegan Paul.
DRAY, W. (1967) 'Singular Hypotheticals and Historical Explanation' in L. GROSS (ed.), *Sociological Theory: Inquiries and Paradigms*, Harper International.
DREEBEN, R. (1967) 'On the Contribution of Schooling to the Learning of Norms', *Harvard Educational Review*, vol. 37, no. 2.
DREITZEL, H. P. (ed.) (1970) *Recent Sociology*, no. 2, Macmillan.
DURKHEIM, E. (1951) *Suicide*, Routledge & Kegan Paul.
DURKHEIM, E. (1958) *Socialism*, Antioch Press.
DURKHEIM, E. (1961) *Moral Education. A Study in the Theory and Application of the Sociology of Education*, Free Press.
DURKHEIM, E. (1965) *Sociology and Education*, Free Press.
EDIE, J. (ed.) (1965) *An Invitation to Phenomenology*, Quadrangle.
EISENSTADT, S. N. (1966) *Modernization, Protest and Change*, Prentice-Hall.
EMMET, D. and MACINTYRE, A. (1970) *Sociological Theory and Philosophical Analysis*, Macmillan.
ENTWISTLE, H. (1970) *Child Centred Education*, Methuen.
ESLAND, G. M. (1971) 'Teaching and Learning as the Organization of Knowledge' in M. F. D. YOUNG (ed.), *Knowledge and Control*.
FILMER, P., PHILLIPSON, M., SILVERMAN, D. and WALSH, D. (1972) *New Directions in Sociological Theory*, Collier-Macmillan.
FLOUD, J., HALSEY, A. H. and MARTIN, F. M. (1956) *Social Class and Educational Opportunity*, Heinemann.
FOSTER, P. (1965) *Education and Social Change in Ghana*, Routledge & Kegan Paul.
FROEBEL, F. (1909) *The Education of Man*, translated and annotated by W. N. Hailmann, Appleton-Century.
GAGE, N. L. (ed.) (1963) *Handbook for Research on Teaching*, Rand

McNally.

GAGE, N. L., *et al.* (1968) 'Explorations of the Teacher's Effectiveness in Explaining', Technical Report no. 4, Centre for Research and Development in Teaching, Stanford University. Reported by B. ROSENSHINE, 'Enthusiastic Teaching: A Research Review', *School Review*, no. 4, 1970.

GARDINER, P. (ed.) (1959) *Theories of History*, Free Press.

GARFINKEL, H. (1967) *Studies in Ethnomethodology*, Prentice-Hall.

GELLNER, E. (1956) 'Explanations in History', *Proceedings of the Aristotelian Society*, supplementary vol. 30, 1956. Reprinted as 'Holism Versus Individualism' in M. BRODBECK (ed.), *Readings in the Philosophy of Science*, Collier-Macmillan, 1968.

GELLNER, E. (1962) 'Concepts and Society', *Transactions of the Fifth World Congress in Sociology*, vol. 1.

GETZELS, J. W. and GUBA, E. G. (1955) 'The Structure of Roles and Role Conflict in the Teaching Situation', *Journal of Educational Sociology*, September.

GETZELS, J. W. and THELEN, H. A. (1960) 'The Classroom Group as a Unique Social System', in B. HENRY (ed.), *The Dynamics of Instructional Groups*, 59th yearbook of the National Society for the Study of Education. Reprinted in part as 'A Conceptual Framework for the Study of the Classroom Group as a Social System,' in A. MORRISON and D. MCINTYRE (eds), *Social Psychology of Teaching*.

GINTIS, H. (1972) 'Towards a Political Economy of Education: A Radical Critique of Ivan Illich's "Deschooling Society"', *Harvard Educational Review*, vol. 42, no. 1, Feb.

GLASER, B. and STRAUSS, A. (1968) *The Discovery of Grounded Theory*, Weidenfeld & Nicolson.

GODELIER, M. (1972) 'Structure and Contradiction in *Capital*', in R. BLACKBURN (ed.), *Ideology in Social Science*, (from *Les Temps Modernes*, no. 246, November 1966).

GOFFMAN, E. (1959) *Presentation of Self in Everyday Life*, Doubleday.

GOFFMAN, E. (1968) *Asylums*, Penguin.

GOLD, R. L. (1958) 'Roles in Sociological Field Observation', *Social Forces*, no. 36, March.

GOLDMAN, L. (1969) *Human Sciences and Philosophy*, Cape.

GOODACRE, E. (1968) *Teachers and their Pupils' Home Background*, NFER.

GOULDNER, A. W. (1958) Introduction to E. DURKHEIM, *Socialism*.

GOULDNER, A. W. (1959) 'Autonomy and Reciprocity in Functional Theory', in L. GROSS (ed.), *Symposium on Sociological Theory*, Harper & Row.

GOULDNER, A. W. (1971) *The Coming Crisis of Western Sociology*, Heinemann.

GRACE, G. (1972) *Role Conflict and the Teacher*, Routledge & Kegan Paul.

GROSS, N. *et al.* (1958) *Explorations in Role Analysis*, Wiley.

GUTTSMAN, W. L. (1965) *The British Political Elite*, MacGibbon & Kee.
HABERMAS, J. (1972) *Knowledge and Human Interests*, Heinemann.
HAGSTROM, W. O. (1965) *The Scientific Community*, Basic Books.
HARGREAVES, D. H. (1967) *Social Relations in a Secondary School*, Routledge & Kegan Paul.
HARGREAVES, D. H. (1972) *Interpersonal Relations and Education*, Routledge & Kegan Paul.
HARGREAVES, D. H. (1972) *Social Differentiation I. Allocation and Differentiation in Schools*, Open University, E. 282, Unit 9.
HILLER, P. (1973) 'Social Reality and Social Stratification', *Sociological Review*, February.
HINDESS, B. (1972) 'The "Phenomenological" Sociology of Alfred Schutz', *Economy and Society*, vol. 1, no. 1, February.
HOLT, J. (1969) *How Children Fail*, Penguin.
HOLZNER, B. (1968) *Reality Construction in Society*, Scherkman.
HMSO (1931) *The Primary School: Report of the Consultative Committee of the Board of Education.*
HMSO (1963) *A Report of the Committee on Higher Education*, (Robbins).
HMSO (1967) *Children and their Primary Schools. Report of the Central Advisory Council for Education (England)*, (Plowden).
HOMANS, G. C. (1964) 'Bringing Men Back In', *American Sociological Review*, vol. 29, no. 5, December.
HOPPER, E. (1970) 'Educational Systems and Selected Consequences of Patterns of Mobility and Non-Mobility in Industrial Societies: A Theoretical Discussion', British Sociological Association Conference Paper.
HORTON, J. (1964) 'The Dehumanization of Anomie and Alienation. A Problem in The Sociology of Knowledge', *British Journal of Sociology*, December.
HORTON, J. (1971) 'The Fetishism of Sociology', in J. D. COLFAX and J. L. ROACH (eds), *Radical Sociology*, Basic Books.
HOWDLE, L. (1968) 'An Inquiry into the Social Factors affecting the Orientation of English Infant Education since the Early Nineteenth Century', unpublished M.A. (Educ.) dissertation, London University, Institute of Education.
HUGHES, E. (1958) *Men and Their Work*, Free Press.
JACKSON, P. W. and LAHADERNE, H. M. (1967) 'Inequalities of Teacher-Pupil Contacts', *Psychology in the Schools*, vol. 4.
JACKSON, P. W. (1968) *Life in Classrooms*, Holt, Rinehart & Winston.
JAHODA, M. (1958) *Current Concepts of Mental Health*, Basic Books.
KAPLAN, A. (1964) *The Conduct of Inquiry*, Chandler.
KEDDIE, N. G. (1970) 'The Social Basis of Classroom Knowledge', M.A. dissertation, London University, Institute of Education.
KEDDIE, N. G. (1971) *The Social Basis of Classroom Knowledge*, in M. F. D. YOUNG, *Knowledge and Control*.
KELSALL, R. K. (1955) *Higher Civil Servants in Britain*, Routledge &

Kegan Paul.

KELSALL, R. K. and KELSALL, H. (1969) *The Schoolteacher in England and the USA*, Pergamon.

KLEIN, J. (1965) *Samples from English Culture*, vols 1 and 2, Routledge & Kegan Paul.

KORSCH, K. (1970) *Marxism and Philosophy*, New Left Books.

KOUNIN, J. S. (1970) *Discipline and Group Management in Classrooms*, Holt, Rinehart & Winston.

KOUNIN, J. S. and GUMP, P. V. (1958) 'The Ripple Effect in Discipline', *Elementary School Journal*, vol. 59.

KOUNIN, J.S. and GUMP, P.V. (1961) 'The Comparative Influence of Punitive and Non-Punitive Teachers upon Children's Conceptions of School Misconduct', *Journal of Educational Psychology*, vol. 52.

KOUNIN, J. S., GUMP, P. V. and RYAN, J. (1961) 'Explorations in Classroom Management', *Journal of Teacher Education*, vol. 12.

KUHN, T. S. (1962) *The Structure of Scientific Revolutions*, University of Chicago Press.

LACEY, C. (1970) *Hightown Grammar: The School as a Social System*, Manchester University Press.

LEMERT, E. M. (1967) *Human Deviance, Social Problems, and Social Control*, Prentice-Hall.

LEWIN, K., LIPPET, R. and WHITE, R. K. (1939) 'Patterns of Aggressive Behaviour in Experimentally created "Social Climates" ', *Journal of Social Psychology*, vol. 10.

LEWIS, W. Arthur (1967) 'Unemployment in Developing Countries', *The World Today*, vol. 23, no. 1.

LICHTMAN, R. (1970) 'Symbolic Interactionism and Social Reality: Some Marxist Queries', *Berkeley Journal of Sociology*, vol. XV.

LIPSET, S. M. and BENDIX, R. (1960) *Social Mobility in Industrial Society*, University of California Press.

LOCKWOOD, D. (1956) 'Some Remarks on the Social System', *British Journal of Sociology*, vol. 7, no. 2.

LOCKWOOD, D. (1964) 'Social Integration and System Integration', in G. K. ZOLLSCHAN and W. HIRSH (eds), *Explorations in Social Change*, Routledge & Kegan Paul.

LUKACS, G. (1971) *History and Class Consciousness. Studies in Marxian Dialectics*, Merlin Press.

LUKES, S. (1968) 'Methodological Individualism Reconsidered', *British Journal of Sociology*, vol. 11.

MACINTYRE, A. (1962) 'A Mistake About Causality in Social Science', in P. LASLETT and W. G. RUNCIMAN (eds) *Philosophy, Politics and Society*, second series, Blackwell.

MCKINNEY, J. C. (1970) 'Sociological Theory and the Process of Typification', in J. C. MCKINNEY and E. A. TIRYAKIAN (eds), *Theoretical Sociology: Perspectives and Developments*, Appleton-Century-Crofts.

MALENBAUM, W. (1957) 'Urban Unemployment in India', *Pacific*

Affairs, vol. 30, no. 2.

MANDELBAUM, M. (1955) 'History and the Social Sciences', *British Journal of Sociology,* vol. 6.

MANIS, J. G. and MELTZER, B. N. (1972) *Symbolic Interaction: a reader in Social Psychology,* Allyn.

MARX, K. and ENGELS, F. (1964) *The German Ideology,* Lawrence & Wishart.

MATZA, D. (1969) *Becoming Deviant,* Prentice-Hall.

MAYS, J. (1962) *Education and the Urban Child,* Liverpool University Press.

MEAD, G. H. (1934) *Mind, Self and Society,* University of Chicago Press.

MERTON, R. (1957) *Social Theory and Social Structure,* Collier-Macmillan.

MÉSZÁROS, I. (1972) *Lukács' Concept of the Totality,* Merlin Press.

MILLER, S. M. and RIESSMAN, R. (1968) *The Mental Health of the Poor,* Basic Books.

MILLS, C. W. (1963) 'Situated Actions and Vocabularies of Motive', in I. L. HOROWITZ (ed.), *Power, Politics and People,* Oxford University Press.

MOGEY, J. (1956) *Family and Neighbourhood,* Oxford University Press.

MOORE, W. E. and TUMIN, M. M. (1949) 'Some Social Functions of Ignorance', *American Sociological Review,* 14 December.

MORRISON, D. and MCINTYRE, D. (eds) (1972) *Social Psychology of Teaching,* Penguin.

MUSGROVE, F. (1961) 'Parents' Expectations of the Junior School', *Sociological Review,* 9, 2.

MUSGROVE, F. and TAYLOR, P. H. (1965) 'Teachers' and Parents' Conceptions of the Teacher's Role', *British Journal of Educational Psychology,* vol. 35.

MUSGROVE, F. and TAYLOR, P. (1969) *Society and the Teacher's Role,* Routledge & Kegan Paul.

MYRDAL, G. (1969) *Asian Drama. An Enquiry into the Poverty of Nations,* Terntieth Century Fund, Pantheon Books.

NASH, R. (1973) *Classrooms Observed: the Teacher's Perception and the Pupil's Performance,* Routledge & Kegan Paul.

NATANSON, M. (ed.) (1963) *Philosophy of the Social Sciences: a Reader,* Random House.

PARSONS, T. (1951) *The Social System,* Routledge & Kegan Paul.

PARSONS, T. (1959) 'The School Class as a Social System. Some of its Functions in American Society', *Harvard Educational Review,* XXIX, Fall.

PARSONS, T. (1963) Introduction to Max Weber, *The Sociology of Religion,* Beacon Press.

PERRY, L. (1965) 'What is an educational situation?', in R. D. ARCHAMBAULT (ed.), *Philosophical Analysis and Education,* Routledge & Kegan Paul.

PLATO (1955 edn) *Republic,* translated and with an introduction by H.

D. P. Lee, Penguin.

PLATT, A. (1969) *The Child Savers*, University of Chicago Press.

RAINWATER, L. (1967) 'The Revolt of the Dirty Workers', *Transaction*, November.

RICKMAN, H. P. (1967) *Understanding and the Social Sciences*, Heinemann Educational.

RIDGEWAY, L. and LAWTON, I. (1965) *Family Grouping in the Infant School*, Ward Lock.

RIESSMAN, F. (1962) *The Culturally Deprived Child*, Harper & Row.

RIST, R. G. (1970) 'Student Social Class and Teacher Expectations: the Self-fulfilling Prophecy in Ghetto Education', *Harvard Educational Review*, vol. 40, no. 3.

ROSE, A. (ed.) (1962) Introduction to *Human Behaviour and Social Processes*, Houghton Mifflin.

ROSENTHAL, R. and JACOBSON, C. (1968) *Pygmalion in the Classroom: Teacher Expectation and Pupils' Intellectual Development*, Holt, Rinehart & Winston.

SARTRE, J. P. (1964) *The Problem of Method*, Methuen.

SCHOOLS COUNCIL (1970) *Cross'd with Adversity*, Working Paper 27, Evans and Methuen Educational.

SCHUR, E. M. (1971) *Labelling Deviant Behaviour: Its Sociological Implications*, Harper & Row.

SCHUTZ, A. (1960) 'The Social World and the Theory of Social Action', *Social Research*, vol. 27, no. 2, Summer.

SCHUTZ, A. (1962, 1964, 1966) *Collected Papers*, vols I, II, and III, Martinus Nijhoff.

SCHUTZ, A. (1962b) 'Common-sense and Scientific Interpretations of Human Action', *Collected Papers*, vol. 1.

SCOTT, J. (1963) 'The Changing Foundation of the Parsonian Action Schema', *American Sociological Review*, no. 28.

SCOTT, M. and LYMAN, M. (1968) 'Accounts', *American Sociological Review*, vol. 33.

SEELEY, J. (1966) 'The "Making" and "Taking" of Problems', *Social Problems*, 14.

SMELSER, N. J. and LIPSET, S. M. (eds) (1966) *Social Structure and Mobility in Economic Development*, Routledge & Kegan Paul.

SPENCER, M. E. (1970) 'Politics and Rhetoric', *Social Research*, vol. 37, no. 4.

STRAUSS, A. (1958) *Mirrors and Masks*, Free Press.

STRAUSS, A. *et al.* (1964) *Psychiatric Ideologies and Institutions*, Collier-Macmillan.

SUDNOW, D. (1968) 'Normal Crimes', in E. RUBINGTON and M. S. WEINBERG (eds), *Deviance: Interactionist Perspective*, Macmillan.

TANNENBAUM, A. (1966) *Dropout or Diploma*, New York, Teachers College Press.

TURNER, R. H. (1961) 'Modes of Social Ascent through Education. Sponsored and Contest Mobility', in A. H. HALSEY, J. FLOUD, and C.

A. ANDERSON, *Education, Economy and Society,* Free Press.

TURNER, R. H. (1962) 'Role Taking: Process versus Conformity', in A. ROSE (ed.), *Human Behaviour and Social Processes.*

VALENTINE, C. (1968) *The Culture of Poverty,* University of Chicago Press.

WATKINS, J. (1959) 'Historical Explanation in the Social Sciences', in P. GARDINER (1959), *Theories of History.*

WEBER, M. (1948) *The Protestant Ethic and the Spirit of Capitalism,* translated by T. Parsons, with a foreword by R. H. Tawney, Allen & Unwin.

WEBER, M. (1949) *The Methodology of the Social Sciences,* Free Press.

WESTERGAARD, J. H. (1965) 'The Withering Away of Class. A Contemporary Myth', in 'New Left Review' (ed.), *Towards Socialism,* Fontana.

WESTERGAARD, J. H. (1970) 'Rediscovery of the cash nexus', *Socialist Register.*

WESTWOOD, L. J. (1967) 'The Role of the Teacher', parts I and II, *Educational Research,* vol. 9, no. 2, February, vol. 10, no. 1, November.

WILLIAMS, R. (1958) *Culture and Society, 1780-1950,* Chatto & Windus.

WINCH, P. (1958) *The Idea of a Social Science,* Routledge & Kegan Paul.

WISEMAN, S. (1964) *Education and Environment,* Manchester University Press.

WITHALL, J. (1949) 'The Development of a Technique for the Measurement of Socio-Educational Climate in Classrooms', *Journal of Experimental Education,* vol. 17.

WITHALL, J. (1960) 'Research Tools: Observing and Recording Behaviour', *Review of Educational Research,* vol. XXX, part 5.

WITTGENSTEIN, L. (1953) *Philosophical Investigations,* Blackwell.

WRONG, D. H. (1961) 'The Oversocialized Concept of Man in Modern Society', *American Sociological Review,* vol. 26, no. 2, April.

YEE, A. H. (ed.) (1971) *Social Interaction in Educational Settings,* Prentice-Hall.

YOUNG, M. F. D. (ed.) (1971) *Knowledge and Control: New Directions in the Sociology of Education,* Collier-Macmillan.

YOUNG, T. R. and BEARDSLEY, P. (1968) 'The Sociology of Classroom Teaching: a microfunctional analysis', *Journal of Educational Thought,* vol. 2, no. 3.

YOUNG, M. and MCGEENEY, P. (1968) *Learning Begins at Home,* Institute of Community Studies, Routledge & Kegan Paul.

Index

accounts, 77, 82, 165, 166f
Adams, R.S., 4, 241
alienation , 237n
Althusser, L., 23, 241
Anderson, R.C., 7, 241
anomie, 235n
anonymization, 119f
anti-humanism, 14
ascribed status, 225

Bachrach, P., 29, 241
background perspective, 73, 134
Baratz, M.S., *see* Bachrach, P.
Beardsley, *see* Young, M.
Becker, H., 20, 69, 125, 241
Beez, W.V., 125, 241
behaviourism, 6, 8, 16
Bendix, R., *see* Lipset, S.M.
Bennet, D.J., 31
Berger, P., 19, 20, 34, 241
Biddle, B.J., *see* Adams, R.S.
Black, M., 16, 241
Boocock, S.S., 4, 242
boundary conditions, 19f
Braybrook, D., 15, 242
Breed, W., 180, 242
Brewster, B., 24, 242
Brodbeck, M., 15, 242
Bruner, J.S., 218, 242
busyness, 121, 122f, 132f, 172f,
    218f; *see also* classroom,

consciousness, pupils, social
    stratification, teachers,
    vocabulary

Callaway, A.C., 222, 242
capitalism, 22, 236-7n
career, 32, 125f, 219, 230; *see
    also* headmaster, pupils,
    teachers
career interests, 181, 188f; *see
    also* headmaster, teachers
causality, 17, 18f
child centred movement, 41f, 62
child centred vocabulary:
    ambiguity of, 166f, 187; key
    concepts in: discovery, 42, ch
    5, freedom, 42, ch 5,
    interests, 41, ch 5, 173,
    needs, 41, 50, 175, play, 42f,
    53, ch 5, readiness, 42f, ch 5,
    170, 175; relation to
    operational problems, 33,
    77f, 118f, 168f; rhetorical
    wage of, 33, 168f; *see also*
    progressive movement,
    rhetoric, social stratification,
    teachers
Cicourel, A., 3, 19, 20, 23, 225,
    242
Clark, B., 222, 242
classroom: management

problems in, 10f, 116f, 130f,
172f, 189f, 191f; deviance in,
130f, 137f; interaction in,
studies of, ch 1; stratification
in, 33, ch 6, ch 7, 123, 172;
see also pupils, social
stratification, teachers,
teachers' perspectives
class structure, 13, 55, 226; *see
also* social stratification
Clegg, A., 195, 225, 242
Clements, R.K., 223, 242
'climates', 7f, 130f
Cohen, P., 29, 243
Coleman, J.S., 223, 243
Collingwood, R.G., 25, 243
commitment, 182f
common sense, 9, ch 5, 127,
167, 171
community schools, 57
compensatory education, 45, 46,
47, 56, 75, 208
conflict, 5, 8, 224; *see also*
material reality, power,
reality
consciousness, 12f, 20-1, 32f,
116-17, 126f, 227; *see also*
false consciousness, meaning,
sociological phenomenology
conservatism, 277
constraints, 22f, 34-5, ch 6,
126, ch 7, 214, 218
contemporary/consociate, 31f,
118f, 132, 218
context of action, 3, 6, 13, 20f,
126f, 167f, 186, 217
control, 5, 22, 28, 32, 122f,
217, 225
cooling out, 225
Copeman, C.H., 223, 243
Craft, M., 196, 243
creativity, 19, 21, 27f
culture, 226

Dahrendorf, R., 25, 28, 243
Daniel, 148-50
Davis, K., 220, 243
deep structure, 82

definition of the situation, 21
deprivation, 45, 61, 62, 71f, 80,
84f, 188; *see also* social
pathology, teachers'
perspectives
deschooling, 227
desist techniques, 8-9
determination, 18, 27f
developmental psychology, 42,
94
deviancy contagion, 10
dialect, 19-20, 23, 30
dirty workers, 176
doctrine, 167, 180f
Douglas, J.B., 196, 242
dramaturgical areas, 200
Dray, W., 25, 243
Dreeben, R., 4, 243
Dreitzel, H., 25, 28, 219, 243
Durkheim, E., 17, 220, 224, 243
dyadic social interchanges, 28

economic man, 7
Edie, J., 19, 243
education: expansion of, 222;
mass demand for, 222f; and
surplus labour, 222f; theory
of in capitalist society, 35,
221
Educationalist Context, 13, 171,
180
Educational Priority Areas, 33
educational theory and policy
orientations, 1
Eisenstadt, S.N., 223, 243
elective affinity, 30-1, 116-17
emergence, 17, 236n
Emmet, D., 15, 243
empiricism, 2, 4, 23, 237n; *see
also* positivism
Entwistle, H., 224, 243
epistemic community, 24, 236n
epistemology, 2f, 18f, 21
equality of opportunity, 13-14,
45, 222-3
Esland, G.M., 3, 243
ethnomethodology, 3-4
exchange theory, 7

existentialism, 34
externality, 27f

false consciousness, 35
feedback effects, 29-30, 116f,
    126, 129f, 188
Filmer, P., 3, 20, 243
fixed abilities, 224
Floud, J., 196, 243
forces of production, 236n
formal curriculum, 79f, 141f,
    167, 173, 184f; see also
    teachers' perspectives
Foster, P., 222, 243
freedom, 26f, 224
Freudianism, 16

Gage, N.C., 4, 244
Gardiner, P., 15, 244
Garfinkel, H., 3, 20, 244
Gellner, E., 21, 24f, 244
Getzels, J.W., 4, 244
Gintis, H., 227, 244
Glazer, B., 216, 244
Glen, 155-8
goal behaviours, 5
Godelier, M., 22, 23, 244
Goffman, E., 127, 180, 244
Gold, R.L., 244
Goldmann, L., 23, 244
Goodacre, E., 196, 244
Gouldner, A.W., 2, 244
'great man' approach, 8
group dynamics, 7
Guttsman, W.C., 223, 248

Habermas, J., 24, 245
Hagstrom, W.O., 180, 245
Hargreaves, D.H., 11f, 245
headmaster perspective, 47f;
    ambiguity, 76, 186-7;
    attitudes to parents, 65f;
    career interests, 180;
    professional experience, 39;
    power, 34-5, ch 9; structural
    pressures on, 76, 180-1
Hegel, viii
hegemony, 5

hermeneutic, 25
hidden curriculum, 218
Hiller, P., 19, 245
Hindess, B., 21, 245
history, 27, 236n
holism, 17, 25; see also
    individualism, reductivism
Homans, G.C., 17, 245
Hopper, E., 222, 245
horticultural model, 76, 179
Horton, J., 218, 244

idealism, ixf, 3, 21f, 34, 226-7
ideal types, 41, ch 6, 129
identity, 1, 3, 10-11, 19f, 33,
    127f, 172, 218
ideological approaches, 5
ideology, 8, 23, 28, 66, 224f
impression management, 200
individualism, 17
individualist epistemology, ix,
    20f, 25
inequality, 11
instruction, theory of, 218; see
    also child centred vocabulary,
    pedagogy
interests, 1, 5, 24, 34, 224; see
    also conflict, material reality,
    power, social stratification
interpretive procedures, 20
intersubjectivity, 30, 31f, 119f

Jackson, P.W., 118, 121, 245
Jacobson, C., see Rosenthal, R.
Jahoda, M., 6, 128f, 171-2,
    180-2, 217, 245
joint actions, 30

Kant, viii, 18
Kaplan, A., 195, 245
Karen, 139-43
Keddie, N.G., 3, 12-13, 34, 171,
    180, 245
Kelsall, R.K., 223, 245
Klein, J., 205, 246
knowing subject, 20f
knowledge-at-hand, 30
Korsch, K., 23, 246

Kounin, J.S., 8, 246
Kuhn, T.S., 1, 181, 246

labelling, 11, 125
language, 33, 34
latent structure, 211–12
leadership, 7–8, 10f
legitimation, 8, 34
Lemert, E.M., 125, 246
levels of analysis, 5, 9, 12, 17f,
    33f, 220
Lewin, K., 6, 7, 246
Lewis, W., 222, 246
liberalism, ixf, 26f
Lichtman, R., 21, 246
Linda, 150–4
Lippet, R., 6, 246
Lipset, S.M., 223, 246
local authority officials, 32
logic-in-use, 195
Luckmann, T., see Berger, P.
Lukács, G., 22, 23, 28, 221, 246
Lukes, S., 25, 246

MacIntyre, A., 18, 246
McIntyre, D., see Morrison, D.
McKinney, J.C., 29, 246
macro-structure, 28f, 66, 220;
    see also power, social
    stratification
maladjustment, 75f, 80, 84f,
    101f, 122; see also
    deprivation, deviancy
    contagion, social pathology
Malenbaum, W., 22, 246
Mandelbaum, M., 25, 247
Mapledean Estate, 30f
Mapledean Lane school:
    description, 36f; ethos, 47f
Marxism, 22, 221, 236n
Mary, 154–5
material reality, 6, 11, 18f, 24f,
    221f
Matza, D., 125, 247
Mays, J.B., 198, 247
Mead, G.H., 3, 347
meaning: objective, 22f;
    subjective, 2, 16f, 172; see

also intersubjectivity
mechanistic theories, 18f; see
    also determinism
mediation, 23, 113, 134
Megson, B., see Clegg, A.
Mészáros, I., 1, 221, 247
methodological individualism,
    25–6; see individualism,
    individualist epistemology
Michael, 137–9
micro contexts, see macro-
    structure
Miller, S.M., 225, 247
Mills, C.W., 34, 166, 247
mind, 24, 31, 237n
mode of production, 236n
Mogey, J., 210, 247
Morrison, D., 4, 247
multiple criterion approaches, 6
Musgrove, F., 198, 247
Myrdal, G., 223, 247

Nash, R., 125, 247
Natanson, M., 15, 247
negotiation, 12, 20f, 28, 35,
    128, 198, 210–11; see also
    intersubjectivity
nomothetic approaches, 5

objectification, 27; see also
    reification
ontology, 17
operational philosophy, 34, 70,
    123, 217
organization theory, 11
oversocialized concept of man, 2

paradigmatic crisis, 1, 181
paradox, 13, 115f, 180f, 217
parents, ch 10; class composition
    of, 37; and compensatory
    education, 208; dimensions
    of 'good parent strategies',
    198f; impression
    management, 200; opposition
    to school, 56f; power
    position of, 212f; status
    assent/dissent, 210f

Parsonian perspective, 4, 16, 22
pedagogy, 7, 8f, 12, 49f, 77f,
    90f, 116, 171, 187f; *see also*
    child centred vocabulary
perspective, definition of, 69
Peter, 145–8
Platt, A., 122, 248
Plowden Report, 40, 42, 45,
    195, 196, 245
positivism, 2, 4, 6; *see also*
    determinism
power, 8, 12, 27f, 32f; in school,
    33, 114f, 165, 177f, 218–19;
    in society, 212, 219f
premature categorization, 12,
    115–16
presentational symbols, 32–3,
    166f, 179
private language, 21–2
progressive movement, 35, 41,
    224f; *see also* child centred
    vocabulary
protestant ethic, 22
psychiatric perspective, 175
psychological reduction, 17
pupils: case studies, 137f;
    deviant pupils, 116f, 130,
    218; ideal pupils, 117, 218;
    identities, 115f; identity
    transformation, 129f; role in
    social stratification, 127,
    128f

rational action, 29
rationality, 8, 27
reality definition, 11f, 29f, 33,
    47, 126
reality tests, 29, 171, 177
reductivism, 7, 17, 236n
reification, 2, 10, 11–12, 13f,
    18f, 24, 26f, 85, 116f, 127,
    172, 204, 212, 218
relativism, 21, 26, 100
rhetoric, 32, 166, 181, 224
Rickman, H.P., 18, 248
Riessman, F., 220, 248
ripple effects, 8f
Rist, R.G., 11, 125, 248

Robbins Report, 223, 245
Robert, 158–62
role conflict, 116; embracement,
    119–20, 207f; segmentation,
    119–20, 208
Rose, A., 19, 248
Rosenthal, R., 11, 125, 248
routine, 82, 118, 175

sanctions, 27f, 213
Sartre, J.-P., 17, 248
scarce resources, 5, 28f, 127
Schur, E.M., 125, 248
Schutz, A., 3, 12, 22, 24, 31,
    119, 248
Scott, J., 17, 248
Scott, M., 181, 248
second order constructs, 22, 121
Seeley, J., 4, 248
self-fulfilling prophecy, 12f,
    125f
Sharon, 162–5
situate, 13, 17, 30, 116, 166f,
    217
Smelser, N.J., 223, 248
social class, 2, 17, 37
social construction of reality, 6,
    11f, 26–7
social distribution: of ignorance,
    221f; of knowledge, 24, 221f;
    of opportunity, 7–8, 27, 220;
    see also equality of
    opportunity, social class,
    social stratification
social forces, vii
social Kantianism, 21
social mobility: in classroom,
    130f; relation to education,
    225; in society 225f
social pathology, 62, 188, 217,
    221
sociological phenomenology,
    viiif, 3, 6, 11, 15, 16f, 114,
    210, 220; critique of, 21f;
    philosophical antecedents,
    235n; in sociology of
    education, ch 1, 235n
sociology of education, viiif, 11,

14, 125
social psychology, 3, 7, 10, 16f
social stratification, 30f, 220,
    222f; in classroom, 117f, 128f,
    137f, 174–5, 218
social workers, 32, 50, 176
society: as objective reality, 21f;
    as process, 18–19, 20f
Spencer, M.E., 166, 248
sponsorship, 132, 185, 218
'star', 179–80
Strauss, A., 19, 34, 69, 216, 248
structural determinants, 6
structural discontinuity, 214–15
structural functionalism, 1, 4f,
    212, 220
Sudnow, P., 125, 248
surface rules, 20
surface structure, 22, 30, 34, 82,
    211
surplus labour, 222
Sylvia, 143–5
symbolic communication, 19
symbolic interaction, 4, 10, 125
system of relevances, 31, 197

taken-for-granted, 13
Tannenbaum, A., 222, 248
Taylor, P.H., see Musgrove, F.
teachers: career interests of,
    189; categorization of pupils,
    115f, 137f; degree of
    autonomy, 33, 166f;
    intersubjectivity with pupils,
    115f, 137f; relation with
    headmaster, 90, 130, 178f,
    182f; relation with other
    teachers, 33, 130, 173f, 181f;
    relation with parents, 34, 85f,
    101, 176f; role in pupil
    processing, 33, 34;
    vocabulary, 166f
teachers' perspectives, 68f; Mrs
    Buchanan, 98–113; Mrs

Carpenter, 70–83; Mrs Lyons,
    83–98
teaching ideology, viif, 12, 33–4,
    40, 49, 66, 68f
Thelen, H.A., see Getzels, J.W.
theoretical displacement, 9
therapeutic perspective, 62, 111,
    112, 217, 225; see also social
    pathology
total institution, 126
Turner, R.H., 2, 248
typifications, 12–13, 21, 24,
    113, 116f, 132f, 197

understanding, 18
unintended consequences, 22,
    31f
universe of meaning, 197f, 203f

Valentine, C., 225, 249
vertical grouping, 44f, 51
videotapes, 4
vocabulary, 34, 166, 177
voluntarism, ix, 19

Watkins, J., 17, 249
Weber, M., 3, 18, 22, 30, 249
welfare assistants, 39
Weltanschauung, 22
we-relationship, 113
Westergaard, J.H., 223, 249
White, R.K., 6, 246
Winch, P., 18, 249
Wiseman, S., 196
Wittgenstein, L., 21
Wrong, D., 2, 17, 249

Yee, A.H., 4, 249
Young, M., 4, 198, 249
Young, M.F.D., 3, 11, 249
youth culture, 11

zero sum, 180